Practical
Risk-Adjusted
Performance
Measurement

For other titles in the Wiley Finance series please see www.wiley.com/finance

Practical Risk-Adjusted Performance Measurement

CARL R. BACON

Second Edition

WILEY

Library of Congress Cataloging-in-Publication Data

Names: Bacon, Carl R., author.
Title: Practical risk-adjusted performance measurement / Carl R. Bacon.
Description: Second edition. | Hoboken, NJ : Wiley, 2022. | Series: Wiley finance series | Includes bibliographical references and index.
Identifiers: LCCN 2021028308 (print) | LCCN 2021028309 (ebook) | ISBN 9781119838845 (cloth) | ISBN 9781119838869 (adobe pdf) | ISBN 9781119838876 (epub) | ISBN 9781119838883 (obook)
Subjects: LCSH: Financial risk management. | Performance standards. | Risk management.
Classification: LCC HD61 .B33 2022 (print) | LCC HD61 (ebook) | DDC 658.15/5—dc23
LC record available at https://lccn.loc.gov/2021028308
LC ebook record available at https://lccn.loc.gov/2021028309

Cover Image: © oxygen/Moment
Cover Design: Wiley

Set in 11/13pt STIXTwoText by Straive, Chennai, India

SKYBED5B39F-FCA5-4828-A72B-26EABDA22B54_092421

This book is dedicated to the staff of Frederick Gent School, South Normanton, Derbyshire. They set me on my way.

Contents

CHAPTER 4
Regression Analysis **75**

CHAPTER 5
Drawdown **107**

CHAPTER 7

CHAPTER 8

Preface

"Beauty is in the eye of the beholder."

Margaret Wolfe Hungerford (1855–1897), *Molly Bawn* 1878

There are many books and articles, perhaps hundreds, written on the subject of portfolio risk, but for the most part they focus on ex-ante risk, tend to be highly academic with authors seemingly in a competition to present the material in as complex a language as possible, prone to *mathiness*[1] and are typically devoid of worked examples. The first edition of this book attempted to fill the gap between practice and theory, written for risk and performance measurement practitioners from a buy side, asset management perspective, focusing on quantitative ex-post measures rather than the qualitative aspects of risk. The first edition provided the material I would have wanted to read, so why a second edition? Well, I've received many useful comments, suggestions and yes, accepted a few corrections or met the need for further clarification. I thank everyone who has contributed, even the innocent question in a training session causing my mind to wander, eventually generating that spark that leads to an epiphany. I've taken the opportunity to add a few new measures, provide additional explanations where the original clearly was not sufficient, corrected a few annoying errors and added six entirely new chapters.

Risk has an undeserved reputation within asset management for being an overly complex, mathematical subject. The purpose of this edition is to simplify the subject and demonstrate with many practical examples that risk is perfectly straightforward and not as complicated as it might seem.

In addition, I wanted to document, with appropriate referencing, as many discrete ex-post risk measures as possible in a structured format, filling gaps,

---

[1]The misuse of mathematics in order to mislead; see Paul Romer (2015) Mathiness in the Theory of Economic Growth. *American Economic Review* 105, 89–93.

encouraging consistency, suggesting new measures and highlighting possible areas of confusion or misrepresentation. In truth many of these measures are rarely used in practice, often for good reason.

This book will not recommend any particular risk measure, although it is difficult to disguise my preferences and prejudices. Risk, like beauty, is very much in the eye of the beholder and different risk measures will suit different investment strategies or asset owner concerns at different times. This book should provide enough information and insight for the reader to determine their own preferences.

In terms of structure **Chapter 1** is naturally an introduction to the subject of risk in the context of asset management firms. In **Chapter 2** the foundations are laid introducing the descriptive statistics that will be used in later chapters. The following chapters are structured according to the type of risk measure being considered: simple performance appraisal measures in **Chapter 3**; regression measures in **Chapter 4**; drawdown in **Chapter 5**; partial moments in **Chapter 6**; a new **Chapter 7** based on prospect theory; extreme risk in **Chapter 8**; risk measures for fixed income instruments in **Chapter 9**; a new **Chapter 10** including miscellaneous risk measures that are difficult to characterise; and risk-adjusted returns in **Chapter 11**.

Chapters 12–16 are entirely new chapters for this edition. **Chapter 12** was really inspired by the background research and writing of the first edition. I wanted to classify all the ex-post risk measures and describe how they are linked; my thoughts came together too late to include the best presentation of this linkage in the first edition, which is, of course, a periodic table of risk measures. **Chapter 13** discusses the use of risk-adjusted performance measures in the context of performance fees. **Chapter 14** discusses dashboard design in the context of risk measures, **Chapter 15** looks at the important subject of how appraisal measures should be used in the context of manager selection and **Chapter 16** introduces the four dimensions of performance and makes the call for ex-ante risk standards.

In the penultimate **Chapter 17** there is a discussion about which risk measures to use and finally **Chapter 18** reviews their application in terms of risk control.

The objective of this edition remains to provide a complete list of ex-post risk measures used by asset managers. Although some have little merit, I've avoided censoring measures I dislike. If a risk measure is not included, maybe I don't fully understand it with enough confidence to write about it, or in a few rare cases I've determined that it literally has no merit.

Acknowledgements

My thanks are owed to many who have contributed to this book, both directly and indirectly – working colleagues over many years, attendees at my various training courses and workshops which I hope will continue, attentive readers of my previous books who have spotted a number of errors and indeed made many good suggestions, numerous fellow GIPS® committee members who have been so insightful and of course the many authors who have laid the foundations of this subject.

I'm particularly thankful to the diligent reviewers of this book, in particular Damian Handzy, Neil Riddles, Paul Giles and Joe Kavanagh for their numerous detailed comments and suggestions; this book is much better for their contribution. Of course, all errors and omissions are my own.

Carl R. Bacon CIPM
Deeping St James
August 2021
carlrbacon@icloud.com

About the Companion Website

This book is accompanied by a companion website:
www.wiley.com\go\bacon\riskadjustedperformance2e

The website includes:

- Excel spreadsheet with supporting data and underlying calculations for all exhibits
- The Periodic Table of Risk Measures

CHAPTER 1

Introduction

"Money is like muck, not good except it be spread."

Francis Bacon (1561–1626)

DEFINITION OF RISK

Risk means very different things to different audiences at different times; risk is truly in the eye of the beholder. In the context of asset management, the *Oxford English Dictionary* provides a surprisingly good definition of risk:

> The potential impact of an event determined by combining the likelihood of the event occurring with the impact should it occur.

Risk is the combination of exposure and uncertainty. As Holton[1] (2004) so eloquently points out it is not risky to jump out of an aircraft without a parachute because death is certain. Holton also points out that we can never operationally define risk; at best, we can operationally define our perception of risk.

Another common and effective, but broader definition of risk is **exposure to uncertainty**.

RISK TYPES

Within asset management firms there are many types of risk that should concern asset managers and senior management. For convenience I've chosen to classify risk into five main categories:

---

[1]Glyn A. Holton (2004) Defining Risk. *Financial Analysts Journal* 60(6), 19–25.

Compliance Risk

Operational Risk

Liquidity Risk

Counterparty Risk

Portfolio Risk

These risks are ranked in my priority order of concern at the point in time I assumed the role of Director of Risk Control at an asset management firm in the late 1990s.[2] What I didn't appreciate fully then, but appreciated much later, is that priorities will vary through time; during the credit crisis I'm sure counterparty risk became the number one priority for many firms.

Although a major concern of all asset managers, reputational risk does not warrant a separate category; a risk failure in any category can cause significant damage to a firm's reputation.

Compliance or regulatory risk is the risk of breaching a regulatory, client or internally imposed guideline, restriction or clear limit. I draw no distinction between internal or external limits; the breach of an internal limit indicates a control failure, which could just as easily have been a regulatory, or client mandated limit. Of course, the financial impact of breaching limits can be significant; in August 1996 Peter Young of Morgan Grenfell Asset Management allegedly cost Deutsche Bank £300 to £400 million in compensation payments to investors in highly regulated authorised unit trusts. Peter Young used Luxembourg listed shell companies to circumvent limits on unlisted and risky holdings.

Operational risk, often defined as a residual catch-all category to include risks not defined elsewhere, actually includes the risk of human error, fraud, system failure, poor controls, management failure and failed trades. Risks of this type are more common but usually less severe. Nevertheless, it is important to continuously monitor errors and near misses of all types, even those that do not result in financial loss. An increase in the frequency of errors regardless of size or sign may indicate a more serious problem that requires further investigation and corrective action. Although typically small in size, operational errors can lead to large losses. In December 2005 a trader at the Japanese brokerage firm Mizuho Securities made a typing error and tried to sell 610,000 shares at 1 yen apiece in recruiting company J-Com Co., which was debuting on the exchange, instead of an intended sale of one share at ¥610,000 – an example of fat-finger syndrome. Mizuho lost approximately

---

[2]In truth I did not identify liquidity risk as a separate risk category at the time.

¥41 billion. In April 2007,[3] a programmer at AXA Rosenberg incorrectly programmed a statistical model, leading to $217 million in losses for clients. A Securities and Exchange Commission (SEC) investigation found that senior management learned in June 2009 of a material error, but instead of disclosing and fixing the error a senior official directed others to keep quiet. The error was kept from senior management until November 2009 and from clients until April 2010. According to the SEC, the firm failed to disclose the error and its impact on client performance, attributed the model's underperformance to market volatility and misrepresented the model's ability to control risk. AXA Rosenberg paid an additional $25 million penalty fine.

Liquidity risk is the risk that assets cannot be traded quickly enough in a market to change asset and risk allocations, realise profits or prevent losses. Perhaps liquidity risk has received less attention than it should in the past but it is capable of causing significant damage. The demise of Long Term Capital Management (LCTM)[4] in 1998 was really a liquidity issue compounded by massive leverage. In less than one year LTCM lost $4.4 billion of its $4.7 billion capital. LTCM was a hedge fund based in Greenwich, Connecticut that used absolute return strategies combined with high leverage. LTCM had been making losses throughout the summer of 1998 which were further compounded by the Russian Debt Crisis in August and September causing a flight to quality. This resulted in the bidding up of the price of the most liquid securities in which LTCM was short and depressing the price of less liquid securities of which LTCM was long. As rumours of LTCM's positions spread, market participants positioned themselves for forced liquidation; eventually LTCM was forced to liquidate at exactly the wrong time, increasing its losses.

A more recent, and extremely relevant, example in the context of today's markets is the liquidity crisis at the LF Woodford Equity Income Fund (WEIF).[5] WEIF, an open-ended investment fund, was forced to suspend dealing in June 2019, to avoid a fire sale of unlisted assets, triggered by the attempted withdrawal of £250 million, or 4%, of the fund's assets by Kent County Council. In the preceding weeks, following a period of poor performance, investors had already withdrawn in excess of £500 million, increasing the already high percentage of unlisted, illiquid assets. The fund had previously circumvented a 10% limit on illiquid assets by bundling up the fund's unlisted assets and listing them on the Guernsey-headquartered International Stock Exchange which

---

[3] AXA Rosenberg Settles Coding-Error Case with SEC. *Morningstar Fund Times*, 3 February 2011.

[4] Roger Lowenstein (2000) *When Genius Failed: The Rise and Fall of Long-Term Capital Management*. Random House.

[5] M. Latham (2019) The Neil Woodford Crisis: An Accident Waiting to Happen? *Funds Europe*, July–August.

had barely any trading activity and was unable to provide sufficient liquidity.[6] Extraordinarily, the Governor of the Bank of England said "These funds are built on a lie which is that you can have daily liquidity for assets that are fundamentally not liquid".[7] WEIF might also be described as a compliance risk failure – for a better comprehension of regulatory arbitrage, pushing the envelope and overpowerful portfolio managers, Owen Walker's *Built on a Lie*[8] is a remarkably good read. Understanding liquidity risk in both normal and turbulent markets is a crucial element of effective risk control; the relatively recently identified phenomenon of crowded exits is a characteristic of those turbulent markets.

Counterparty risk occurs when counterparties are unwilling or unable to fulfil their contractual obligations, at its most basic through corporate failure. Counterparty exposure could include profits on an OTC derivatives contract, unsettled transactions, cash management, administrators, custodians, prime brokers and – even with the comfort of appropriate collateral – the failure to return stock that has been used for stock lending. Perhaps the most obvious example of counterparty risk is the failure of Lehman Brothers[9] in September 2008.

In the middle office of asset management firms, we are most concerned with portfolio risk, which I define as the uncertainty of meeting asset owner[10] expectations. Is the portfolio of assets managed in line with the asset owner's investment objectives? The consequences of not meeting asset owner expectations can be quite severe. Early in 2001,[11] the Unilever Superannuation Fund sued Merrill Lynch for damages of £130 million claiming negligence in that Merrill Lynch had not sufficiently considered the risk of underperformance. Ultimately the case was settled out of court for an undisclosed sum, believed to be £70 million, the perception to many being that Unilever won.

Credit risk (or issuer risk) as opposed to counterparty risk is a type of portfolio risk. Credit risk or default risk is the investor's risk of a borrower failing

---

[6]N. Corbishley (2019) Liquidity Crisis at Woodford Equity Fund is Symptomatic of Systemic Problem, Bank of England Warns. *Wolf Street*, 12 July.

[7]J. Booth (2019) Carney Warns that Woodford-style Funds Are "Built on a Lie". *City A.M.*, 26 June.

[8]Owen Walker (2021) *Built on a Lie*. Penguin Random House.

[9]R. Z. Wiggins, T. Piontek and A. Metrick (2014) The Lehman Brothers Bankruptcy. *Yale Program on Financial Stability Case Study* 2014-3A-V1.

[10]Asset owners are investors, typically pension funds, endowments, sovereign wealth funds, boards of investment trusts and high net wealth individuals.

[11]A. F. Perold and R. Alloway (2003) *The Unilever Superannuation Fund vs. Merrill Lynch*. Harvard Business School Publishing.

to meet their financial commitments in full. The higher the risk of default the higher the rate of interest investors will demand to lend their capital. Therefore, the reward or returns in terms of higher yields must offset the increased risk of default. Similarly, market, currency and interest rate risks taken by asset managers in the pursuit of asset owner objectives would constitute portfolio risks in this context.

I'm sure readers can quickly add to this brief list of risks and extend through various subdivisions, but I'm fairly certain any risk I've not mentioned so far can be allocated to one or more of the above categories.

RISK MANAGEMENT VERSUS RISK CONTROL

It is useful to distinguish between the ways portfolio managers[12] and risk professionals see risk. For this purpose, let us refer to portfolio managers as "risk managers" and to risk professionals as "risk controllers". Then there is a clear distinction between risk management and risk control. As risk managers, portfolio managers are paid to take risk, they need to take risk in order to achieve higher returns. For the risk manager "Risk is good".

Risk controllers on the other hand are paid to monitor risk; their role is to measure risk and make transparent to the entire firm how much risk is being taken by the portfolio manager (and often from their perspective to reduce risk). The risk controller's objective is to reduce the probability or eliminate entirely a major loss event on their watch. For the risk controller "Risk is bad".

Risk managers' and risk controllers' objectives are in conflict leading to a natural tension between them. To resolve this conflict, we need measures that assess the quality of return and answer the question, "Are we achieving sufficient return for the risk taken?"

RISK AVERSION

It is helpful to assume that asset owners are risk averse, that is to say, that given portfolios with equal rates of return they will prefer the portfolio with the lowest risk.

Asset owners will only accept additional risk if they are compensated by the prospect of higher returns.

---

[12] In this book the terms portfolio manager and asset manager are to some degree interchangeable. I use the term portfolio manager in the context of individual managers employed by asset managers charged with the management of a portfolio of assets.

EX POST AND EX ANTE

Risk is calculated in two fundamentally different ways: ex post and ex ante. Ex-post or historical risk is the analysis of risk after the event; it answers the question how risky the portfolio has been in the past.

On the other hand, ex-ante risk or prospective risk is forward looking, based on a snapshot of the current securities and instruments within the portfolio and their historical relationship with each other; it is an estimate or forecast of the future risk of the portfolio. Obviously, the use of historical returns and correlations to forecast future risk is problematic, particularly for extreme, low probability events. Increasing the length of the historical track record or increasing the frequency of observations does not always result in an improvement because of the changing nature of markets and underlying securities. Older returns may be less reliable for future predictions, but on the other hand more recent observations may not include the more extreme results.

Ex-post risk calculations and ex-ante risk forecasts are substantially different and therefore can lead to completely different results and conclusions. Differences between ex-post risk calculations and ex-ante risk forecasts provide significant additional information which should be monitored continuously.

DISPERSION

For the most part risk managers and risk controllers use dispersion measures of return as a proxy for their perception of risk.

There are several measures of return dispersion that will be discussed in this book and they all measure some aspect of the range of portfolio returns experienced in a particular time period. They all report on what has *actually happened* during the time period of interest. Even from an ex-post perspective, one can ask whether the return variability truly represents how much risk the asset manager took during the time period or whether one needs to explore the range of possible returns that *might have (realistically) happened* during the time period.

This is an interesting question but one that is outside the scope of this book. Primarily this book is focused on historical portfolio return dispersion.

CHAPTER 2

Descriptive Statistics

"I am always doing that which I cannot do, in order that I might learn how to do it."

Pablo Picasso (1881–1973)

"Do not worry about your difficulties in Mathematics. I can assure you mine are still greater."

Albert Einstein (1879–1955)

Ex-post performance measurement is two dimensional; we are concerned with both the return of the asset manager over a period of time and the risk of that return measured by the variability of return or another dispersion measure. Both the return and the shape of the return distribution are of interest to asset owners. We need descriptive statistics to help understand the underlying distribution of returns. The classic descriptive statistics are the mean, variance, skewness and kurtosis known as the first, second, third and fourth moments of the return distribution. These descriptive statistics are the basic components of many of the ex-post risk measures we shall encounter later in this book.

MEAN (OR ARITHMETIC MEAN)

The mean is the sum of returns divided by the total number of returns:

$$\text{Mean } \bar{r} = \frac{\sum\limits_{i=1}^{i=n} r_i}{n} \tag{2.1}$$

Where:

n = total number of returns, and

r_i = return in period i.

For example, one might calculate the average monthly return over a 2-year period using 24 returns ($n = 24$) where each r_i is the monthly return.

Note this mean (or average) return is calculated arithmetically which should not be confused with the annualised return which is calculated geometrically. The average is a measure of central tendency; the median and the mode are also average measures. The mode is the most frequently occurring return and the median is the middle ranked when returns are ranked in order of size.

The annual arithmetic mean return ($\bar{r}_A$) or annual average return is simply the mean of annual returns over the time period being evaluated.

ANNUALISED RETURN

The annualised return is the annual return which compounded with itself will generate the cumulative return of the portfolio over multiple years.

$$\text{Annualised return} \quad \tilde{r} = \left(\prod (1 + r_i) \right)^{\frac{t}{n}} - 1 \tag{2.2}$$

Where:

t = frequency of underlying data. For monthly $t = 12$ and quarterly $t = 4$ etc.

n = total number of returns

Note the annualised return will always be lower than or equal to the annual arithmetic mean return and better reflects the return achieved by the portfolio manager. Typically, annualised rather than cumulative returns are used to present performance over multiple years.

> ⚠ **Caution**
>
> It is bad performance measurement practice to annualise periods for less than one year since that implies that the rate of return achieved so far in the year will be maintained, which is not a valid assumption.

CONTINUOUSLY COMPOUNDED RETURNS (OR LOG RETURNS)

The returns used in this book are all simple returns as opposed to continuously compounded returns (or log returns). Ideally for all statistical calculations, continuously compounded returns should be used, but in practice, simple returns are more typically used. Hudert, Schmitt and von Thanden[1] (2018/2019) usefully explore the methodical, practical and regulatory issues of using continuously compounded returns in some detail.

Positive simple returns are simply not equivalent in absolute impact to negative simple returns of the same absolute size; for example, if a positive return of 10% is followed by a negative return of 10% the combined return over both periods is $(1.1 \times 0.9) - 1 = -1.0\%$ not 0.0%. In other words, and somewhat counter-intuitively, if a portfolio increases by a given (relative) return and then drops by that same (relative) return, it does *not* return to its starting value. This is because the second "equivalent" return starts from a higher absolute base and therefore does not result in the same absolute change.

On the other hand, positive and negative *continuously* compounded returns *are* equivalent. Simple returns are positively biased. The continuously compounded or log return is derived as follows:

$$r_{\log} = \log(1 + r) \tag{2.3}$$

Simple returns compound through time as follows:

$$r_c = (1 + r_1) \times (1 + r_2) \times (1 + r_3) \ldots \ldots \times (1 + r_n) \tag{2.4}$$

Where:
r_c = cumulative return over the entire n periods

Continuously compounded returns add through time as follows:

$$r_{c \log} = r_{1 \log} + r_{2 \log} + r_{3 \log} \ldots \ldots r_{n \log} \tag{2.5}$$

In practice given other issues such as accuracy of data, annualisation of risk numbers and other assumptions, the decision to use simple rather than continuous returns is perhaps less of an oversight than it first appears. For example,

---

[1] R. Hudert, M. G. Schmitt and M. von Thanden (2018/2019) Portfolio Performance Evaluation: What Difference Do Logarithmic Returns Make?, *Journal of Performance Measurement,* Winter, 8–15.

the simple annualised return is equivalent to the arithmetic mean of continuously compounded returns and the geometric excess return is equivalent to the continuously compounded arithmetic excess return. It is of much greater importance that risk measures are calculated consistently for comparison purposes.

 Note

Many risk management applications prefer continuously compounded returns as a basis for subsequent calculations because that permits end-of-period asset values to be expressed as an exponential function of returns and start-of-period asset values like $V_{end} = V_{start} \times e^{rt}$. The exponential function has several desirable mathematical properties that make it a logical choice for quants.[2]

WINSORISED MEAN

The Winsorised mean (named after Charles P. Winsor) adjusts for extreme returns (or outliers) that might impact the mean calculation. Both the extreme high and low returns are replaced with the next highest and next lowest or a fixed percentage of high and low returns are replaced.

In other industries it may be appropriate to adjust for extreme values, assuming they are measurement errors. However, in finance this is almost never the case; extreme returns are rarely measurement errors and on the contrary are of great interest to potential investors, portfolio managers and risk controllers.

A trimmed[3] or truncated mean is similar to a Winsorised mean except that the extreme returns are simply removed from the calculation rather than replaced.

---

[2] Experts in the use of mathematical models and statistics.
[3] Before its scheduled demise in late 2021, LIBOR – an interest rate benchmark – used a trimmed mean in its calculation. SONIA, its replacement in the UK, will continue to be calculated using a trimmed mean.

Note

Winsorisation, like all forms of
outlier treatment, is a subjective
manipulation of raw data that
should always be disclosed.

MEAN ABSOLUTE DEVIATION (OR MEAN DEVIATION)

The mean of the distribution of returns provides useful information but as
investors we are also interested in the deviation or dispersion of returns from
the mean as shown in Figure 2.1.

If one were to simply sum up all the positive and negative deviations from
the mean, they would cancel each other out. By using the absolute difference
(i.e. ignoring the sign), we are able to calculate the mean or average *absolute*
deviation as follows:

$$\text{Mean absolute deviation } MAD = \frac{\sum_{i=1}^{i=n} |r_i - \bar{r}|}{n} \tag{2.6}$$

The mean absolute deviation is the average *absolute* deviation of returns
from the mean and penalises positive and negative deviations equally.

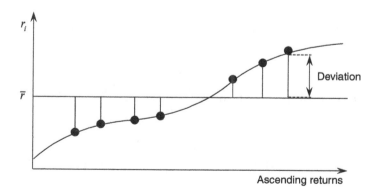

FIGURE 2.1   Deviation from the mean

VARIANCE

The variance of returns is the average *squared* deviation of returns from the mean.

$$\text{Variance } \sigma^2 = \frac{\sum\limits_{i=1}^{i=n} (r_i - \bar{r})^2}{n} \tag{2.7}$$

Squaring the deviations from the mean avoids the problem of negative deviations cancelling with positive deviations and also penalises larger deviations from the mean. It provides a kind of weighted average deviation in which large deviations carry more weight (because the square of the difference is larger). It is a more accepted method for measuring deviation, hence the name "standard deviation", which is the square root of the variance.

Variance is a measure of variability (or dispersion) of returns from the average or mean return. Winsorised and trimmed variances can be calculated in just the same way as Winsorised and trimmed means.

Table 2.1 contains 36 monthly portfolio returns. We will return to this standard portfolio data many times during the course of this book. The mean, annualised return, mean absolute deviation and variance for this portfolio are calculated in Exhibit 2.1.

EXHIBIT 2.1   Portfolio mean and variance

$$\text{Mean } \bar{r} = \frac{\sum\limits_{i=1}^{i=n} r_i}{n} = \frac{39.6\%}{36} = 1.1\%$$

$$\text{Annualised return } \tilde{r} = \left(\frac{145.4}{100.0}\right)^{\frac{12}{36}} - 1 = 13.29\%$$

$$\text{Mean absolute deviation} = \frac{\sum\limits_{i=1}^{i=n} |r_i - \bar{r}|}{n} = \frac{90.8\%}{36} = 2.52\%$$

$$\text{Variance } \sigma^2 = \frac{\sum\limits_{i=1}^{i=n} (r_i - \bar{r})^2}{n} = \frac{396.18}{36} = 11.0\%$$

TABLE 2.1 Portfolio variability

Portfolio Monthly Return (%) r_i	Unit Price	Absolute Deviation $\|r_i - \bar{r}\|$	Deviation Squared $(r_i - \bar{r})^2$
	100.00		
0.3	100.30	0.8	0.64
2.6	102.91	1.5	2.25
1.1	104.04	0.0	0.00
−0.9	103.10	2.0	4.00
1.4	104.55	0.3	0.09
2.4	107.06	1.3	1.69
1.5	108.66	0.4	0.16
6.6	115.83	5.5	30.25
−1.4	114.21	2.5	6.25
3.9	118.67	2.8	7.84
−0.5	118.07	1.6	2.56
8.1	127.64	7.0	49.00
4.0	132.74	2.9	8.41
−3.7	127.83	4.8	23.04
−6.1	120.03	7.2	51.84
1.4	121.71	0.3	0.09
−4.9	115.75	6.0	36.00
−2.1	113.32	3.2	10.24
6.2	120.34	5.1	26.01
5.8	127.32	4.7	22.09
−6.4	119.18	7.5	56.25
1.7	121.20	0.6	0.36
−0.4	120.72	1.5	2.25
−0.2	120.48	1.3	1.69
−2.1	117.95	3.2	10.24
1.1	119.24	0.0	0.00
4.7	124.85	3.6	12.96
2.4	127.84	1.3	1.69
3.3	132.06	2.2	4.84
−0.7	131.14	1.8	3.24
4.7	137.30	3.6	12.96
0.6	138.13	0.5	0.25
1.0	139.51	0.1	0.01
−0.2	139.23	1.3	1.69
3.4	143.96	2.3	5.29
1.0	145.40	0.1	0.01
Total $\sum\limits_{i=1}^{i=n} r_i = 39.6$		**Total** $\sum\limits_{i=1}^{i=n} \|r_i - \bar{r}\| = 90.8$	**Total** $\sum\limits_{i=1}^{i=n} (r_i - \bar{r})^2 = 396.18$

Table 2.2 contains 36 months of benchmark returns associated with the portfolio in Table 2.1. The mean, annualised return, mean absolute deviation and variance for this benchmark are calculated in Exhibit 2.2.

EXHIBIT 2.2   Benchmark mean and variance

$$\text{Mean } \bar{b} = \frac{\sum\limits_{i=1}^{i=n} b_i}{n} = \frac{43.2\%}{36} = 1.2\%$$

$$\text{Annualised return } \tilde{b} = \left(\frac{150.59}{100.0}\right)^{\frac{12}{36}} - 1 = 14.62\%$$

$$\text{Mean absolute deviation} = \frac{\sum\limits_{i=1}^{i=n} |b_i - \bar{b}|}{n} = \frac{92.8\%}{36} = 2.58\%$$

$$\text{Variance } \sigma^2 = \frac{\sum\limits_{i=1}^{i=n} (b_i - \bar{b})^2}{n} = \frac{406.92\%}{36} = 11.3\%$$

TABLE 2.2   Benchmark variability

Benchmark Monthly Return (%) b_i	Benchmark Value	Absolute Deviation $|b_i - \bar{b}|$	Deviation Squared $(b_i - \bar{b})^2$
	100		
0.2	100.20	1.0	1.00
2.5	102.71	1.3	1.69
1.8	104.55	0.6	0.36
−1.1	103.40	2.3	5.29
1.4	104.85	0.2	0.04
2.3	107.26	1.1	1.21
1.4	108.76	0.2	0.04
6.5	115.83	5.3	28.09

(Continued)

TABLE 2.2 (*Continued*)

Benchmark Monthly Return (%) b_i	Benchmark Value	Absolute Deviation $\lvert b_i - \bar{b} \rvert$	Deviation Squared $(b_i - \bar{b})^2$
−1.5	114.10	2.7	7.29
4.2	118.89	3.0	9.00
−0.3	118.53	1.5	2.25
8.3	128.37	7.1	50.41
3.9	133.38	2.7	7.29
−3.8	128.31	5.0	25.00
−6.2	120.35	7.4	54.76
1.5	122.16	0.3	0.09
−4.8	116.29	6.0	36.00
−2.0	113.97	3.2	10.24
6.0	120.81	4.8	23.04
5.6	127.57	4.4	19.36
−6.7	119.03	7.9	62.41
1.9	121.29	0.7	0.49
−0.3	120.92	1.5	2.25
−0.1	120.80	1.3	1.69
−2.6	117.66	3.8	14.44
0.7	118.48	0.5	0.25
4.3	123.58	3.1	9.61
2.9	127.16	1.7	2.89
3.8	132.00	2.6	6.76
−0.2	131.73	1.4	1.96
5.1	138.45	3.9	15.21
1.4	140.39	0.2	0.04
1.3	142.21	0.1	0.01
0.3	142.64	0.9	0.81
3.4	147.49	2.2	4.84
2.1	150.59	0.9	0.81
Total		**Total**	**Total**
$\sum_{i=1}^{i=n} b_i = 43.2$		$\sum_{i=1}^{i=n} \lvert b_i - \bar{b} \rvert = 92.8$	$\sum_{i=1}^{i=n} (b_i - \bar{b})^2 = 406.92$

MEAN DIFFERENCE (ABSOLUTE MEAN DIFFERENCE OR GINI MEAN DIFFERENCE)

Mean difference, defined below, is a measure of variability developed by Corrado Gini[4] in 1912 which is the absolute mean of the difference between each pair of returns rather than the mean of the deviations from the mean. Mean difference is a more appropriate, but rarely used measure for the dispersion of non-normal return distributions. Gini is perhaps better known for the related statistic, the Gini coefficient which measures income disparity.

Gini disliked variance and mean absolute deviation because they were linked to the mean and he argued that these measures were distinct and not linked and therefore proposed pair wise deviations between all returns as a measure of variability.

$$\text{Mean difference } MD = \frac{\sum\limits_{i=1}^{i=n}\sum\limits_{j=1}^{j=n}|r_i - r_j|}{n \times (n-1)} \quad i,j = 1,2\ldots\ldots n, i \neq j \tag{2.8}$$

The denominator in the mean difference is of course the total number of paired returns in the distribution.

RELATIVE MEAN DIFFERENCE

The mean difference is normalised by dividing by the arithmetic mean.[5]

$$\text{Relative mean difference } RMD = \frac{\sum\limits_{i=1}^{i=n}\sum\limits_{j=1}^{j=n}|r_i - r_j|}{n \times (n-1) \times \bar{r}} \quad i,j = 1,2\ldots\ldots n, i \neq j \tag{2.9}$$

BESSEL'S CORRECTION (POPULATION OR SAMPLE, n OR $n-1$)

It might seem obvious that we should use n in the denominator of the calculation of variance, but if we are using sample data to estimate the variance of the population, the sample mean will typically differ from the real mean of the population μ and as a consequence underestimate variance.

---

[4]Variability and mutability (Variabilità e mutabilità).
[5]The Gini coefficient is half the relative mean difference where the variables are cumulative proportions, say income and population. It can range from 0 to 1, with 0 corresponding to complete equality.

For example, using the original data in Table 2.1 we can use the returns of the first, second and third month of each quarter as shown in Table 2.3 to calculate sample means for three groups, each of 12 months of portfolio returns and then calculate variances in Exhibit 2.3 using both the sample mean and the true population mean of the total population of 36 months.

EXHIBIT 2.3   Bessel's correction

FIRST MONTH IN EACH QUARTER

Sample mean $\dfrac{22.9}{12} = 1.91$

Variance using the true mean of the population $\dfrac{74.09}{12} = 6.17$

Variance using the sample mean of the month 1 sample $\dfrac{66.25}{12} = 5.52$

SECOND MONTH IN EACH QUARTER

Sample mean $\dfrac{15.3}{12} = 1.28$

Variance using the true mean of the population $\dfrac{128.91}{12} = 10.74$

Variance using the sample mean of the month 1 sample $\dfrac{128.54}{12} = 10.71$

THIRD MONTH IN EACH QUARTER

Sample mean $\dfrac{1.4}{12} = 0.12$

Variance using the true mean of the population $\dfrac{193.18}{12} = 16.1$

Variance using the sample mean of the month 1 sample $\dfrac{181.58}{12} = 15.13$

For each different sample the variance using the sample mean underestimates the variance calculated using the true mean.

TABLE 2.3 Bessel's correction

Monthly Portfolio Return	Deviation from Population Average	Deviation Squared	Deviation from Sample Average	Deviation Squared
		First Monthly Return in Each Quarter		
0.3	−0.8	0.64	−1.61	2.59
−0.9	−2.0	4.0	−2.81	7.89
1.5	0.4	0.16	−0.41	0.17
3.9	2.8	7.84	1.99	3.97
4.0	2.9	8.41	2.09	4.38
1.4	0.3	0.09	−0.51	0.26
6.2	5.1	26.01	4.29	18.42
1.7	0.6	0.36	−0.21	0.04
−2.1	−3.2	10.24	−4.01	16.07
2.4	1.3	1.69	0.49	0.24
4.7	3.6	12.96	2.79	7.79
−0.2	−1.3	1.69	−2.11	4.45
			Sample Average	
Total = 22.9		**Total = 74.09**	22.9/12 = 1.91	**Total = 66.25**
		Second Monthly Return in Each Quarter		
2.6	1.5	2.25	1.33	1.76
1.4	0.3	0.09	0.13	0.02
6.6	5.5	30.25	5.33	28.36
−0.5	−1.6	2.56	−1.78	3.15
−3.7	−4.8	23.04	−4.98	24.75
−4.9	−6.0	36.00	−6.18	38.13
5.8	4.7	22.09	4.53	20.48
−0.4	−1.5	2.25	−1.68	2.81
1.1	0.0	0.00	−0.18	0.03
3.3	2.2	4.84	2.03	4.10
0.6	−0.5	0.25	−0.68	0.46
3.4	2.3	5.29	2.13	4.52
			Sample Average	
Total = 15.3		**Total = 128.91**	15.3/12 = 1.275	**Total = 128.54**

(Continued)

TABLE 2.3 (*Continued*)

Monthly Portfolio Return	Deviation from Population Average	Deviation Squared	Deviation from Sample Average	Deviation Squared
Third Monthly Return in Each Quarter				
1.1	0.0	0.00	0.98	0.97
2.4	1.3	1.69	2.28	5.21
−1.4	−2.5	6.25	−1.52	2.30
8.1	7.0	49.00	7.98	63.73
−6.1	−7.2	51.84	−6.22	38.65
−2.1	−3.2	10.24	−2.22	4.91
−6.4	−7.5	56.25	−6.52	42.47
−0.2	−1.3	1.69	−0.32	0.10
4.7	3.6	12.96	4.58	21.01
−0.7	−1.8	3.24	−0.82	0.67
1.0	−0.1	0.01	0.88	0.78
1.0	−0.1	0.01	0.88	0.78
Total = 1.4		Total = 193.18	Sample Average 1.4/12 = 0.12	Total = 181.58

Bessel's correction helps correct this underestimation by multiplying by the term $\frac{n}{n-1}$.

For a more detailed discussion on Bessel's correction see So[6] (2008).

It is a moot point whether or not the mean of the full period of 36 months is a sample of the portfolio manager's returns or the true mean of the population being analysed – I incline to the full population. In any event, for large n there is little practical difference and the industry standard is n not $(n-1)$. This is sensible from the performance measurer's ex-post perspective; it is easy to appreciate from the risk controller's more conservative ex-ante perspective that $(n-1)$ might be chosen.

The CFA Institute (previously the Association for Investment Management and Research) effectively reinforced the standard use of n in the 1997,

---

[6]Stephen So (2008) *Why Is the Sample Variance a Biased Estimator?* Signal and Processing Laboratory, Griffith School of Engineering, Griffith University, Brisbane, Queensland, Australia, 11 September.

second edition of the *AIMR Performance Presentation Standards Handbook*, stating:

> *The use of* n *in the denominator of standard deviation (as opposed to* n − 1*) is supported because using n yields the maximum likelihood estimate of standard deviation. The use of* n − 1 *in the denominator of the sample variance makes sample variance, an unbiased estimate of the true variance. When the square root of sample variance is taken to obtain the sample standard deviation, however, the result is not an unbiased estimate of population standard deviation. The seldom used unbiased estimate of standard deviation has a cumbersome constant based on sample size, which needs to be calculated. Because the unbiased estimate of standard deviation is not practical, it is wise to use the maximum likelihood estimate of standard deviation.*
>
> *Further compounding the issue is the fact that the use of* n − 1 *(unbiased) hinges on the assumptions that random and independent samples are taken from a normal distribution. The sample data (in this case, the manager's returns) are not random, arguably not independent, and may not be normally distributed.*

SAMPLE VARIANCE

Multiplying Equation 2.7 by Bessel's correction $\frac{n}{n-1}$ provides the formula for sample variance:

$$\text{Sample variance } \hat{\sigma}^2 = \frac{\sum_{i=1}^{i=n}(r_i - \bar{r})^2}{n-1} \tag{2.10}$$

STANDARD DEVIATION (VARIABILITY OR VOLATILITY)

For the analysis of portfolio variability, it is more convenient to use our original non-squared units of return; therefore, we take the square root of the variance to obtain the standard deviation:

$$\text{Standard deviation } \sigma = \sqrt{\frac{\sum_{i=1}^{i=n}(r_i - \bar{r})^2}{n}} \tag{2.11}$$

The term "standard deviation" was first coined by the statistician Karl Pearson in 1894.[7] It is perhaps convenient to interpret standard deviation as a standardised measure of variance or even just a standard measure. A higher standard deviation would indicate greater uncertainty, variability or risk. Mean absolute deviation and standard deviation are related measures of variability. The standard deviation of portfolio returns is frequently (but less accurately) described as volatility; variability is a more appropriate term. Sample standard deviation is simply:

$$\text{Sample standard deviation } \hat{\sigma} = \sqrt{\frac{\sum\limits_{i=1}^{i=n} (r_i - \bar{r})^2}{n-1}} \qquad (2.12)$$

❓ Interpretation

Many risk practitioners warn about interpreting a portfolio's standard deviation (also known as volatility) as a proper measure of "risk". Their reasoning is as follows: a portfolio's volatility is a measure of the portfolio's *usual* deviation from its average return and is therefore not a measure of how bad a performance can be generated by the portfolio. Most investors are concerned about large losses, not the usual deviation from the average return.

📄 Note

The annualised return and the arithmetic average annual return are linked by the formula:

$$\bar{r} \cong \bar{r}_A - \frac{\sigma^2}{2}$$

The annualised return is always less than the annual arithmetic average; the greater the variability of the returns the greater the difference.

---

[7]K. Pearson (1894) On the Dissection of Asymmetrical Frequency-curves. *Philosophical Transactions of the Royal Society of London* 185, 71–110.

ANNUALISED RISK (OR TIME AGGREGATION)

Equations 2.11 and 2.12 calculate standard deviation based on the periodicity of the data used, daily, monthly, quarterly and so on. For comparison of portfolio returns standard deviation or variability is normally annualised for presentation purposes.

To annualise standard deviation we need to multiply by the square root of the number of observations in the year.

$$\text{Annualised standard deviation } \tilde{\sigma} = \sqrt{t} \times \sigma \qquad (2.13)$$

Where:

t = number of observations in year, quarterly = 4, monthly = 12, weekly = 52 etc.

For example, to annualise a monthly standard deviation, regardless of the number of monthly observations, multiply by $\sqrt{12}$; for quarterly standard deviation multiply by $\sqrt{4}$ or 2.

 Note

Because of weekends and public holidays, to annualise a daily standard deviation, a range of 250 to 260 (52 × 5 weekdays) observations in the year is typically used. The number itself is less important, rather that the number chosen should be used consistently for comparison.

This calculation requires the assumption that each periodic return is independent and hence not correlated with other returns. Making this assumption the variance over one year is simply:

$$\sigma^2_{12 \text{ months}} = \sigma^2_{\text{Month } 1} + \sigma^2_{\text{Month } 2} + \cdots \cdots + \sigma^2_{\text{Month } 12} \qquad (2.14)$$

If we now assume that the variance of each month is the same then the variance over the year is simply 12 times the variance over one month.

$$\sigma^2_{12 \text{ months}} = 12 \times \sigma^2 \qquad (2.15)$$

Taking the square root leads to Equation 2.16 which ultimately leads to Equation 2.13:

$$\sigma_{12 \text{ months}} = \sqrt{12} \times \sigma \qquad (2.16)$$

 Note

The typical annualised standard deviation of worldwide equities is about 16%, corresponding to a typical daily standard deviation of about 1% $\sqrt{252} \times 1.0\% \approx 16\%$ as there are about 252 trading days per calendar year. This means that a 1% daily move in equities is normal: equities generate daily returns of ±1% about two-thirds (68%) of the time.

THE CENTRAL LIMIT THEOREM

To annualise risk we must, in part, rely on the Central Limit Theorem, which states that if a number of observations of an independent random variable are taken:

i) The mean of the resulting sample mean is equal to the mean of the underlying population.
ii) The standard deviation of the resulting sample mean is the standard deviation of the underlying population divided by the square root of the number of observations.
iii) Even if the underlying distribution is strongly non-normal the sampling distribution of means will increasingly approximate to a normal distribution as the sample size increases.

FREQUENCY AND NUMBER OF DATA POINTS

If variability is stable then clearly the more observations, the higher number of data points the better, to maximise the accuracy of the estimation process. If variability is not stable then we must find a balance between long measurement periods that are more accurate but slow to reflect structural changes and short recent measurement periods that reflect recent market conditions but are less accurate.

⚠ Caution

The industry standard requires a minimum of 36 monthly periods and 20 quarterly periods. If absolutely pushed I would provide risk statistics calculated using 24 months of monthly data but never less; the resulting information is less meaningful and potentially misleading.

Daily information is too noisy for long-term investment portfolios and should be ignored for standard risk measures (but not extreme risk measures, see Chapter 8) although very tempting for short time periods for which there are an insufficient number of observations. On the other hand, the standard for ex-ante value at risk (VaR) calculations is to use a 100-day (5-month) or 252-day (1-year) window of daily returns. Far better to refuse to calculate risk measures, for which there are insufficient data points, than to provide misleading information.

⚠ Caution

Although it is easy to calculate annualised standard deviations, it is never appropriate to compare portfolios with risk statistics calculated using different frequencies. For daily valued mutual funds, you may wish to calculate the daily, weekly, monthly and quarterly annualised standard deviations say over 5 years and note the range of annualised standard deviations that result from the same data.

Using the data from Table 2.1 and Table 2.2 the standard deviation, sample standard deviation and annualised standard deviation are calculated in Exhibit 2.4 for both the portfolio and benchmark respectively.

EXHIBIT 2.4 Standard deviation

$$\text{Portfolio standard deviation } \sigma = \sqrt{\frac{\sum\limits_{i=1}^{i=n}(r_i - \bar{r})^2}{n}} = \sqrt{\frac{396.18\%}{36}} = 3.32\%$$

$$\text{Sample standard deviation } \hat{\sigma} = \sqrt{\frac{\sum\limits_{i=1}^{i=n}(r_i - \bar{r})^2}{n-1}} = \sqrt{\frac{396.18\%}{35}} = 3.36\%$$

$$\text{Annualised standard deviation } \tilde{\sigma} = \sqrt{t} \times \sigma = \sqrt{12} \times 3.32\% = 11.49\%$$

$$\text{Benchmark standard deviation } \sigma_b = \sqrt{\frac{\sum\limits_{i=1}^{i=n}(b_i - \bar{b})^2}{n}} = \sqrt{\frac{406.92\%}{36}} = 3.36\%$$

$$\text{Sample standard deviation } \hat{\sigma}_b = \sqrt{\frac{\sum\limits_{i=1}^{i=n}(b_i - \bar{b})^2}{n-1}} = \sqrt{\frac{406.92\%}{35}} = 3.41\%$$

$$\text{Annualised standard deviation } \tilde{\sigma}_b = \sqrt{t} \times \sigma_b = \sqrt{12} \times 3.36\% = 11.65\%$$

ALTERNATIVE RISK ANNUALISATION METHODS

Although applied universally, Janssen[8] points out that the traditional method used to annualise standard deviation (even if returns are independent) is a crude approximation of annualised risk and takes no account of compounding. Janssen suggests a more precise formula for the annualisation of standard deviation:

$$\tilde{\sigma}' = (1 + \bar{r}) \times \sqrt{t} \times \sigma$$

$$\text{Recall } \bar{r} = \text{annualised return} \tag{2.17}$$

---

[8] Dr Bart Janssen, *Annualizing Standard Deviations* (undated).

Kaplen[9] (2012/2013) and Weber[10] (2017) both make the same point as Jannsen and offer an alternative method to annualise standard deviation:

$$\tilde{\sigma}'' = \sqrt{(\sigma^2 + (1 + \bar{r})^2)^t - (1 + \bar{r})^{2t}} \qquad (2.18)$$

Notwithstanding the greater precision of the above formulae the more important requirement is that risk is annualised consistently for comparison purposes. This type of annualisation is far from industry standard and is perhaps an overcomplication. Alternative annualised standard deviations are calculated in Exhibit 2.5.

EXHIBIT 2.5 Alternative annualised standard deviation

Janssen annualisation

$$\tilde{\sigma}' = (1 + \bar{r}) \times \sqrt{t} \times \sigma = (1 + 13.29\%) \times \sqrt{12} \times 3.32\% = 13.02\%$$

Kaplan annualisation:

$$\tilde{\sigma}'' = \sqrt{(\sigma^2 + (1 + \bar{r})^2)^t - (1 + \bar{r})^{2t}}$$

$$= \sqrt{(3.32\%^2 + (1 + 1.1\%)^2)^{12} - (1 + 1.1\%)^{24}} = 13.00\%$$

NORMAL (OR GAUSSIAN) DISTRIBUTION

A distribution is said to be normal if there is a high probability that an observation will be close to the average and a low probability that an observation is far away from the average tailing away symmetrically. A normal distribution curve peaks at the average value. Returns are equally likely to lie above or below the mean. Normal distributions, sometimes called the "Bell Curve",

[9]Paul Kaplan (2012/2013) What Is Wrong with Multiplying by the Square Root of Twelve? *Journal of Performance Measurement,* Winter, 16–24.
[10]A. Weber (2017) Annual Risk Measures and Related Statistics. *Journal of Performance Measurement,* Spring, 50–64.

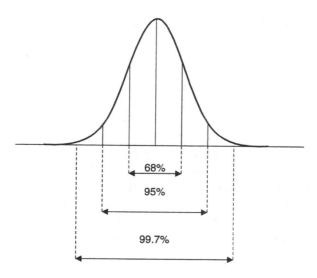

FIGURE 2.2   Normal distribution

are more formally known as Gaussian distributions, named after the German mathematician Carl Friedrich Gauss.

A normal distribution (see Figure 2.2) has special properties that are useful to asset management. If returns are normally distributed, then we can use the average return and variability or standard deviation of returns to describe the distribution of returns, such that:

Approximately 68% of returns will be within a range of one standard deviation above and below the average return.

Approximately 95% of returns will be within a range of 2 standard deviations above and below the average return.

Approximately 99.7% of returns will be within a range of 3 standard deviations above and below the average return.[11]

This property is obviously very useful for calculating the probability of an event occurring outside a specified range of returns. Normal distributions

---

[11]The "Empirical or 68-95-99.7" Rule; actually, more accurately 68.2689%, 95.4499% and 99.7300%.

are popular because of these statistical properties and because many random events can be approximated by a normal distribution.

⚠️ **Caution**

Although it's tempting to use a mathematical function like the normal curve because it has convenient properties, care must be taken to ensure that it properly models the data. Equity returns are often shown to follow the normal curve within about 2 standard deviations but outside this range show a higher frequency of extreme returns than the normal curve implies. Equities exhibit so-called "fat tails" precisely for this reason: their return distributions have more weight (i.e. are fatter) for large returns. This means that large losses (and gains) occur more frequently that the normal curve implies.

HISTOGRAMS

Histograms were first introduced by Pearson[12] to provide a graphical representation of the distribution of data and are ideal for illustrating the distribution of returns of an asset manager's track record. A histogram of the example data from the portfolio in Table 2.1 is shown in Figure 2.3. The horizontal axis is split into consecutive intervals of return, or bins, and the vertical axis represents the frequency in which periodic returns fall within the bin. A normal distribution curve is imposed on the histogram to show that in this particular case the distribution of returns is quite normal. The term histogram is derived from the Greek *histos*, anything set upright such as the vertical bars on a graph and *gramma*, drawing.

SKEWNESS (FISHER'S OR MOMENT SKEWNESS)

Not all distributions are normally distributed; if there are more extreme returns extending to the right tail of a distribution it is said to be positively skewed

---

[12]K. Pearson (1895) Contributions to the Mathematical Theory of Evolution. II. Skew Variation in Homogeneous Material. *Philosophical Transactions of the Royal Society of London* 186, 343–424.

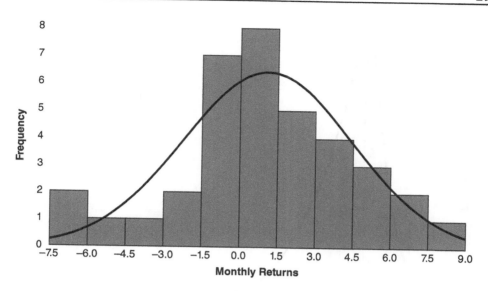

FIGURE 2.3   Histogram of portfolio returns

and if there are more returns extending to the left it is said to be negatively skewed.

We can measure the degree of skewness (or more accurately Fisher's skewness) in the following formula:

$$\text{Skewness } \varsigma = \sum_{i=1}^{i=n} \left(\frac{r_i - \bar{r}}{\sigma} \right)^3 \times \frac{1}{n} \tag{2.19}$$

A normal distribution will have a skewness of 0. Note in Equation 2.19 that extreme values carry greater weight as they are cubed whilst maintaining their initial sign positive or negative. Note also that the difference from the mean return is standardised by dividing by the standard deviation of returns. Skewness is a measure of asymmetry of the return distribution.

Positive and negative skew are illustrated in Figures 2.4 and 2.5 respectively.

We can use skewness in making a judgement about the possibility of large negative or positive outliers when comparing portfolio returns. Skewness provides more information about the shape of return distribution, where deviations from the mean are greater in one direction than the other; this measure will deviate from zero in the direction of the larger deviations.

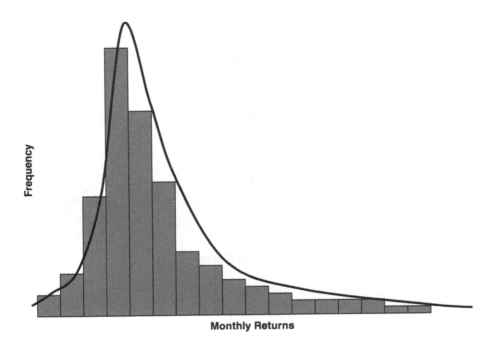

FIGURE 2.4   Positive skew

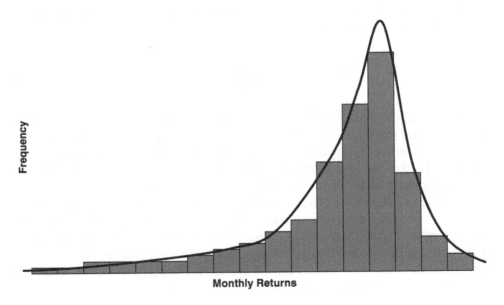

FIGURE 2.5   Negative skew

SAMPLE SKEWNESS

Sample skewness is calculated using Bessel's correction as follows:

$$\text{Sample skewness } \hat{\varsigma} = \sum_{i=1}^{i=n} \left(\frac{r_i - \bar{r}}{\hat{\sigma}} \right)^3 \times \frac{n}{(n-1) \times (n-2)} \qquad (2.20)$$

 Note

The standard Excel® function called skewness is in fact sample skewness.

KURTOSIS (PEARSON'S KURTOSIS)

Kurtosis[13] (or more correctly Pearson's kurtosis) provides additional information about the shape of a return distribution; formally, it measures the weight of returns in the tails of the distribution relative to standard deviation but is more often associated as a measure of flatness or peakedness of the return distribution. Actually, DeCarlo[14] correctly points out that both tailedness and peakedness are components of kurtosis.

$$\text{Kurtosis} \quad \kappa = \sum_{i=1}^{i=n} \left(\frac{r_i - \bar{r}}{\sigma} \right)^4 \times \frac{1}{n} \qquad (2.21)$$

Note in Equation 2.21 extreme results of either sign make very large positive contributions to kurtosis. Just like the formula for skewness the difference from the mean is again standardised by dividing by the standard deviation of returns.

The kurtosis of a normal distribution is 3 (called *mesokurtic*); greater than 3 may indicate a peaked distribution with fat tails (called *leptokurtic*) and less

[13] K. Pearson (1905) Das Fehlergesetz und seine Verallgemeinerungen durch Fechner und Pearson: A Rejoinder. *Biometrika* 4, 169–212.

[14] L. T. DeCarlo (1997) On the Meaning and Use of Kurtosis. *Psychological Methods* 2(3), 292–307.

than 3 may indicate a less peaked distribution with thin tails (called *platykurtic*). The word kurtosis is derived from the Greek word for bulge, *kurtos*. *Platy* comes from the Greek word *platus* for broad or flat. *Leptos* is Greek for thin or slender describing the shape of the peak not the tails. For symmetric distributions with skewness close to zero, kurtosis greater than 3 could indicate an excess of returns either in the tails, or the centre, or both.

 Note

Generally speaking, investors prefer platykurtic distributions with a kurtosis less than 3, less peaked but with fewer extreme returns.

A leptokurtic distribution is shown in Figure 2.6 and a platykurtic distribution in Figure 2.7.

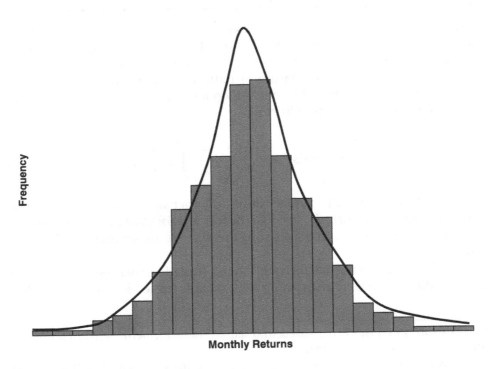

FIGURE 2.6   Kurtosis >3, thin peak with fat tails

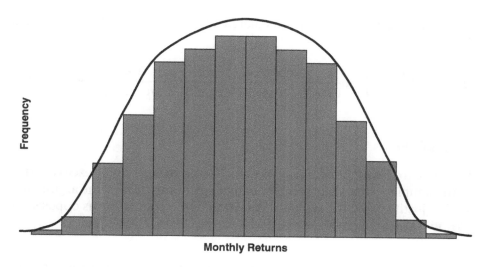

FIGURE 2.7   Kurtosis <3, broad peak with thin tails

EXCESS KURTOSIS (OR FISHER'S KURTOSIS)

Subtracting 3 from Equation 2.21 we obtain a measure of excess kurtosis (or Fisher's kurtosis). The terms kurtosis and excess kurtosis are often confused.

$$\text{Excess kurtosis } \kappa_E = \sum_{i=1}^{i=n} \left(\frac{r_i - \bar{r}}{\sigma} \right)^4 \times \frac{1}{n} - 3 \qquad (2.22)$$

> ⚠ **Caution**
>
> Care needs to be taken whenever calculating kurtosis to ensure that it's clear whether the calculation is excess kurtosis (subtracting 3) or not.

SAMPLE KURTOSIS

Sample kurtosis is calculated using Bessel's correction as follows:

$$\text{Sample kurtosis } \hat{\kappa} = \sum_{i=1}^{i=n} \left(\frac{r_i - \bar{r}}{\hat{\sigma}} \right)^4 \times \frac{n \times (n+1)}{(n-1) \times (n-2) \times (n-3)} \qquad (2.23)$$

Sample excess kurtosis is calculated also using Bessel's correction as follows:

$$\hat{\kappa}_E = \sum_{i=1}^{i=n} \left(\frac{r_i - \bar{r}}{\hat{\sigma}}\right)^4 \times \frac{n \times (n+1)}{(n-1) \times (n-2) \times (n-3)} - \frac{3 \times (n-1)^2}{(n-2) \times (n-3)} \quad (2.24)$$

⚠ Caution

The standard Excel® function labelled kurtosis is in fact sample excess kurtosis (or sample Fisher's kurtosis if I am more generous). The same arguments used to justify using the standard deviation of the population as opposed to a sample also apply to skewness and kurtosis.

A better understanding of the shape of the distribution of returns will aid in assessing the relative qualities of asset manager return distributions. Whether we prefer higher or lower kurtosis (or for that matter positive or negative skewness) will depend on the type of return series we want to see.

Equity markets tend to have fat tails; when markets fall asset managers tend to sell and when markets rise asset managers tend to buy, and there is a higher probability of extreme events than the normal distribution would suggest. Therefore, any risk measure calculated using normal assumptions may well underestimate risk, especially outside the 2-standard deviation bands.

🗊 Note

Investors will naturally prefer positive skew and lower kurtosis with thinner tails.

BERA–JARQUE STATISTIC (OR JARQUE–BERA)

Since normal distributions should have skewness near 0 and kurtosis near 3, we can test for normality using the Bera–Jarque[15] test.

$$\text{Bera–Jarque statistic } BJ = \frac{n}{6} \times \left(\varsigma^2 + \frac{\kappa_E^2}{4}\right) \quad (2.25)$$

---

[15]C. M. Jarque and A. K. Bera (1987) A Test for Normality of Observations and Regression Residuals. *International Statistics Review* 55, 163–177.

With a confidence level of 95% we will reject the hypothesis that a distribution is normal if the Bera–Jarque statistic exceeds 5.99, and with a confidence level of 99% if it exceeds 9.21.

> **Note**
>
> Perfectly normal distributions will have a $BJ = 0$

Portfolio skewness, kurtosis and the Bera–Jarque statistic of the portfolio data first shown in Table 2.1 are calculated in Exhibit 2.6 from summarised data contained in Table 2.4.

Skewness and kurtosis for the benchmark data in Table 2.2 are calculated in Exhibit 2.7 from the summarised data in Table 2.5.

COVARIANCE

Covariance is a descriptive statistic that measures the tendency of two return streams to move together relative to their averages – for example, this could be the covariance between two portfolios, two indices or, most commonly, between a portfolio and its benchmark.

$$\text{Covariance} = \frac{\sum_{i=1}^{i=n} (r_i - \bar{r}) \times (b_i - \bar{b})}{n} \tag{2.26}$$

Where:

b_i = benchmark return in period i

$\bar{b}$ = mean benchmark return

Equation 2.26 multiplies the period portfolio return difference from the mean portfolio return with the same period benchmark return difference from the mean benchmark return. If both are positive or negative this will make a positive contribution to covariance, if they are of different signs, it will make a negative contribution to covariance.

Therefore, a total positive covariance indicates the returns are associated, they move together. A total negative covariance indicates the returns move in opposite directions. A low or near zero covariance would indicate little relationship between portfolio and benchmark returns.

EXHIBIT 2.6   Skewness, kurtosis and the Bera–Jarque hypothesis test

$$\text{Skewness } \varsigma = \sum_{i=1}^{i=n} \left(\frac{r_i - \bar{r}}{\sigma} \right)^3 \times \frac{1}{n} = \frac{-312.79}{3.32^3} \times \frac{1}{36} = -0.24$$

$$\text{Kurtosis } \kappa = \sum_{i=1}^{i=n} \left(\frac{r_i - \bar{r}}{\sigma} \right)^4 \times \frac{1}{n} = \frac{12982.39}{3.32^4} \times \frac{1}{36} = 2.98$$

Excess kurtosis $\kappa_E = \kappa - 3 = 2.98 - 3 = -0.02$

$$\text{Bera–Jarque statistic} = \frac{n}{6} \times \left(\varsigma^2 + \frac{\kappa_E^2}{4} \right) = \frac{36}{6} \times \left(-0.24^2 + \frac{-0.02^2}{4} \right) = 0.34$$

It would appear this return distribution is close to normal.

Sample skewness

$$\hat{\varsigma} = \sum_{i=1}^{i=n} \left(\frac{r_i - \vec{r}}{\hat{\sigma}} \right)^3 \times \frac{n}{(n-1) \times (n-2)}$$

$$= \frac{-312.79}{3.36^3} \times \frac{36}{(36-1) \times (36-2)} = -0.25$$

Sample kurtosis

$$\hat{\kappa} = \sum_{i=1}^{i=n} \left(\frac{r_i - \bar{r}}{\hat{\sigma}} \right)^4 \times \frac{n \times (n+1)}{(n-1) \times (n-2) \times (n-3)}$$

$$= \frac{12982.39}{3.36^4} \times \frac{36 \times (36+1)}{(36-1) \times (36-2) \times (36-3)} = 3.44$$

Sample excess kurtosis

$$\hat{\kappa}_E = \hat{\kappa} - \frac{3 \times (n-1)^2}{(n-2) \times (n-3)} = 3.44 - \frac{3 \times (36-1)^2}{(36-2) \times (36-3)} = 0.16$$

TABLE 2.4 Portfolio skewness and kurtosis

Monthly Return (%) r_i	Deviation Cubed $(r_i - \bar{r})^3$	4th Power Deviation $(r_i - \bar{r})^4$
0.3	-0.51	0.41
2.6	3.38	5.06
1.1	0.00	0.00
−0.9	−8.00	16.00
1.4	0.03	0.01
2.4	2.20	2.86
1.5	0.06	0.03
6.6	166.38	915.06
−1.4	−15.63	39.06
3.9	21.95	61.47
−0.5	−4.10	6.55
8.1	343.00	2401.00
4.0	24.39	70.73
−3.7	−110.59	530.84
−6.1	−373.25	2687.39
1.4	0.03	0.01
−4.9	−216.00	1296.00
−2.1	−32.77	104.86
6.2	132.65	676.52
5.8	103.82	487.97
−6.4	−421.88	3164.06
1.7	0.22	0.13
−0.4	−3.38	5.06
−0.2	−2.20	2.86
−2.1	−32.77	104.86
1.1	0.00	0.00
4.7	46.66	167.96
2.4	2.20	2.86
3.3	10.65	23.43
−0.7	−5.83	10.50
4.7	46.66	167.96
0.6	−0.13	0.06
1.0	0.00	0.00
−0.2	−2.20	2.86
3.4	12.17	27.98
1.0	0.00	0.00
	Total	**Total**
	$\sum_{i=1}^{i=n} (r_i - \bar{r})^3 = -312.79$	$\sum_{i=1}^{i=n} (r_i - \bar{r})^4 = 12982.39$

EXHIBIT 2.7   Benchmark skewness and kurtosis

$$\text{Skewness } \varsigma_b = \sum_{i=1}^{i=n} \left(\frac{b_i - \overline{b}}{\sigma_b} \right)^3 \times \frac{1}{n} = \frac{-495.94}{3.36^3} \times \frac{1}{36} = -0.36$$

$$\text{Kurtosis } \kappa_b = \sum_{i=1}^{i=n} \left(\frac{b_i - \overline{b}}{\sigma_b} \right)^4 \times \frac{1}{n} = \frac{14004.25}{3.36^4} \times \frac{1}{36} = 3.04$$

Excess kurtosis $\kappa_{Eb} = \kappa_b - 3 = 3.04 - 3 = 0.04$

Sample skewness

$$\hat{\varsigma} = i = \sum_{i=1}^{i=n} \left(\frac{b_i - \overline{b}}{\hat{\sigma}_b} \right)^3 \times \frac{n}{(n-1) \times (n-2)}$$

$$= \frac{-495.94}{3.41^3} \times \frac{36}{(36-1) \times (36-2)} = -0.38$$

Sample kurtosis

$$\hat{\kappa} = \sum_{i=1}^{i=n} \left(\frac{b_i - \overline{b}}{\hat{\sigma}_b} \right)^4 \times \frac{n \times (n+1)}{(n-1) \times (n-2) \times (n-3)}$$

$$= \frac{14004.25}{3.41^4} \times \frac{36 \times (36+1)}{(36-1) \times (36-2) \times (36-3)} = 3.51$$

Sample excess kurtosis

$$\hat{\kappa}_E = \hat{\kappa} - \frac{3 \times (n-1)^2}{(n-2) \times (n-3)} = 3.51 - \frac{3 \times (36-1)^2}{(36-2) \times (36-3)} = 0.24$$

TABLE 2.5 Benchmark skewness and kurtosis

Monthly Return (%) b_i	Deviation Cubed $(b_i - \bar{b})^3$	4th Power Deviation $(b_i - \bar{b})^4$
0.2	−1.00	1.00
2.5	2.20	2.86
1.8	0.22	0.13
−1.1	−12.17	27.98
1.4	0.01	0.00
2.3	1.33	1.46
1.4	0.01	0.00
6.5	148.88	789.05
−1.5	−19.68	53.14
4.2	27.00	81.00
−0.3	−3.38	5.06
8.3	357.91	2541.17
3.9	19.68	53.14
−3.8	−125.00	625.00
−6.2	−405.22	2998.66
1.5	0.03	0.01
−4.8	−216.00	1296.00
−2.0	−32.77	104.86
6.0	110.59	530.84
5.6	85.18	374.81
−6.7	−493.04	3895.01
1.9	0.34	0.24
−0.3	−3.38	5.06
−0.1	−2.20	2.86
−2.6	−54.87	208.51
0.7	−0.13	0.06
4.3	29.79	92.35
2.9	4.91	8.35
3.8	17.58	45.70
−0.2	−2.74	3.84
5.1	59.32	231.34
1.4	0.01	0.00
1.3	0.00	0.00
0.3	−0.73	0.66
3.4	10.65	23.43
2.1	0.73	0.66
Total		
	$\sum_{i=1}^{i=n} (b_i - \bar{b})^3 = -495.94$	$\sum_{i=1}^{i=n} (b_i - \bar{b})^4 = 14004.25$

SAMPLE COVARIANCE

Sample covariance is calculated using Bessel's correction as follows:

$$\text{Sample covariance} = \frac{\sum_{i=1}^{i=n}(r_i - \bar{r}) \times (b_i - \bar{b})}{n-1} \qquad (2.27)$$

CORRELATION (ρ)

In isolation, covariance is a difficult statistic to interpret because it measures the "co-dispersion" relative to both the portfolio and its benchmark, which can be of unknown size. For example, is a covariance of 3 large or small? The answer depends on the standard deviations of both the portfolio and the benchmark.

We can standardise the covariance to a value between 1 and –1 by dividing by the product of the portfolio standard deviation and the benchmark standard deviation as follows:

$$\text{Correlation } \rho_{r,b} = \frac{\text{Covariance}}{\sigma \times \sigma_b} \qquad (2.28)$$

Where $\rho_{r,b}$ is the coefficient of correlation between the portfolio return and benchmark return. The closer the correlation is to one the stronger the linear relationship.

This standardisation has the very helpful feature that it allows us to compare the correlations between disparate portfolios and benchmarks on an apples-to-apples basis.

⚠ Caution

Interpreting correlation can sometimes be tricky. If a portfolio and its benchmark have a high correlation (for example, above 0.9) then it can be tempting to believe that the portfolio will move up (or down) as much as the benchmark. In such a case, if the benchmark moves up 1% it is NOT correct to expect the portfolio to move up by 1%.

The correlation measures the tendency of the portfolio to move up or down *relative to its own average and volatility* but not as an absolute measure. In the example above, if the portfolio has a very small standard deviation, the expectation should be for it to move up just a little when the benchmark moves up by 1%.

SAMPLE CORRELATION

Bessel's correction applies equally to covariance and the product of the portfolio and benchmark standard deviations and therefore the correction in the numerator cancels with the correction in the denominator, eliminating the need to calculate sample correlation.

Covariance and correlation are calculated in Exhibit 2.8 from the standard portfolio data shown in Table 2.6.

EXHIBIT 2.8 Covariance and correlation

$$\text{Covariance} = \frac{\sum_{i=1}^{i=n}(r_i - \bar{r}) \times (b_i - \bar{b})}{n} = \frac{399.37}{36} = 11.09$$

$$\text{Correlation } \rho_{r,b} = \frac{\text{Covariance}}{\sigma \times \sigma_b} = \frac{11.09}{3.32 \times 3.36} = 0.995$$

AUTOCOVARIANCE

Autocovariance is the covariance of a lagged return with itself. A step in the calculation of autocorrelation, it is useful in determining if there is a pattern in the return series; in other words, if there is a close linear relationship.

$$\text{Autocovariance} = \frac{\sum_{i=1}^{i=n}(r_i - \bar{r}) \times (r_{i+1} - \bar{r})}{n} \qquad (2.29)$$

AUTOCORRELATION (OR SERIAL CORRELATION)

Autocorrelation or serial correlation is the correlation of a lagged return with itself:

$$\text{Autocorrelation } \rho_{r,r+1} = \frac{\text{Autocovariance}}{\sigma^2_r} \qquad (2.30)$$

If returns are positively autocorrelated they exhibit mean aversion, if negatively autocorrelated they exhibit mean reversion. Zero autocorrelation means

TABLE 2.6   Covariance and correlation

Portfolio Monthly Return (%) r_i	Deviation from Average $(r_i - \bar{r})$	Benchmark Monthly Return b_i	Deviation from Average $(b_i - \bar{b})$	Portfolio Deviation × Benchmark Deviation $(r_i - \bar{r}) \times (b_i - \bar{b})$
0.3	−0.8	0.2	−1.0	0.80
2.6	1.5	2.5	1.3	1.95
1.1	0.0	1.8	0.6	0.00
−0.9	−2.0	−1.1	−2.3	4.60
1.4	0.3	1.4	0.2	0.06
2.4	1.3	2.3	1.1	1.43
1.5	0.4	1.4	0.2	0.08
6.6	5.5	6.5	5.3	29.15
−1.4	−2.5	−1.5	−2.7	6.75
3.9	2.8	4.2	3.0	8.40
−0.5	−1.6	−0.3	−1.5	2.40
8.1	7.0	8.3	7.1	49.70
4.0	2.9	3.9	2.7	7.83
−3.7	−4.8	−3.8	−5.0	24.00
−6.1	−7.2	−6.2	−7.4	53.28
1.4	0.3	1.5	0.3	0.09
−4.9	−6.0	−4.8	−6.0	36.00
−2.1	−3.2	−2.0	−3.2	10.24
6.2	5.1	6.0	4.8	24.48
5.8	4.7	5.6	4.4	20.68
−6.4	−7.5	−6.7	−7.9	59.25
1.7	0.6	1.9	0.7	0.42
−0.4	−1.5	−0.3	−1.5	2.25
−0.2	−1.3	−0.1	−1.3	1.69
−2.1	−3.2	−2.6	−3.8	12.16
1.1	0.0	0.7	−0.5	0.00
4.7	3.6	4.3	3.1	11.16
2.4	1.3	2.9	1.7	2.21
3.3	2.2	3.8	2.6	5.72
−0.7	−1.8	−0.2	−1.4	2.52
4.7	3.6	5.1	3.9	14.04
0.6	−0.5	1.4	0.2	−0.10
1.0	−0.1	1.3	0.1	−0.01
−0.2	−1.3	0.3	−0.9	1.17
3.4	2.3	3.4	2.2	5.06
1.0	−0.1	2.1	0.9	−0.09
				Total

$$\sum_{i=1}^{i=n}(r_i - \bar{r}) \times (b_i - \bar{b}) = 399.37$$

there is no close linear relationship but it does not necessarily mean independence.

The standard deviation and the mean of the time series r to $n - 1$ and $r + 1$ to n is very slightly different but can be ignored for the purpose of this calculation.

> ⚠ **Caution**
>
> For a strongly mean reverting or mean averting return series it may be appropriate to adjust the resulting variability calculations.

Autocovariance and autocorrelation are calculated in Exhibit 2.9 from the standard portfolio data shown in Table 2.7.

EXHIBIT 2.9 Autocovariance and autocorrelation

$$\text{Autocovariance} = \frac{\sum\limits_{i=1}^{i=n}(r_i - \bar{r}) \times (r_{i+1} - \bar{r})}{n} = \frac{-13.57}{11.32} = -0.39$$

$$\text{Autocorrelation } \rho_{r,r+1} = \frac{\text{Autocovariance}}{\sigma_r^2} = \frac{-0.39}{11.32} = -0.034$$

ANNUALISED VARIABILITY IF RETURNS ARE AUTOCORRELATED

1. Lo[16] (2002) demonstrates how to annualise risk if returns are not independent and identically distributed by introducing the following scaling factor:

$$\eta(t) = \sqrt{1 + \frac{2 \times \rho_{r,r+1}}{1 - \rho_{r,r+1}} \times \left(1 - \frac{1 - \rho_{r,r+1}^t}{t \times (1 - \rho_{r,r+1})}\right)} \qquad (2.31)$$

---

[16]A. W. Lo (2002) The Statistics of Sharpe Ratios, *Financial Analysts Journal* 58(4), 36–52.

TABLE 2.7 Autocovariance and autocorrelation

Portfolio Monthly Return r_i	Deviation from Average $(r_i - \bar{r})$	Following Month Portfolio Return r_{i+1}	Deviation from Average $(r_{i+1} - \bar{r})$	Portfolio Deviation × Following Month Deviation $(r_i - \bar{r}) \times (r_{i+1} - \bar{r})$
0.3	−0.8	2.6	1.5	−1.19
2.6	1.5	1.1	0.0	−0.03
1.1	0.0	−0.9	−2.0	0.01
−0.9	−2.0	1.4	0.3	−0.56
1.4	0.3	2.4	1.3	0.38
2.4	1.3	1.5	0.4	0.49
1.5	0.4	6.6	5.5	2.18
6.6	5.5	−1.4	−2.5	−13.87
−1.4	−2.5	3.9	2.8	−6.95
3.9	2.8	−0.5	−1.6	−4.54
−0.5	−1.6	8.1	7.0	−11.18
8.1	7.0	4.0	2.9	20.13
4.0	2.9	−3.7	−4.8	−13.97
−3.7	−4.8	−6.1	−7.2	34.69
−6.1	−7.2	1.4	0.3	−2.00
1.4	0.3	−4.9	−6.0	−1.79
−4.9	−6.0	−2.1	−3.2	19.35
−2.1	−3.2	6.2	5.1	−16.26
6.2	5.1	5.8	4.7	23.84
5.8	4.7	−6.4	−7.5	−35.34
−6.4	−7.5	1.7	0.6	−4.33
1.7	0.6	−0.4	−1.5	−0.91
−0.4	−1.5	−0.2	−1.3	1.99
−0.2	−1.3	−2.1	−3.2	4.20
−2.1	−3.2	1.1	0.0	0.07
1.1	0.0	4.7	3.6	−0.01
4.7	3.6	2.4	1.3	4.59
2.4	1.3	3.3	2.2	2.82
3.3	2.2	−0.7	−1.8	−4.01
−0.7	−1.8	4.7	3.6	−6.45
4.7	3.6	0.6	−0.5	−1.88
0.6	−0.5	1	−0.1	0.06
1.0	−0.1	−0.2	−1.3	0.14
−0.2	−1.3	3.4	2.3	−2.97
3.4	2.3	1.0	−0.1	−0.28

Total

$$\sum_{i=1}^{i=n} (r_i - \bar{r}) \times (r_{i+1} - \bar{r}) = -13.57$$

Where:

$\eta(t)$ = factor used to scale risk

$\rho_{r,r+1}$ = autocorrelation coefficient

If autocorrelation is 0, note that this factor reduces to 1; if positive it generates a factor greater than 1 and if negative it generates a factor less than 1. Adjusted annualised standard deviation is now:

$$\sigma^{\tilde{}\prime\prime\prime} = \eta(t) \times \tilde{\sigma} \qquad (2.32)$$

Clearly, if returns are positively autocorrelated (mean averting) this adjustment will increase the calculated annualised variability and if returns are negatively autocorrelated (mean reverting) this adjustment will reduce the calculated annualised variability. Persistent returns may understate risk.

Lo suggests a number of causes of positive autocorrelation, in particular smoothing, which naturally occurs in illiquid assets such as real estate, private equity or infrastructure.

⚠ Caution

The ability to adjust annualised variability for smoothing might suggest it is appropriate to compare risk statistics of illiquid and liquid assets after appropriate adjustment. I take the view that it is never appropriate to compare risk statistics of liquid and illiquid assets; the hidden variability of the natural smoothing of illiquid assets is the main reason but there are others including:

- the quality and independence of valuations
- investment style, investment objective and time horizon
- control of external cash flow and
- return methodology.

Most analysts simply assume that returns are independent and autocorrelation is zero. The underlying assumption that forms the basis of much of modern portfolio theory is that security returns are "independently and identically distributed" – the so-called "i.i.d. assumption".

⚠ **Caution**

The assumption that stock returns, in particular, are independent of one another, is contradicted by a significant phenomenon in the investment industry: the concept of momentum – that winning stocks tend to keep winning. Momentum[17] would not be possible if returns were truly independent of one another. However, the i.i.d. assumption is still made in practice because it is required for much of the mathematics that is regularly used.

Adjusted annualised standard deviation for the standard portfolio data is calculated in Exhibit 2.10.

EXHIBIT 2.10   Annualised variability adjusted for autocorrelation

$$\eta(12) = \sqrt{1 + \frac{2 \times \rho}{1 - \rho} \times \left(1 - \frac{1 - \rho^{12}}{12 \times (1 - \rho)}\right)}$$

$$= \sqrt{1 + \frac{2 \times -0.035}{1 + 0.035} \times \left(\frac{1 - -0.035^{12}}{12 \times (1 + 0.035)}\right)} = 0.9693$$

Adjusted annualised standard deviation

$$\tilde{\sigma}''' = \eta(12) \times \tilde{\sigma} = 0.9693 \times 11.49\% = 11.14\%$$

Note in this case the returns are very mildly mean reverting therefore reducing the calculation of annualised variability marginally.

---

[17]Whether, or not, momentum actually exists is beyond the scope of this book; despite numerous studies it is not entirely clear why momentum exists.

CHAPTER 3

Performance Appraisal Measures

"Take calculated risks. That is quite different from being rash."

–George S Patton (1885–1945)

"Mathematics, rightly viewed, possesses not only truth, but supreme beauty – a beauty cold and austere, like that of sculpture."

–Bertrand Russell (1872–1970)

PERFORMANCE APPRAISAL

Asset owners are risk averse; given the same return they would prefer the portfolio with less risk or less variability of return. Therefore, how do we evaluate portfolios with different returns and different levels of risks? We need composite risk measures that determine if the risk undertaken by the asset manager has been justified by the reward received.

A reviewer of the first edition of this book made a very strong case for naming this chapter "Performance Appraisal Measures" rather than "Simple Risk Measures". I didn't take his advice in the first edition; belatedly in this edition I will. In many ways, performance appraisal is a better term than risk measure; we are doing exactly that – appraising the performance of the asset manager by combining a measure of risk with a measure of reward ex post. The dispersion, variability and tendency measures in Chapter 2 are truly risk measures. Many of the measures that follow in subsequent chapters are not particularly complex and many could also be described as simple.

Attempting to interpret a portfolio's performance without taking into account its risk is a misguided venture. Is an annualised performance of 8% a good return? One way to compare that number is relative to what other portfolios returned. Another, potentially more nuanced way, is to compare it to its own risk: a portfolio that delivers an 8% return while taking only 4% risk is clearly superior to a portfolio that delivers the same 8% return while taking 16% risk.

One way of thinking about the relationship between return and risk is that risk is one of the *costs* of investing. It is a *potential* cost that may (or may not) be realised and therefore should be interpreted probabilistically. Not taking it into account is a dangerous game.

SHARPE RATIO (REWARD TO VARIABILITY, SHARPE INDEX)

With two variables it is natural to resort to a graphical representation with return represented by the vertical axis and risk represented by the horizontal axis as shown in Figure 3.1 using data from Table 3.1.

A straight line is drawn from a fixed point on the vertical axis to points A and B representing the annualised returns and annualised variability (risk) of portfolios A and B respectively.

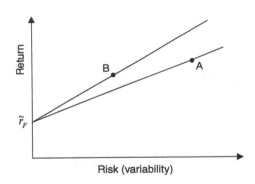

FIGURE 3.1   Sharpe ratio

TABLE 3.1   Sharpe ratio

	Portfolio A	**Portfolio B**	**Benchmark**
Annualised return	7.9%	6.9%	7.5%
Annualised risk	5.5%	3.2%	4.5%
Sharpe ratio (Risk-free rate = 2%) $SR = \dfrac{\tilde{r} - \tilde{r}_F}{\tilde{\sigma}}$	$\dfrac{7.9\% - 2.0\%}{5.5\%} = 1.07$	$\dfrac{6.9\% - 2.0\%}{3.2\%} = 1.53$	$\dfrac{7.5\% - 2.0\%}{4.5\%} = 1.22$

This fixed point represents the natural starting point for all investors; the risk-free rate. The risk-free rate represents the return we should expect on a riskless asset; for example, the interest return on cash or treasury bills. An investor can achieve this return without any variability or risk.

> ⚠ **Caution**
>
> It is important to ensure that the same risk-free rate is used for all portfolios for comparison purposes.

Clearly the investor will prefer to be in the top left-hand quadrant of this graph representing high return and low risk. The gradient of the line determines how far toward the top left-hand quadrant each portfolio is positioned. The steeper the gradient, the further to the top left-hand side.

This gradient is called the Sharpe ratio named after William Sharpe[1] (1966) and calculated as follows:

$$SR = \frac{\tilde{r} - \tilde{r}_F}{\tilde{\sigma}} \tag{3.1}$$

Where:

$\tilde{r}$ = annualised portfolio return

$\tilde{r}_F$ = annualised risk-free rate

$\tilde{\sigma}$ = annualised portfolio risk (variability, standard deviation of return)

The greater the Sharpe ratio, the steeper the gradient and hence a better combination of risk and return. The Sharpe ratio can be described as the return (or reward) per unit of variability (or risk).

Both graphically in Figure 3.1 and in the Sharpe ratios calculated in Table 3.1 we can see that portfolio B has a better risk-*adjusted* performance than either portfolio A or the benchmark even though portfolio B has a lower absolute return than both portfolio A and the benchmark.

> ❓ **Interpretation**
>
> Negative returns will generate negative Sharpe ratios, which despite the views of some commentators still retain meaning. Perversely for negative returns it is better to be more variable not least because the chance of returning into positive territory is higher than when variability is low!

---

[1]W. F. Sharpe (1966) Mutual Fund Performance. *Journal of Business* 39, 119–138.

Although the concept of the Sharpe ratio is based on CAPM and the assumption that excess returns from risky assets cannot be negative (otherwise investors can simply invest in a risk-free asset), comparing two portfolios that both have a negative Sharpe ratio may still be meaningful in a way that a portfolio with a "less negative" Sharpe ratio has generated a smaller loss per unit of risk incurred. Akeda[2] (2003) concludes that the Sharpe ratio can be used as an indicator of performance evaluation, irrespective of its sign. For those who think higher variability is always less desirable, negative Sharpe ratios are difficult statistics to interpret. Some commentators[3] have suggested squaring the Sharpe ratio (or squaring the numerator of the Sharpe ratio) to eliminate negative ratios. Apart from not recognising the need to adjust for negative Sharpe ratios in the first place, I can see no merit in squaring the Sharpe ratio and therefore it is not listed in this book.

Annualised portfolio and risk-free returns are used in the numerator rather than the arithmetic means, primarily because as performance measurers we are more concerned with annualised returns and in any event the mean of continuously compounded returns are equivalent to the annualised simple returns.

> ### ❓ Interpretation
>
> Sharpe ratios, like returns, are best used for comparison against the Sharpe ratios of benchmarks or other portfolios rather than analysed in isolation.

ROY RATIO

The Sharpe ratio is regarded, quite correctly, as the grandfather of all risk-adjusted performance measures, despite the fact that the Treynor ratio (see Equation 4.34 in Chapter 4) predates the Sharpe by one year, and that Arthur Roy[4] suggested a similar measure as early as 1952:

$$\text{Roy ratio } RR = \frac{\bar{r} - \bar{r}_T}{\bar{\sigma}} \tag{3.2}$$

---

[2]Y. Akeda (2003) Interpretation of Negative Sharpe Ratio. *Journal of Performance Measurement*, Spring, 19–23.

[3]See K. Dowd (2000) Adjusting for Risk: An Improved Sharpe Ratio. International Review of Economics and Finance 9(3), 209–222; and D. Kidd (2011) *The Sharpe Ratio and the Information Ratio*. CFA Institute.

[4]A. D. Roy (1952) Safety First and the Holding of Assets. *Econometrica*, July, 431–450.

Where:

$\tilde{r}_T$ = annualised minimum target return or "Disaster Level"

Minimum target return is discussed in more detail in Chapter 6.

RISK-FREE RATE

The risk-free rate of return is defined as the rate of return an investor can expect from a theoretically risk-free investment. Of course, no investments are genuinely risk free and even cash returns will display some variability. Investors' perceptions of the risk-free rate of return will differ, ranging from short-term rates of interest, long-term interest rates or even real risk-free rates adjusted for inflation. In the context of the reward-to-risk ratios covered in this chapter, the actual choice of risk-free rate is not as crucial as might be imagined. Consider a magnet attached to the risk-free rate that allows movement up and down the vertical axis – although the calculated ratio may differ with different risk-free rates, the ranking of portfolios is not significantly impacted.

> **Caution**
>
> When comparing the Sharpe ratios of portfolios, it is important to ensure risk-free rates are consistent.

Risk-free rates will vary depending on investor preferences, typically across currencies, and as we have observed in recent years may even be negative.

> **Caution**
>
> Negative interest rates still represent the natural starting point for investors – do not be tempted to replace negative rates with zero.

ALTERNATIVE SHARPE RATIO

In the alternative Sharpe ratio the variability of the risk-free rate is explicitly considered.

$$\text{Alternative Sharpe ratio } r = \frac{\tilde{r} - \tilde{r}_T}{\tilde{\sigma} - \tilde{\sigma}_F} \qquad (3.3)$$

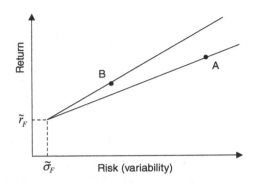

FIGURE 3.2   Alternative Sharpe ratio

Where:

$\tilde{\sigma}_F$ = the annualised variability of the risk-free rate.

Even after allowing the risk-free rate anchor point to move away from the vertical axis to the right as shown in Figure 3.2, the natural starting point of investors will still inhabit a region close to the vertical access with low risk and relatively low return (if the risk-free rate of return is too high investors will not be incentivised to take any risk). The gradients of the Sharpe ratio (or alternative Sharpe ratio) lines will vary without a significant impact on rankings.

Although acknowledging that there is some variability in the risk-free rate, this version of the Sharpe ratio is rarely, if ever, used.

REVISED SHARPE RATIO

Sharpe revised his ratio in 1994,[5] acknowledging that the risk-free rate is not constant and varies over time as follows:

$$\text{Revised Sharpe ratio} = \frac{\tilde{r} - \tilde{r}_F}{\tilde{\sigma}(r_i - r_{Fi})} \tag{3.4}$$

The denominator of the revised Sharpe ratio is the variability of return above the risk-free rate, which of course will not be significantly different from the variability of the portfolio return if the variability of the risk-free rate is low.

---

[5]W. F. Sharpe (1994) The Sharpe Ratio. *Journal of Portfolio Management*, Fall, 49–58.

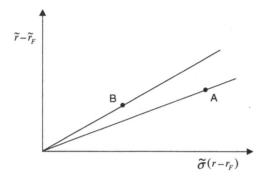

FIGURE 3.3   Revised Sharpe ratio

Although technically more appropriate than the original version of the Sharpe ratio, this revised Sharpe ratio is not often used because the original is so ingrained and universal. The revised Sharpe ratio is shown in Figure 3.3; note the revised Sharpe ratio lines are now anchored through the origin because the *x*-axis has effectively been redefined to ensure zero offset.

ADJUSTED SHARPE RATIO

Pezier and White[6] (2006) suggest using the adjusted Sharpe ratio (ASR) which explicitly adjusts for skewness and kurtosis by incorporating a penalty factor for negative skewness and excess kurtosis as follows:

$$\text{Adjusted Sharpe ratio } ASR = SR \times \left[1 + \left(\frac{S}{6}\right) \times SR - \left(\frac{\kappa - 3}{24}\right) \times SR^2\right] \quad (3.5)$$

❓ Interpretation

The adjusted Sharpe ratio rewards positive skew and kurtosis less than 3 and penalises negative skew and kurtosis greater than 3.

---

[6]J. Pezier and A. White (2006) The Relative Merits of Investable Hedge Fund Indices and of Funds of Hedge Funds in Optimal Passive Portfolios. *ICMA Centre Discussion Papers in Finance*, icma-dp2006-10, Henley Business School, Reading University.

Note

Any time variability, variance or
standard deviation are used in a
formula, there is an implicit
assumption that returns are
normally distributed, which we
empirically know is not a
particularly good assumption. For
this reason, any analytic that
adjusts for skewness and kurtosis
will be an improvement on that
analytic.

 Interpretation

Although rarely used, the adjusted Sharpe ratio addresses the issue that
portfolio returns are not normally distributed and it is fairly easy to calculate. In my view it should be used more often – it is demonstrably better than
the Sharpe ratio.

SKEW-ADJUSTED SHARPE RATIO

A slightly easier calculation would adjust for skewness only in the skew-
adjusted Sharpe ratio ignoring kurtosis which, frankly, in most cases makes
very little difference anyway:

$$\text{Skew-adjusted Sharpe ratio SASR} = \text{SR} \times \left[1 + \left(\frac{\varsigma}{6}\right) \times SR\right] \qquad (3.6)$$

The Sharpe ratio, alternative Sharpe ratio, adjusted Sharpe ratio and
skew-adjusted Sharpe ratio for the standard portfolio data shown in Tables 2.1
and 2.4 together with the monthly risk-free rates in Table 3.2 are calculated in
Exhibit 3.1. Revised Sharpe ratios are calculated in Exhibit 3.2 using data from
Table 3.3.

TABLE 3.2 Risk free rate variability

Portfolio Monthly Return (%) r_i	Monthly Risk-Free Rate (%) r_{Fi}	Absolute Deviation $\lvert r_{Fi} - \bar{r}_F \rvert$	Deviation Squared $(r_{Fi} - \bar{r}_F)^2$
0.3	0.1	0.10	0.01
2.6	0.1	0.10	0.01
1.1	0.2	0.00	0.00
−0.9	0.2	0.00	0.00
1.4	0.2	0.00	0.00
2.4	0.2	0.00	0.00
1.5	0.2	0.00	0.00
6.6	0.3	0.10	0.01
−1.4	0.3	0.10	0.01
3.9	0.4	0.20	0.04
−0.5	0.4	0.20	0.04
8.1	0.3	0.10	0.01
4.0	0.3	0.10	0.01
−3.7	0.3	0.10	0.01
−6.1	0.3	0.10	0.01
1.4	0.4	0.20	0.04
−4.9	0.2	0.00	0.00
−2.1	0.2	0.00	0.00
6.2	0.2	0.00	0.00
5.8	0.1	0.10	0.01
−6.4	0.1	0.10	0.01
1.7	0.1	0.10	0.01
−0.4	0.1	0.10	0.01
−0.2	0.1	0.10	0.01
−2.1	0.1	0.10	0.01
1.1	0.1	0.10	0.01
4.7	0.1	0.10	0.01
2.4	0.1	0.10	0.01
3.3	0.1	0.10	0.01
−0.7	0.2	0.00	0.00
4.7	0.2	0.00	0.00
0.6	0.2	0.00	0.00
1.0	0.2	0.00	0.00
−0.2	0.2	0.00	0.00
3.4	0.2	0.00	0.00
1.0	0.2	0.00	0.00
Total $\sum\limits_{i=1}^{i=n} r_i = 39.6$	**Total** $\sum\limits_{i=1}^{i=n} r_{Fi} = 7.2$	**Total** $\sum\limits_{i=1}^{i=n} \lvert r_{Fi} - \bar{r}_F \rvert = 2.4$	**Total** $\sum\limits_{i=1}^{i=n} (r_{Fi} - \bar{r}_F)^2 = 0.3$

$$\bar{r}_F = \frac{7.2\%}{36} = 0.2$$

$$\tilde{r}_F = 2.43$$

EXHIBIT 3.1 Sharpe, alternative, skew-adjusted and adjusted Sharpe ratios

$$\text{Sharpe ratio} = \frac{\bar{r} - \bar{r}_F}{\tilde{\sigma}} = \frac{13.29\% - 2.43\%}{11.49\%} = 0.94$$

Note the annualised risk-free rate is 2.43%.

$$\text{Alternative Sharpe ratio} = \frac{\bar{r} - \bar{r}_F}{\tilde{\sigma} - \tilde{\sigma}_F} = \frac{13.29\% - 2.43\%}{11.49\% - 0.23\%} = 0.97$$

Skew-adjusted Sharpe ratio:

$$SASR = SR \times \left[1 + \left(\frac{\varsigma}{6}\right) \times SR\right] = 0.94 \times \left[1 + \frac{-0.24}{6} \times 0.94\right] = 0.91$$

Adjusted Sharpe ratio:

$$ASR = SR \times \left[1 + \left(\frac{\varsigma}{6}\right) \times SR - \left(\frac{\kappa - 3}{24}\right) \times SR^2\right]$$

$$= 0.94 \times \left[1 + \frac{-0.24}{6} \times 0.94 - \left(\frac{2.98 - 3}{24}\right) \times 0.94^2\right] = 0.91$$

In this example the adjusted Sharpe ratio is less good, primarily because of the negative skewness of the return distribution. There is a tiny benefit from kurtosis just less than 3. The adjustment is small because the return distribution is close to normal with a slight negative skew.

EXHIBIT 3.2 Revised Sharpe ratio

Standard deviation of excess return above risk free rate

$$\sigma(r_i - r_{Fi}) = \sqrt{\frac{\sum\limits_{i=1}^{i=n} ((r_i - r_{Fi}) - (\bar{r} - \bar{r}_F))^2}{n}} = \sqrt{\frac{395.62\%}{36}} = 3.315\%$$

$$\tilde{\sigma}(r_i - r_{Fi}) = 3.315\% \times \sqrt{12} = 11.48\%$$

$$\text{Revised Sharpe ratio} = \frac{\bar{r} - \bar{r}_F}{\tilde{\sigma}(r_i - r_{Fi})} = \frac{13.29\% - 2.43\%}{11.48\%} = 0.95$$

In this example the difference between the Sharpe ratio and the revised Sharpe ratio is so small because of the stability of the risk-free rate.

TABLE 3.3 Variability of portfolio excess return above risk free rate

Portfolio Monthly Return (%) r_i	Monthly Risk-Free Rate (%) r_{Fi}	Excess Return (%) (Risk-Free Rate) $(r_i - r_{Fi})$	Deviation $(r_i - r_{Fi}) - (\bar{r} - \bar{r}_F)$	Deviation Squared $[(r_i - r_{Fi}) - (\bar{r} - \bar{r}_F)]^2$
0.3	0.1	0.2	−0.7	0.49
2.6	0.1	2.5	1.6	2.56
1.1	0.2	0.9	0.0	0.00
−0.9	0.2	−1.1	−2.0	4.00
1.4	0.2	1.2	0.3	0.09
2.4	0.2	2.2	1.3	1.69
1.5	0.2	1.3	0.4	0.16
6.6	0.3	6.3	5.4	29.16
−1.4	0.3	−1.7	−2.6	6.76
3.9	0.4	3.5	2.6	6.76
−0.5	0.4	−0.9	−1.8	3.24
8.1	0.3	7.8	6.9	47.61
4.0	0.3	3.7	2.8	7.84
−3.7	0.3	−4.0	−4.9	24.01
−6.1	0.3	−6.4	−7.3	53.29
1.4	0.4	1.0	0.1	0.01
−4.9	0.2	−5.1	−6.0	36.00
−2.1	0.2	−2.3	−3.2	10.24
6.2	0.2	6.0	5.1	26.01
5.8	0.1	5.7	4.8	23.04
−6.4	0.1	−6.5	−7.4	54.76
1.7	0.1	1.6	0.7	0.49
−0.4	0.1	−0.5	−1.4	1.96
−0.2	0.1	−0.3	−1.2	1.44
−2.1	0.1	−2.2	−3.1	9.61
1.1	0.1	1.0	0.1	0.01
4.7	0.1	4.6	3.7	13.69
2.4	0.1	2.3	1.4	1.96
3.3	0.1	3.2	2.3	5.29
−0.7	0.2	−0.9	−1.8	3.24
4.7	0.2	4.5	3.6	12.96
0.6	0.2	0.4	−0.5	0.25
1.0	0.2	0.8	−0.1	0.01
−0.2	0.2	−0.4	−1.3	1.69
3.4	0.2	3.2	2.3	5.29
1.0	0.2	0.8	−0.1	0.01
Total $\sum_{i=1}^{i=n} r_i = 39.6$	**Total** $\sum_{i=1}^{i=n} r_{Fi} = 7.2$			**Total = 395.62**

$$\bar{r} - \bar{r}_F = \frac{39.6\% - 7.2\%}{36} = 0.9$$

> **Interpretation**
>
> The adjusted Sharpe ratio emphasises that the first moment of the return distribution is the most important, followed by the second moment, then the third moment, with the fourth moment having the least impact.

SKEWNESS–KURTOSIS RATIO

Watanabe[7] (2006) also explicitly adjusts for skewness and kurtosis by suggesting using the skewness–kurtosis ratio in conjunction with the Sharpe ratio, ranking portfolios using the sum of the two rather than the Sharpe ratio in isolation. Again, higher rather than lower ratios are preferred.

$$\text{Skewness–kurtosis ratio} = \frac{\varsigma}{\kappa} \tag{3.7}$$

> **Note**
>
> Although also adjusting for skewness and kurtosis, for me, the adjusted Sharpe ratio is by far the superior to the skewness–kurtosis ratio.

ALTERNATIVE ADJUSTED SHARPE RATIOS

Less useful adjusted Sharpe ratios are also suggested by Watanabe[8] (2014) and are included for completeness.

For positive skewness ($\varsigma \geq 0$):

$$\text{Alternative skew-adjusted Sharpe ratio} = \frac{\bar{r} - \bar{r}_F}{\sqrt{\bar{\sigma}^2 + \left(\frac{1}{1+\varsigma}\right)^2}} \tag{3.8}$$

---

[7]Y. Watanabe (2006) Is Sharpe Ratio Still Effective? *Journal of Performance Measurement,* Fall, 55–66.

[8]Y. Watanabe (2014) New Prospect Ratio: Application to Hedge Funds with Higher Order Moments. *Journal of Performance Measurement,* Fall, 41–53.

For negative skewness ($\varsigma < 0$):

$$\text{Alternative skew-adjusted Sharpe ratio} = \frac{\tilde{r} - \tilde{r}_F}{\sqrt{\tilde{\sigma}^2 + (\varsigma - 1)^2}} \qquad (3.9)$$

And including kurtosis for positive skewness ($\varsigma \geq 0$):

$$\text{Alternative adjusted Sharpe ratio} = \frac{\tilde{r} - \tilde{r}_F}{\sqrt{\tilde{\sigma}^2 + \left(\dfrac{1}{1+\varsigma}\right)^2 + \kappa^2}} \qquad (3.10)$$

Including kurtosis for negative skewness ($\varsigma < 0$):

$$\text{Alternative adjusted Sharpe ratio} = \frac{\tilde{r} - \tilde{r}_F}{\sqrt{\tilde{\sigma}^2 + (\varsigma - 1)^2 + \kappa^2}} \qquad (3.11)$$

> **Note**
>
> These ratios clearly also reward positive skew, penalise negative skew and reward lower kurtosis and may meet investor expectations but in my view for ease of calculation and effectiveness I prefer the adjusted Sharpe ratio suggested by Pezier and White.

SMOOTHING-ADJUSTED SHARPE RATIO

Lo[9] (2002) suggests a smoothing-adjusted (or perhaps more appropriately named autocorrelation-adjusted) Sharpe ratio exchanging annualised standard deviation in the denominator of the Sharpe ratio with (smoothing) adjusted annualised standard deviation:

$$\text{Smoothing-adjusted Sharpe ratio } SASR = \frac{\tilde{r} - \tilde{r}_F}{\tilde{\sigma}''} \qquad (3.12)$$

---

[9]A.W. Lo (2002) The Statistics of Sharpe Ratios. *Financial Analysts Journal* 58(4), 36–52.

EXHIBIT 3.3 Smoothing-adjusted Sharpe ratio

$$\text{Smoothing-adjusted Sharpe ratio} = \frac{\tilde{r} - \tilde{r}_F}{\tilde{\sigma}''} = \frac{13.29\% - 2.43\%}{11.14\%} = 0.97$$

Where:

$\tilde{\sigma}''$ = adjusted annualised standard deviation (or smoothing-adjusted annualised standard deviation)

The smoothing-adjusted Sharpe ratio is calculated in Exhibit 3.3 using the adjusted annualised standard deviation from Exhibit 2.9.

MAD RATIO

The MAD ratio suggested by Konno and Yamazaki[10] in 1991 is similar to the Sharpe ratio but uses mean absolute deviation in the denominator (or the horizontal axis in the graph) rather than standard deviation. This ratio is less sensitive to extreme returns than the Sharpe ratio.

$$\text{MAD ratio} = \frac{\tilde{r} - \tilde{r}_F}{\text{MAD}} \tag{3.13}$$

GINI RATIO

The Gini ratio suggested by Yitzhaki[11] in 1982 is again similar to the Sharpe ratio but uses mean difference in the denominator rather than standard deviation. This ratio is more appropriate for non-normal distributions.

$$\text{Gini ratio} = \frac{\tilde{r} - \tilde{r}_F}{\text{MD}} \tag{3.14}$$

The MAD and Gini ratios are largely unknown and therefore hardly used at all.

---

[10]H. Konno and H. Yamazaki (1991) Mean–Absolute Deviation Portfolio Optimization Model and its Application to Tokyo Stock Market. *Management Science* 37(5), 519–531.
[11]S. Yitzhaki (1982) Stochastic Dominance, Mean Variance and Gini's Mean Difference. *American Economic Review* 72(1), 178–185.

RELATIVE RISK

The appraisal measures we have discussed so far are examples of absolute rather than relative risk measures; that is to say, the returns and risks of the portfolio and benchmark are calculated separately and then used for comparison.

Relative risk measures, on the other hand, focus on the excess return of the portfolio against the benchmark. The variability of excess return calculated using standard deviation is called tracking error, tracking risk, relative risk or active risk.[12]

Tracking error is by far the most common of these terms used in the traditional asset management industry but it's probably not the best. The term is also used by the exchange traded funds (ETF)[13] industry in particular and passive asset managers in general, but it means something slightly different. In the context of ETFs, the tracking error is the difference in the ETF's return from the index the fund is intending to "track". Any difference is of course an error, so in this context the language "tracking error" make sense. In the context of the volatility of excess return the language is less convincing.

❓ Interpretation

I prefer the term relative risk, which is appropriately descriptive, but I will continue to use the term *tracking error* in this book because it is so familiar.

⚠ Caution

Of course, in isolation, low tracking error is not necessarily a good thing; it is a measure of consistency and might imply consistent under-performance.

TRACKING ERROR (OR TRACKING RISK, RELATIVE RISK, ACTIVE RISK)

Tracking error is often forecast and since the calculation methods and meaning are quite different it is essential to clearly label if you are using an ex-post or ex-ante tracking error.

---

[12]At this point I should perhaps introduce "Bacon's Law": the more alternative names for a risk statistic or appraisal measure the more useful it is.

[13]An ETF is an investment fund traded on stock exchanges. Most ETFs are designed to "track" a specific index.

$$\text{Tracking error } \sigma_A = \sqrt{\frac{\sum\limits_{i=1}^{i=n} (a_i - \overline{a})^2}{n}} \tag{3.15}$$

Where:

σ_A = ex-post tracking error of arithmetic excess return
a_i = arithmetic excess return in month i, $(r_i - b_i)$
$\overline{a}$ = mean arithmetic excess return

Or if you prefer geometric excess returns:

$$\text{Tracking error } \sigma_G = \sqrt{\frac{\sum\limits_{i=1}^{i=n} (g_i - \overline{g})^2}{n}} \tag{3.16}$$

Where:

σ_G = ex-post tracking of geometric excess return
g_i = geometric excess return in month i, $\left(\dfrac{1 + r_i}{1 + b_i}\right) - 1$
$\overline{g}$ = mean of geometric excess returns

For an analysis of the differences between arithmetic and geometric excess return and an explanation of why geometric excess returns are preferred see Bacon[14] (2008).

The arithmetic subtraction of continuously compounded or log returns is equivalent to the geometric excess of simple returns. Therefore, the geometric excess return is equivalent to the continuously compounded arithmetic difference and is thus more appropriate for use in a statistical context.

RELATIVE SKEWNESS

Relative skewness is simply the skewness of excess return.

For arithmetic excess returns:

$$\text{Relative skewness (arithmetic) } \varsigma_A = \sum\limits_{i=1}^{i=n} \left(\frac{a_i - \overline{a}}{\sigma_A}\right)^3 \times \frac{1}{n} \tag{3.17}$$

---

[14]C. R. Bacon (2008) *Practical Portfolio Performance Measurement and Attribution*, 2nd edn. John Wiley & Sons, 51–55.

Or again if you prefer geometric excess returns:

$$\text{Relative skewness (geometric)} \quad \varsigma_G = \sum_{i=1}^{i=n}\left(\frac{g_i - \bar{g}}{\sigma_G}\right)^3 \times \frac{1}{n} \qquad (3.18)$$

RELATIVE KURTOSIS

Relative kurtosis is simply the kurtosis of excess return.
For arithmetic excess returns:

$$\text{Relative kurtosis (arithmetic)} \quad \kappa_A = \sum_{i=1}^{i=n}\left(\frac{a_i - \bar{a}}{\sigma_A}\right)^4 \times \frac{1}{n} \qquad (3.19)$$

Or again if you prefer geometric excess returns:

$$\text{Relative kurtosis (geometric)} \quad \kappa_G = \sum_{i=1}^{i=n}\left(\frac{g_i - \bar{g}}{\sigma_G}\right)^4 \times \frac{1}{n} \qquad (3.20)$$

INFORMATION RATIO

In exactly the same way we compared absolute return and absolute risk in the Sharpe ratio you can compare excess return and tracking error (the standard deviation of excess return) graphically: see Figure 3.4.

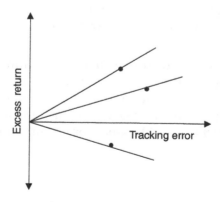

FIGURE 3.4 Information ratio

The information ratio is similar to the Sharpe ratio except that instead of absolute return on the vertical axis we have excess return, and instead of absolute risk on the horizontal axis we have tracking error or relative risk, the standard deviation of excess return.

We have no need for a risk-free rate since we are dealing with excess returns; the natural starting point is the benchmark. The information ratio lines, therefore, must always originate from the origin. The gradient of the line is simply the ratio of excess return and tracking error as follows:

$$\text{Information ratio} \, \text{IR}_A = \frac{\tilde{a}}{\tilde{\sigma}_A} = \frac{\text{Annualised Excess Return}}{\text{Annualised Tracking Error}} \qquad (3.21)$$

Where:

IR_A = Information ratio using arithmetic excess return

$\tilde{a}$ = annualised arithmetic excess return

$\tilde{\sigma}_A$ = annualised ex-post tracking error of arithmetic excess return.

The information ratio is directly related to the revised Sharpe ratio, simply replacing the risk-free rate with the benchmark.

GEOMETRIC INFORMATION RATIO

Using geometric excess returns we get the geometric information ratio:

$$\text{Information ratio} \, \text{IR}_G = \frac{\tilde{g}}{\tilde{\sigma}_G} \qquad (3.22)$$

Where:

$\tilde{g}$ = annualised geometric excess return

$\tilde{\sigma}_G$ = annualised ex-post tracking error of geometric excess return.

Normally information ratios are calculated using annualised excess returns and annualised tracking errors. To aid comparison it is absolutely essential to disclose the method of calculation, that is, frequency of data, overall time period, arithmetic or geometric excess returns, arithmetic or geometric means, population or sample (n or $n - 1$), ex-post or ex-ante, simple or continuously compounded returns.

⚠ **Caution**

When comparing information ratios, it is important to ensure that they are calculated using the same methodology and the same type of data.

For the record, my preference is monthly data, over three years using the geometric excess return, assuming a full population, calculated ex post using simple returns – monthly returns because month-end valuations are typically of better quality and daily data can be a bit noisy; three years because that is long enough with monthly data to be statistically significant and short enough to reflect recent history; full population rather than a sample because we know the exact mean of the population we are analysing; and using simple returns because they are commonly used and in truth we have bigger problems with the data than whether or not to use simple or continuously compounded returns.

If ex-ante tracking errors are used in the denominator please remember it is only a forecast based on a current snapshot of the portfolio. The portfolio manager will be able to "window dress"[15] the portfolio by reducing any "bets" at the point of measurement thus reducing the forecast tracking error and therefore apparently improving the information ratio.

 Note

Information ratio is a key statistic, used extensively by institutional asset managers; it is often described as the measure of a portfolio manager's skill. Called the information ratio because it holds so much information, like many financial statistics it is borrowed from other industries. Engineers might recognise it as the "Signal to Noise" ratio.

Views vary on what constitutes a good information ratio. In his research commentary Thomas Goodwin[16] (1998) quotes Grinold and Kahn[17] (1994) stating that an information ratio of 0.5 is good, 0.75 is very good and 1.0 is exceptional; there is ample evidence to suggest that anything substantially above

---

[15]"Window dressing" refers to actions taken by a portfolio manager prior to publication of portfolio information in order to (temporarily or artificially) improve the appearance of that information.

[16]Thomas Goodwin (1998) The Information Ratio: More Than You Ever Wanted to Know About One Performance Measure, *Russell Research Commentary*.

[17]R. C. Grinold and R. N. Khan (1994) *Active Portfolio Management: Quantitative Theory and Applications*. McGraw-Hill.

1.0 is unsustainable or fraudulent. These numbers certainly accord with my personal experience if sustained over a substantial period (three to five years). Clearly a positive information ratio indicates outperformance and a negative information ratio indicates underperformance. Unlike the Sharpe ratio there is more consensus that if you are going to underperform, consistent under-performance (as indicated by a low tracking error) is worse than inconsistent underperformance (high tracking error).

It is quite easy to obtain a good information ratio for a single period; like all statistics the development of the information ratio should be viewed over time. Goodwin suggests that sustaining a high information ratio above 0.5 is more difficult than Grinold and Kahn suggest.

Of course, this statistic is most useful measuring the performance of port-folios that are specifically required to outperform a benchmark.

Tracking error and information ratios are calculated in Exhibit 3.4 – for our standard example data in Table 3.4 arithmetic and Table 3.5 geometric.

EXHIBIT 3.4 Arithmetic and geometric information ratios

Arithmetic tracking error $\sigma_A = \sqrt{\dfrac{\sum\limits_{i=1}^{i=n}(a_i - \overline{a})^2}{n}} = \sqrt{\dfrac{4.36}{36}} = 0.348\%$

Annualised arithmetic tracking error $\tilde{\sigma}_A = \sqrt{12} \times 0.348\% = 1.21\%$

Annualised portfolio return $\tilde{r} = 13.29\%$

Annualised benchmark return $\tilde{b} = 14.62\%$

Annualised arithmetic excess return $\tilde{a} = 13.29\% - 14.62\% = -1.33\%$

Information ratio $IR_A = \dfrac{\tilde{a}}{\tilde{\sigma}_A} = \dfrac{-1.33\%}{1.21\%} = -1.1$

Geometric tracking error $\sigma_G = \sqrt{\dfrac{\sum\limits_{i=1}^{i=n}(g_i - \overline{g})^2}{n}} = \sqrt{\dfrac{4.24}{36}} = 0.343\%$

Annualised geometric tracking error $\tilde{\sigma}_G = \sqrt{12} \times 0.343\% = 1.19\%$

Annualised geometric excess return

$\tilde{g} = \left(\dfrac{1+\tilde{r}}{1+\tilde{b}}\right) - 1 = \left(\dfrac{1.1329}{1.1462}\right) - 1 = -1.16\%$

Geometric information ratio $IR_G = \dfrac{\tilde{g}}{\tilde{\sigma}_G} = \dfrac{-1.16\%}{1.19\%} = -0.98$

TABLE 3.4 Information ratio arithmetic excess return

Portfolio Monthly Return (%) r_i	Benchmark Monthly Return (%) b_i	Arithmetic Excess Return $a_i = r_i - b_i$	Deviation from Average $(a_i - \bar{a})$	Deviation Squared $(a_i - \bar{a})^2$
0.3	0.2	0.1	0.2	0.04
2.6	2.5	0.1	0.2	0.04
1.1	1.8	−0.7	−0.6	0.36
−0.9	−1.1	0.2	0.3	0.09
1.4	1.4	0.0	0.1	0.01
2.4	2.3	0.1	0.2	0.04
1.5	1.4	0.1	0.2	0.04
6.6	6.5	0.1	0.2	0.04
−1.4	−1.5	0.1	0.2	0.04
3.9	4.2	−0.3	−0.2	0.04
−0.5	−0.3	−0.2	−0.1	0.01
8.1	8.3	−0.2	−0.1	0.01
4.0	3.9	0.1	0.2	0.04
−3.7	−3.8	0.1	0.2	0.04
−6.1	−6.2	0.1	0.2	0.04
1.4	1.5	−0.1	0.0	0.00
−4.9	−4.8	−0.1	0.0	0.00
−2.1	−2.0	−0.1	0.0	0.00
6.2	6.0	0.2	0.3	0.09
5.8	5.6	0.2	0.3	0.09
−6.4	−6.7	0.3	0.4	0.16
1.7	1.9	−0.2	−0.1	0.01
−0.4	−0.3	−0.1	0.0	0.00
−0.2	−0.1	−0.1	0.0	0.00
−2.1	−2.6	0.5	0.6	0.36
1.1	0.7	0.4	0.5	0.25
4.7	4.3	0.4	0.5	0.25
2.4	2.9	−0.5	−0.4	0.16
3.3	3.8	−0.5	−0.4	0.16
−0.7	−0.2	−0.5	−0.4	0.16
4.7	5.1	−0.4	−0.3	0.09
0.6	1.4	−0.8	−0.7	0.49
1.0	1.3	−0.3	−0.2	0.04
−0.2	0.3	−0.5	−0.4	0.16
3.4	3.4	0.0	0.1	0.01
1.0	2.1	−1.1	−1.0	1.00

Total

$$\sum_{i=1}^{i=n} (a_i - \bar{a})^2 = 4.36$$

TABLE 3.5   Information ratio geometric excess return

Portfolio Monthly Return (%) r_i	Benchmark Monthly Return (%) b_i	Geometric Excess Return $g_i = \left(\dfrac{1+r_i}{1+b_i}\right) - 1$	Deviation from Average $(g_i - \overline{g})$	Deviation Squared $(g_i - \overline{g})^2$
0.3	0.2	0.10	0.2	0.04
2.6	2.5	0.10	0.19	0.04
1.1	1.8	−0.69	−0.59	0.35
−0.9	−1.1	0.20	0.30	0.09
1.4	1.4	0.00	0.10	0.01
2.4	2.3	0.10	0.19	0.04
1.5	1.4	0.10	0.20	0.04
6.6	6.5	0.09	0.19	0.04
−1.4	−1.5	0.10	0.20	0.04
3.9	4.2	−0.29	−0.19	0.04
−0.5	−0.3	−0.20	−0.10	0.01
8.1	8.3	−0.18	−0.09	0.01
4.0	3.9	0.10	0.19	0.04
−3.7	−3.8	0.10	0.20	0.04
−6.1	−6.2	0.11	0.20	0.04
1.4	1.5	−0.10	0.00	0.00
−4.9	−4.8	−0.11	−0.01	0.00
−2.1	−2.0	−0.10	−0.01	0.00
6.2	6.0	0.19	0.29	0.08
5.8	5.6	0.19	0.29	0.08
−6.4	−6.7	0.32	0.42	0.17
1.7	1.9	−0.20	−0.10	0.01
−0.4	−0.3	−0.10	0.00	0.00
−0.2	−0.1	−0.10	0.00	0.00
−2.1	−2.6	0.51	0.61	0.37
1.1	0.7	0.40	0.49	0.24
4.7	4.3	0.38	0.48	0.23
2.4	2.9	−0.49	−0.39	0.15
3.3	3.8	−0.48	−0.38	0.15
−0.7	−0.2	−0.50	−0.40	0.16
4.7	5.1	−0.38	−0.28	0.08
0.6	1.4	−0.79	−0.69	0.48
1.0	1.3	−0.30	−0.20	0.04
−0.2	0.3	−0.50	−0.40	0.16
3.4	3.4	0.00	0.10	0.01
1.0	2.1	−1.08	−0.98	0.96

Total

$$\sum_{i=1}^{i=n} (g_i - \overline{g})^2 = 4.24$$

MODIFIED INFORMATION RATIO

Some commentators would suggest that negative Sharpe and information ratios have no value, pointing out that if performance is negative the respective ratios actually reward higher variability and higher tracking error. While it's true that negative Sharpe and information ratios require a more nuanced interpretation, I disagree that they provide no value. It seems self-evident, to me at least, that if you are going to underperform it is better to underperform inconsistently rather than underperform consistently.

The modified information ratio suggested by Israelsen[18] (2005) adjusts the information ratio to ensure that higher tracking errors are always penalised:

$$\text{Modified information ratio MIR}_A = \frac{\tilde{a}}{\tilde{\sigma}_A^{\frac{a}{|a|}}} \tag{3.23}$$

For negative excess return Equation 3.23 means that the excess return is multiplied by the tracking error rather than divided as in the unmodified information ratio.

$$\text{Modified information ratio (−ve returns) MIR}_A^- = \tilde{a} \times \tilde{\sigma}_A \tag{3.24}$$

Obviously for geometric excess returns:

$$\text{Modified information ratio MIR}_G = \frac{\tilde{g}}{\tilde{\sigma}_G^{\frac{g}{|g|}}} \tag{3.25}$$

and for negative geometric excess return:

$$\text{Modified information ratio (−ve returns) MIR}_G^- = \tilde{g} \times \tilde{\sigma}_G \tag{3.26}$$

⚠ Caution

I hesitate to mention it, given my dislike of the modified information ratio, but there is also a modified Sharpe ratio[19] which applies the same concept to absolute returns. Please do not confuse with the more legitimate modified Sharpe ratio discussed in Chapter 8 based on modified value at risk.

---

[18] C. L. Israelsen (2005) A Refinement to the Sharpe Ratio and Information Ratio. *Journal of Asset Management* 5(6), 423–427.
[19] Equation 8.17.

ADJUSTED INFORMATION RATIO

The information ratio can be adjusted in a similar way as suggested by Pezier for the Sharpe ratio, penalising negative skewness and positive excess kurtosis in the tracking error as follows:

For arithmetic excess returns:

Adjusted information ratio (arithmetic)

$$= IR_A \times \left[1 + \left(\frac{\varsigma_A}{6} \right) \times IR_A - \left(\frac{\kappa_A - 3}{24} \right) \times IR_A^2 \right] \qquad (3.27)$$

For geometric excess returns:

Adjusted information ratio (geometric)

$$= IR_G \times \left[1 + \left(\frac{\varsigma_G}{6} \right) \times IR_G - \left(\frac{\kappa_G - 3}{24} \right) \times IR_G^2 \right] \qquad (3.28)$$

SKEW-ADJUSTED INFORMATION RATIO

Just as for the skew-adjusted Sharpe ratio the information ratio could be adjusted for just skewness as follows:

For arithmetic excess returns:

Skew-adjusted information ratio (arithmetic)

$$= IR_A \times \left[1 + \left(\frac{\varsigma_A}{6} \right) \times IR_A \right] \qquad (3.29)$$

For geometric excess returns:

Skew-adjusted information ratio (geometric)

$$= IR_G \times \left[1 + \left(\frac{\varsigma_G}{6} \right) \times IR_G \right] \qquad (3.30)$$

Relative skewness, relative kurtosis, skew-adjusted and adjusted information ratios are calculated from arithmetic and geometric data in Tables 3.6 and 3.7 in Exhibit 3.5.

TABLE 3.6   Arithmetic relative skewness and kurtosis

Arithmetic Excess a_i	Deviation Cubed $(a_i - \overline{a})^3$	4th Power Deviation $(a_i - \overline{a})^4$
0.1	0.01	0.00
0.1	0.01	0.00
−0.7	−0.22	0.13
0.2	0.03	0.01
0.0	0.00	0.00
0.1	0.01	0.00
0.1	0.01	0.00
0.1	0.01	0.00
0.1	0.01	0.00
−0.3	−0.01	0.00
−0.2	0.00	0.00
−0.2	0.00	0.00
0.1	0.01	0.00
0.1	0.01	0.00
0.1	0.01	0.00
−0.1	0.00	0.00
−0.1	0.00	0.00
−0.1	0.00	0.00
0.2	0.03	0.01
0.2	0.03	0.01
0.3	0.06	0.03
−0.2	0.00	0.00
−0.1	0.00	0.00
−0.1	0.00	0.00
0.5	0.22	0.13
0.4	0.13	0.06
0.4	0.13	0.06
−0.5	−0.06	0.03
−0.5	−0.06	0.03
−0.5	−0.06	0.03
−0.4	−0.03	0.01
−0.8	−0.34	0.24
−0.3	−0.01	0.00
−0.5	−0.06	0.03
0.0	0.00	0.00
−1.1	−1.00	1.00
	Total	**Total**
	$\sum_{i=1}^{i=n} (a_i - \overline{a})^3 = -1.18$	$\sum_{i=1}^{i=n} (a_i - \overline{a})^4 = 1.8$

TABLE 3.7   Geometric relative skewness and kurtosis

Geometric Excess g_i	Deviation Cubed $(g_i - \bar{g})^3$	4th Power Deviation $(g_i - \bar{g})^4$
0.10	0.01	0.00
0.10	0.01	0.00
−0.69	−0.21	0.12
0.20	0.03	0.01
0.00	0.00	0.00
0.10	0.01	0.00
0.10	0.01	0.00
0.09	0.01	0.00
0.10	0.01	0.00
−0.29	−0.01	0.00
−0.20	0.00	0.00
−0.18	0.00	0.00
0.10	0.01	0.00
0.10	0.01	0.00
0.11	0.01	0.00
−0.10	0.00	0.00
−0.11	0.00	0.00
−0.10	0.00	0.00
0.19	0.02	0.01
0.19	0.02	0.01
0.32	0.07	0.03
−0.20	0.00	0.00
−0.10	0.00	0.00
−0.10	0.00	0.00
0.51	0.23	0.14
0.40	0.12	0.06
0.38	0.11	0.05
−0.49	−0.06	0.02
−0.48	−0.06	0.02
−0.50	−0.07	0.03
−0.38	−0.02	0.01
−0.79	−0.33	0.23
−0.30	−0.01	0.00
−0.50	−0.06	0.03
0.00	0.00	0.00
−1.08	−0.94	0.92
	Total	**Total**
	$\sum_{i=1}^{i=n} (g_i - \bar{g})^3 = -1.09$	$\sum_{i=1}^{i=n} (g_i - \bar{g})^4 = 1.7$

EXHIBIT 3.5   Relative skewness, kurtosis and adjusted information ratio

Arithmetic relative skewness

$$\varsigma_A = \sum_{i=1}^{i=n} \left(\frac{a_i - \bar{a}}{\sigma_A} \right)^3 \times \frac{1}{n} = \frac{-1.18}{0.348^3} \times \frac{1}{36} = -0.775$$

Arithmetic relative kurtosis

$$\kappa_A = \sum_{i=1}^{i=n} \left(\frac{a_i - \bar{a}}{\sigma_A} \right)^4 \times \frac{1}{n} = \frac{1.8}{0.348^4} \times \frac{1}{36} = 3.414$$

Adjusted information ratio (arithmetic)

$$= IR_A \times \left[1 + \left(\frac{\varsigma_A}{6} \right) \times IR_A - \left(\frac{\kappa_A - 3}{24} \right) \times IR_A^2 \right]$$

$$= -1.1 \times \left[1 + \frac{-0.775}{6} \times -1.1 - \left(\frac{3.414 - 3}{24} \right) \times 1.1^2 \right] = -1.24$$

Geometric relative skewness

$$\varsigma_A = \sum_{i=1}^{i=n} \left(\frac{g_i - \bar{g}}{\sigma_G} \right)^3 \times \frac{1}{n} = \frac{-1.09}{0.343^3} \times \frac{1}{36} = -0.752$$

Geometric relative kurtosis

$$\kappa_G = \sum_{i=1}^{i=n} \left(\frac{g_i - \bar{g}}{\sigma_G} \right)^4 \times \frac{1}{36} = \frac{1.7}{0.343^4} \times \frac{1}{36} = 3.405$$

Adjusted information ratio (geometric)

$$= IR_G \times \left[1 + \left(\frac{\varsigma_G}{6} \right) \times IR_G - \left(\frac{\kappa_G - 3}{24} \right) \times IR_G^2 \right]$$

$$= -0.98 \times \left[1 + \frac{-0.752}{6} \times -0.98 - \left(\frac{3.405 - 3}{24} \right) \times -0.98^2 \right] = -1.08$$

For both arithmetic and geometric versions, the adjusted information ratio is worse than the unadjusted information ratio because of both negative skewness and slightly higher kurtosis indicating fatter tails than a normal distribution.

CHAPTER 4

Regression Analysis

"I've come loaded with statistics, for I've noticed a man can't prove anything without statistics."

Mark Twain (1835–1910)

"If you torture the data long enough, it will confess."

Ronald Coase (1910–2013)

Regression analysis is a statistical tool used for the investigation of relationships between variables. Regression analysis with a single explanatory variable is termed simple regression and multiple regression is a technique that allows additional factors to enter the analysis separately so that the effect of each can be estimated.

We can gain further information from a portfolio by plotting the portfolio returns against the corresponding benchmark returns in a scatter diagram (see Figure 4.1).

We might expect portfolio returns to move in line with benchmark returns. If so, we can draw a line of best fit through these points, the aim of which is to minimise the (squares of) vertical distances of any one point from this line.

REGRESSION EQUATION

The formula of any straight line on a graph is given by the slope or gradient of the line plus the intercept with the vertical axis. Thus, the return of the portfolio might be described as:

$$r = \alpha_R + \beta_R \times b + \varepsilon_R \tag{4.1}$$

75

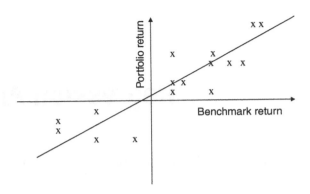

FIGURE 4.1   Regression analysis

This equation is called the "regression equation". The term regression was first coined by Francis Galton[1] in the nineteenth century to describe the biological phenomenon of the heights of tall ancestors to *regress* down towards a more normal average.

REGRESSION *ALPHA*

The regression *alpha* α_R is the intercept of the regression equation with the vertical axis:

$$\text{Regression } alpha \; \alpha_R = \bar{r} - \beta_R \times \bar{b} \tag{4.2}$$

REGRESSION *BETA*

The regression *beta* β_R is the slope or gradient of the regression equation.
The slope of the regression equation is given by:

$$\beta_R = \frac{\sum\limits_{i=1}^{i=n} \left[(r_i - \bar{r}) \times (b_i - \bar{b}) \right]}{\sum\limits_{i=1}^{i=n} (b_i - \bar{b})^2} = \frac{\text{Covariance}}{\sigma_b^2} \tag{4.3}$$

---

[1]Francis Galton (reprinted 1989) Kinship and Correlation. *Statistical Science* 4(2), 80–86.

REGRESSION *EPSILON*

The regression *epsilon* ε_R is an error term measuring the vertical distance between the return predicted by the equation and the real result.

$$\text{Regression } epsilon \; \varepsilon_{Ri} = r_i - \alpha_{Ri} - \beta_R \times b_i \qquad (4.4)$$

The regression *alpha* and *beta* for the standard portfolio and benchmark data calculated in Exhibit 2.4 and Exhibit 2.7 are calculated in Exhibit 4.1.

EXHIBIT 4.1   Regression *alpha* and *beta*

$$\text{Covariance} = \frac{\displaystyle\sum_{i=1}^{i=n}(r_i - \bar{r}) \times (b_i - \bar{b})}{n} = \frac{399.37\%}{36} = 11.09\%$$

$$\text{Benchmark variance } \sigma_b^2 = \frac{\displaystyle\sum_{i=1}^{i=n}(b_i - \bar{b})^2}{n} = \frac{406.92\%}{36} = 11.30\%$$

$$\text{Regression } beta \; \beta_R = \frac{\displaystyle\sum_{i=1}^{i=n}[(r_i - \bar{r}) \times (b_i - \bar{b})]}{\displaystyle\sum_{i=1}^{i=n}(b_i - \bar{b})^2}$$

$$= \frac{\text{Covariance}}{\sigma_b^2} = \frac{11.09\%}{11.30\%} = 0.9814$$

$$\text{Regression } alpha \; \alpha_R = \bar{r} - \beta_R \times \bar{b} = 1.1\% - 0.9814 \times 1.2\%$$

$$= -0.078\%$$

CAPITAL ASSET PRICING MODEL (CAPM)

The capital asset pricing model (CAPM) links expected return with systematic risk. The CAPM was published by Sharpe[2] in 1964 and states that the expected return of the portfolio is:

$$r = r_F + \beta \times (b - r_F) \qquad (4.5)$$

The CAPM starts with the risk-free rate r_F, however described, to which is added the premium $(b - r_F)$ multiplied by volatility β or systematic risk.

The CAPM in Equation 4.5 describes theoretical return. Any return above this theoretical return, the intercept with the vertical access, is *alpha* and is the result of specific risk. Incorporating the risk-free rate, we can use the following revised regression equation to calculate *beta* and a new *alpha* (Jensen's *alpha*[3])

$$r - r_F = \alpha + \beta \times (b - r_F) + \varepsilon \qquad (4.6)$$

⚠ Caution

You may have noticed the underlying assumption of linearity in the CAPM. While some portfolios exhibit a linear relationship with their benchmarks (especially index tracking funds), many portfolios do not. This is a significant source of criticism of the CAPM and its biggest limitation.

BETA (β) (SYSTEMATIC RISK OR VOLATILITY)

Beta was originally described as volatility and in some quarters may still be called volatility but these days volatility is more likely to refer to standard deviation, which is a real shame because I prefer the term variability in the context of standard deviation.

In the context of the CAPM model we should compare the excess return of the portfolio against the risk-free rate with the excess return of benchmark

---

[2]William Sharpe (1964) Capital Asset Prices: A Theory of Market Equilibrium Under Conditions of Risk. *Journal of Finance* 19(3), 425–442.

[3]Michael Jensen (1968) The Performance of Mutual Funds 1945–1964. *Journal of Finance* 23(2), 389–416.

against the same risk-free rate as follows:

$$\beta = \frac{\displaystyle\sum_{i=1}^{i=n}\left[((r_i - r_{Fi}) - (\bar{r} - \bar{r}_F)) \times ((b_i - r_{Fi}) - (\bar{b} - \bar{r}_F))\right]}{\displaystyle\sum_{i=1}^{i=n}\left((b_i - r_{Fi}) - (\bar{b} - \bar{r}_F)\right)^2} \qquad (4.7)$$

Where:

$\bar{r}_F$ = mean risk-free rate
r_{Fi} = risk-free rate in month i
$\bar{b}$ = mean benchmark return

The result will be not too different from the regression *beta* (and indeed regression *betas* are often calculated because calculating the CAPM *beta* is perhaps a little tedious for little added value, particularly in a low interest rate environment) but technically we should consider the risk-free rate.

JENSEN'S *ALPHA* (JENSEN'S MEASURE OR JENSEN'S DIFFERENTIAL RETURN OR EX-POST *ALPHA*)

Jensen's *alpha* is the intercept of the regression equation in the CAPM and is in effect the excess return adjusted for systematic risk.

Ignoring the error term for ex-post calculations and using Equation 4.6:

$$\text{Jensen's } alpha \ \alpha = \bar{r} - \bar{r}_F - \beta \times (\bar{b} - \bar{r}_F) \qquad (4.8)$$

Note the similarities to the related formula for differential return given in Equation 11.6 in Chapter 11 (Risk-adjusted returns) hence the alternative name, Jensen's differential return.

Portfolio managers often talk in terms of *alpha* to describe their added value but rarely are they referring to either the regression or even Jensen's *alpha*. In all probability they are referring to their excess return above the benchmark. Confusingly, academics also frequently refer to excess return as the return above the risk-free rate.

In fact, both these terms are frequently abused; *beta* is often used by the financial media and portfolio managers alike to describe market returns when of course it is in fact the systematic risk relative to the market.

Due to the rise of passive investments, this changing terminology has become even more frequent. Today, beta is often used to indicate passive investment returns that take no skill to generate while alpha is used to indicate manager skill, justifying the fees charged by active managers.

Note that subtracting the benchmark return from both sides of Equation 4.5 we can see the arithmetic excess return can be expressed by:

$$r - b = \alpha + (\beta - 1) \times (b - r_F) \tag{4.9}$$

Note: $b = r_F + (b - r_F)$

ANNUALISED ALPHA

The *alpha* calculated in the regression equations is linked to the periodicity of the underlying data.

The annualised *alpha* can be calculated directly from annualised data as follows:

$$\text{Annualised regression } alpha \; \tilde{\alpha}_R = \tilde{r} - \beta_R \times \tilde{b} \tag{4.10}$$

$$\text{Annualised Jensen's } alpha \; \tilde{\alpha} = \tilde{r} - \tilde{r}_F - \beta(\tilde{b} - \tilde{r}_F) \tag{4.11}$$

Alternatively, and less accurately, *alpha* can be annualised either by multiplying by the periodicity of the data or taking the power of the periodicity as follows:

$$\tilde{\alpha} = t \times \alpha \tag{4.12}$$

or

$$\tilde{\alpha} = (1 + \alpha)^t - 1 \tag{4.13}$$

Revised CAPM *beta* and Jensen's *alpha* are calculated in Exhibit 4.2 using data from Table 4.2 and Table 4.3. For completeness the underlying data required to calculate the variability of portfolio returns above the risk-free rate is shown in Table 4.1.

EXHIBIT 4.2   CAPM *beta* and Jensen's *alpha*

$$\text{Beta } \beta = \frac{\sum\limits_{i=1}^{i=n}[((r_i - r_{Fi}) - (\bar{r} - \bar{r}F)) \times ((b_i - r_{Fi}) - (\bar{b} - \bar{r}_F))]}{\sum\limits_{i=1}^{i=n}((b_i - r_{Fi}) - (\bar{b} - \bar{r}_F))^2}$$

$$= \frac{398.66}{406.06} = 0.982$$

$$\text{Jensen's } alpha \; \alpha = \bar{r} - \bar{r}_F - \beta \times (\bar{b} - \bar{r}_F) = 0.9 - 0.982 \times 1.0 = -0.082$$

TABLE 4.1   Portfolio excess return variability

Portfolio Monthly Return (%) r_i	Risk-Free Rate (%) r_{Fi}	Excess Return (Above Risk-Free Rate) $(r_i - r_{Fi})$	Deviation $(r_i - r_{Fi}) - (\bar{r} - \bar{r}_F)$	Deviation Squared $[(r_i - r_{Fi}) - (\bar{r} - \bar{r}_F)]^2$
0.3	0.1	0.2	−0.7	0.49
2.6	0.1	2.5	1.6	2.56
1.1	0.2	0.9	0.0	0.00
−0.9	0.2	−1.1	−2.0	4.00
1.4	0.2	1.2	0.3	0.09
2.4	0.2	2.2	1.3	1.69
1.5	0.2	1.3	0.4	0.16
6.6	0.3	6.3	5.4	29.16
−1.4	0.3	−1.7	−2.6	6.76
3.9	0.4	3.5	2.6	6.76
−0.5	0.4	−0.9	−1.8	3.24
8.1	0.3	7.8	6.9	47.61
4.0	0.3	3.7	2.8	7.84
−3.7	0.3	−4.0	−4.9	24.01
−6.1	0.3	−6.4	−7.3	53.29
1.4	0.4	1.0	0.1	0.01
−4.9	0.2	−5.1	−6.0	36.00
−2.1	0.2	−2.3	−3.2	10.24
6.2	0.2	6.0	5.1	26.01
5.8	0.1	5.7	4.8	23.04
−6.4	0.1	−6.5	−7.4	54.76
1.7	0.1	1.6	0.7	0.49
−0.4	0.1	−0.5	−1.4	1.96
−0.2	0.1	−0.3	−1.2	1.44
−2.1	0.1	−2.2	−3.1	9.61
1.1	0.1	1.0	0.1	0.01
4.7	0.1	4.6	3.7	13.69
2.4	0.1	2.3	1.4	1.96
3.3	0.1	3.2	2.3	5.29
−0.7	0.2	−0.9	−1.8	3.24
4.7	0.2	4.5	3.6	12.96
0.6	0.2	0.4	−0.5	0.25
1.0	0.2	0.8	−0.1	0.01
−0.2	0.2	−0.4	−1.3	1.69
3.4	0.2	3.2	2.3	5.29
1.0	0.2	0.8	−0.1	0.01
		Total		**Total**
		$\displaystyle\sum_{i=1}^{i=n}(r_i - r_{Fi}) = 32.4$		**395.62**

$$(\bar{r} - \bar{r}_F) = \frac{32.4}{36} = 0.9$$

TABLE 4.2   Benchmark excess return variability

Benchmark Monthly Return (%) b_i	Risk-Free Rate (%) r_{Fi}	Excess Return $(b - r_{Fi})$	Deviation $(b_i - r_{Fi}) - (\bar{b} - \bar{r}_F)$	Deviation Squared $[(b_i - r_{Fi}) - (\bar{b} - \bar{r}_F)]^2$
0.2	0.1	0.1	−0.9	0.81
2.5	0.1	2.4	1.4	1.96
1.8	0.2	1.6	0.6	0.36
−1.1	0.2	−1.3	−2.3	5.29
1.4	0.2	1.2	0.2	0.04
2.3	0.2	2.1	1.1	1.21
1.4	0.2	1.2	0.2	0.04
6.5	0.3	6.2	5.2	27.04
−1.5	0.3	−1.8	−2.8	7.84
4.2	0.4	3.8	2.8	7.84
−0.3	0.4	−0.7	−1.7	2.89
8.3	0.3	8.0	7.0	49.00
3.9	0.3	3.6	2.6	6.76
−3.8	0.3	−4.1	−5.1	26.01
−6.2	0.3	−6.5	−7.5	56.25
1.5	0.4	1.1	0.1	0.01
−4.8	0.2	−5.0	−6.0	36.00
−2.0	0.2	−2.2	−3.2	10.24
6.0	0.2	5.8	4.8	23.04
5.6	0.1	5.5	4.5	20.25
−6.7	0.1	−6.8	−7.8	60.84
1.9	0.1	1.8	0.8	0.64
−0.3	0.1	−0.4	−1.4	1.96
−0.1	0.1	−0.2	−1.2	1.44
−2.6	0.1	−2.7	−3.7	13.69
0.7	0.1	0.6	−0.4	0.16
4.3	0.1	4.2	3.2	10.24
2.9	0.1	2.8	1.8	3.24
3.8	0.1	3.7	2.7	7.29
−0.2	0.2	−0.4	−1.4	1.96
5.1	0.2	4.9	3.9	15.21
1.4	0.2	1.2	0.2	0.04
1.3	0.2	1.1	0.1	0.01
0.3	0.2	0.1	−0.9	0.81
3.4	0.2	3.2	2.2	4.84
2.1	0.2	1.9	0.9	0.81
		Total		**Total**
		$\sum_{i=1}^{i=n}(b_i - r_{Fi}) = 36.0$		**406.06**
		$(\bar{b} - \bar{r}_F) = \frac{36.0}{36} = 1.0$		

TABLE 4.3 CAPM covariance

Portfolio Monthly Excess Return (%) $(r_i - r_{Fi})$	Deviation from Average $(r_i - r_{Fi}) - (\bar{r} - \bar{r}_F)$	Benchmark Monthly Excess Return (%) $(b - r_{Fi})$	Deviation from Average $(b_i - r_{Fi}) - (\bar{b} - \bar{r}_F)$	Portfolio Deviation $\times$ Benchmark Deviation $(r_i - r_{Fi}) - (\bar{r} - \bar{r}_F) \times (b_i - r_{Fi}) - (\bar{b} - \bar{r}_F)$
0.2	−0.7	0.1	−0.9	0.63
2.5	1.6	2.4	1.4	2.24
0.9	0.0	1.6	0.6	0.00
−1.1	−2.0	−1.3	−2.3	4.60
1.2	0.3	1.2	0.2	0.06
2.2	1.3	2.1	1.1	1.43
1.3	0.4	1.2	0.2	0.08
6.3	5.4	6.2	5.2	28.08
−1.7	−2.6	−1.8	−2.8	7.28
3.5	2.6	3.8	2.8	7.28
−0.9	−1.8	−0.7	−1.7	3.06
7.8	6.9	8.0	7.0	48.30
3.7	2.8	3.6	2.6	7.28
−4.0	−4.9	−4.1	−5.1	24.99
−6.4	−7.3	−6.5	−7.5	54.75
1.0	0.1	1.1	0.1	0.01
−5.1	−6.0	−5.0	−6.0	36.00
−2.3	−3.2	−2.2	−3.2	10.24
6.0	5.1	5.8	4.8	24.48
5.7	4.8	5.5	4.5	21.60
−6.5	−7.4	−6.8	−7.8	57.72
1.6	0.7	1.8	0.8	0.56
−0.5	−1.4	−0.4	−1.4	1.96
−0.3	−1.2	−0.2	−1.2	1.44
−2.2	−3.1	−2.7	−3.7	11.47
1.0	0.1	0.6	−0.4	−0.04
4.6	3.7	4.2	3.2	11.84
2.3	1.4	2.8	1.8	2.52
3.2	2.3	3.7	2.7	6.21
−0.9	−1.8	−0.4	−1.4	2.52
4.5	3.6	4.9	3.9	14.04
0.4	−0.5	1.2	0.2	−0.10
0.8	−0.1	1.1	0.1	−0.01
−0.4	−1.3	0.1	−0.9	1.17
3.2	2.3	3.2	2.2	5.06
0.8	−0.1	1.9	0.9	−0.09
				Total
				398.66

BULL *BETA* (β^+)

We need not restrict ourselves to fitting lines of best fit to all benchmark (or market) returns, both positive and negative. If we calculate a regression equation for only positive benchmark returns we gain information on the behaviour of the portfolio in positive or "bull" markets.

BEAR *BETA* (β^-)

The *beta* for negative benchmark (or market) returns is described as the "bear" *beta*.

 Note

Bull and bear betas are useful if you believe some stocks have persistently different betas depending on the direction of the market.

BETA TIMING RATIO

Ideally, we would prefer a portfolio manager with a *beta* greater than 1 in rising markets and less than 1 in falling markets. In all likelihood such a manager would be a good timer of asset allocation decisions. Figure 4.2 demonstrates these two lines of best fit with a steeper gradient for positive benchmark returns

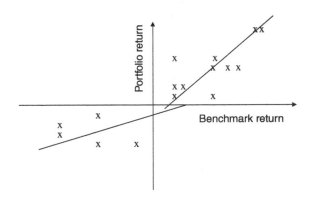

FIGURE 4.2   *Beta* timing ratio

than for negative benchmark returns. One measure of this desirable property of convexity would the *beta* timing ratio.

$$\text{Beta timing ratio} = \frac{\beta^+}{\beta^-} \tag{4.14}$$

Bull and bear *betas* and the *beta* timing ratio are calculated from the data in Tables 4.5, 4.6 and 4.7 in Exhibit 4.3.

EXHIBIT 4.3   *Beta* timing ratio

$$\text{Bull } beta \ \beta^+ = \frac{104.17}{100.62} = 1.035$$

$$\text{Bear } beta \ \beta^- = \frac{59.11}{62.34} = 0.948$$

$$beta \text{ timing ratio} = \frac{\beta^+}{\beta^-} = \frac{1.035}{0.948} = 1.092$$

> 📄 **Note**
>
> The bull *beta* need not be greater than 1 to generate a desirable *beta* timing ratio greater than 1; it is sufficient for the bull *beta* to be greater than the bear *beta*.

MARKET TIMING

There are additional methods to calculate market timing skill that utilise multiple regression. Henriksson and Merton[4] (1981) performed a multiple regression in which the portfolio excess return is regressed against the benchmark and up-market returns as follows:

$$r - r_F = \sigma_{MH} + \beta_{MH} \times (b - r_F) + \gamma_{MH} \times \max(0, b - r_F) + \varepsilon_{MH} \tag{4.15}$$

Where
α_{MH} = intercept or *alpha*
β_{MH} = market sensitivity
γ_{MH} = market timing abilities
ε_{MH} = error term

---

[4] R. D. Henriksson and R. C. Merton (1981) On Market Timing and Investment Performance. II. Statistical Procedures for Evaluating Forecast Skills. *Journal of Business* 54, 513–533.

TABLE 4.4 Bull and bear deviations

Benchmark Monthly Excess Return	Bull Deviation	Bull Deviation Squared	Bear Deviation	Bear Deviation Squared
0.1	−2.74	7.49		
2.4	−0.44	0.19		
1.6	−1.24	1.53		
−1.3			1.38	1.89
1.2	−1.64	2.68		
2.1	−0.74	0.54		
1.2	−1.64	2.68		
6.2	3.36	11.31		
−1.8			0.87	0.77
3.8	0.96	0.93		
−0.7			1.98	3.90
8.0	5.16	26.65		
3.6	0.76	0.58		
−4.1			−1.43	2.03
−6.5			−3.83	14.63
1.1	−1.74	3.02		
−5.0			−2.33	5.41
−2.2			0.47	0.23
5.8	2.96	8.78		
5.5	2.66	7.09		
−6.8			−4.13	17.02
1.8	−1.04	1.08		
−0.4			2.28	5.18
−0.2			2.48	6.13
−2.7			−0.03	0.00
0.6	−2.24	5.01		
4.2	1.36	1.86		
2.8	−0.04	0.00		
3.7	0.86	0.74		
−0.4			2.28	5.18
4.9	2.06	4.25		
1.2	−1.64	2.68		
1.1	−1.74	3.02		
0.1	−2.74	7.49		
3.2	0.36	0.13		
1.9	−0.94	0.88		
		Total		**Total**
		100.62		**62.34**

TABLE 4.5 Bull covariance

Month	Portfolio Monthly Excess Return	Deviation from Average	Benchmark Monthly Excess Return	Deviation from Average	Portfolio Deviation × Benchmark Deviation
1	0.2	−2.48	0.1	−2.74	6.79
2	2.5	−0.18	2.4	−0.44	0.08
3	0.9	−1.78	1.6	−1.24	2.20
4					
5	1.2	−1.48	1.2	−1.64	2.42
6	2.2	−0.48	2.1	−0.74	0.35
7	1.3	−1.38	1.2	−1.64	2.26
8	6.3	3.62	6.2	3.36	12.18
9					
10	3.5	0.82	3.8	0.96	0.79
11					
12	7.8	5.12	8.0	5.16	26.44
13	3.7	1.02	3.6	0.76	0.78
14					
15					
16	1.0	−1.68	1.1	−1.74	2.92
17					
18					
19	6.0	3.32	5.8	2.96	9.84
20	5.7	3.02	5.5	2.66	8.04
21					
22	1.6	−1.08	1.8	−1.04	1.12
23					
24					
25					
26	1.0	−1.68	0.6	−2.24	3.76
27	4.6	1.92	4.2	1.36	2.62
28	2.3	−0.38	2.8	−0.04	0.01
29	3.2	0.52	3.7	0.86	0.45
30					
31	4.5	1.82	4.9	2.06	3.76
32	0.4	−2.28	1.2	−1.64	3.73
33	0.8	−1.88	1.1	−1.74	3.27
34	−0.4	−3.08	0.1	−2.74	8.43
35	3.2	0.52	3.2	0.36	0.19
36	0.8	−1.88	1.9	−0.94	1.76
					Total 104.17

TABLE 4.6   Bear covariance

Month	Portfolio Monthly Excess Return	Deviation from Average	Benchmark Monthly Excess Return	Deviation from Average	Portfolio Deviation × Benchmark Deviation
1					
2					
3					
4	−1.1	1.56	−1.3	1.38	2.14
5					
6					
7					
8					
9	−1.7	0.96	−1.8	0.87	0.84
10					
11	−0.9	1.76	−0.7	1.98	3.47
12					
13					
14	−4.0	−1.34	−4.1	−1.43	1.91
15	−6.4	−3.74	−6.5	−3.83	14.31
16					
17	−5.1	−2.44	−5.0	−2.33	5.68
18	−2.3	0.36	−2.2	0.47	0.17
19					
20					
21	−6.5	−3.84	−6.8	−4.13	15.85
22					
23	−0.5	2.16	−0.4	2.28	4.91
24	−0.3	2.36	−0.2	2.48	5.84
25	−2.2	0.46	−2.7	−0.03	−0.01
26					
27					
28					
29					
30	−0.9	1.76	−0.4	2.28	4.00
31					
32					
33					
34					
35					
36					
					Total 59.11

If γ_{MH} is positive then the portfolio manager is demonstrating good market timing ability.

Treynor and Mazuy[5] also utilised multiple regression to analyse market timing skill with essentially a quadratic extension of the CAPM model. The first term is again the benchmark and the second term is the value of excess return squared as follows:

$$r - r_F = \alpha_{TM} + \beta_{TM} \times (b - r_F) + \gamma_{TM} \times (b - r_F)^2 + \varepsilon_{TM} \qquad (4.16)$$

Where:

α_{TM} = intercept or *alpha*
β_{TM} = market sensitivity
γ_{TM} = market timing abilities
ε_{TM} = error term

If γ_{TM} is positive then the estimated equation describes a convex upward-sloping regression curve demonstrating good market timing skill (see Figure 4.3).

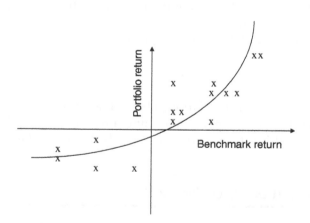

FIGURE 4.3 Market timing

[5]J. L. Treynor and K. Mazuy (1966) Can Mutual Funds Outguess the Market? *Harvard Business Review* 44, 131–136.

SYSTEMATIC RISK

Michael Jensen[6] (1969) described *beta* as systematic risk. If we multiply *beta* by market risk, we obtain a measure of systematic risk calculated in the same units as variability. In my view this is a better definition of systematic risk.

$$\text{Systematic risk } \sigma_S = \beta_R \times \sigma_b \tag{4.17}$$

Either the regression or CAPM *beta* can be used.

CORRELATION

Correlation can also be derived by:

$$\rho_{r,b} = \frac{\text{Systematic risk}}{\text{Total risk}}$$

$$\text{or} \qquad \rho_{r,b} = \frac{\beta \times \sigma_b}{\sigma} \tag{4.18}$$

Therefore, *beta* and correlation are linked by the formula:

$$\beta_R = \rho_{r,b} \times \frac{\sigma}{\sigma_b} \tag{4.19}$$

Correlation measures the variability in the portfolio that is systematic compared to the total variability.

If the correlation is high enough, we can approximate it with 1, leading to:

$$\beta_R \approx \frac{\sigma}{\sigma_b} \tag{4.20}$$

With sufficiently high correlation, a beta above 1 indicates that the portfolio is more volatile than the benchmark and a beta below 1 indicates it is less volatile. Note that this interpretation only holds if the correlation is very close to 1.

R^2 (OR COEFFICIENT OF DETERMINATION)

R^2 is the proportion of variance in fund returns that is related to the variance of benchmark returns; it is a measure of portfolio diversification. Note variance is the square of standard deviation or variability.

---

[6]Michael Jensen (1969) Risk, the Pricing of Capital Assets, and the Evaluation of Investment Portfolios. *Journal of Business* 42(2), 167–247.

The closer R^2 is to 1 the more portfolio variance is explained by benchmark variance. A low R^2 would indicate that returns are more scattered and would indicate a less reliable line of best fit leading to unstable *alphas* and *betas*. Therefore, if a portfolio has a low R^2, say much less than 0.7, then any *alphas* and *betas* and their derivative statistics should probably be ignored.

> ⚠ **Caution**
>
> While alpha and beta are often calculated and quoted in reports, R^2 is often left out, possibly because it requires deeper understanding of regressions and statistics or possibly because analysts are concerned that the readers of the report will not know how to interpret R^2. In practice, this can lead (and has led) to making portfolio decisions based on unsupported measures because of low R^2 values. I repeat the above warning: the only appropriate thing to do when R^2 is lower than about 0.7 is to ignore the associated *alpha* and *beta* measure and any appraisal measure derived from them.

$$R^2 = \frac{\sigma_S^2}{\sigma^2} = \frac{\beta_R^2 \times \sigma_b^2}{\sigma^2} = \rho_{r,b}^2 \qquad (4.21)$$

R^2 in this context is correlation (ρ) squared.
Correlation and R^2 are calculated in Exhibit 4.4.

EXHIBIT 4.4 Correlation and R^2

$$\text{Correlation } \rho_{r,b} = \frac{\beta_R \times \sigma_b}{\sigma} = \frac{0.981 \times 3.36}{3.32} = 0.995$$

or

$$\text{Correlation } \rho_{r,b} = \frac{\text{Covariance}}{\sigma \times \sigma_b} = \frac{11.09}{3.32 \times 3.36} = 0.995$$

$$R^2 = \frac{\sigma_S^2}{\sigma^2} = \frac{\beta_R^2 \times \sigma_b^2}{\sigma^2} = 0.989$$

SPECIFIC (OR RESIDUAL) RISK

Residual or specific risk is not attributed to general market movements but is unique to the particular portfolio under consideration. It is represented by the standard deviation of the error term in the regression equation σ_ε.

Since specific risk and systematic risk are by definition independent, we can calculate total risk by using Pythagoras's equation.[7]

$$\text{Total risk}^2 = \text{Systematic risk}^2 + \text{Specific risk}^2$$

$$\sigma^2 = \sigma_S^2 + \sigma_\varepsilon^2 = \beta_R^2 \times \sigma_b^2 + \sigma_\varepsilon^2 \tag{4.22}$$

It follows that:

$$\tilde{\sigma}^2 = \beta_R^2 \times \tilde{\sigma}_b^2 + \tilde{\sigma}_\varepsilon^2 \tag{4.23}$$

Rearranging Equation 4.22, specific risk and total risk can be calculated directly from:

$$\sigma_\varepsilon = \sqrt{\sigma^2 - \sigma_S^2} \tag{4.24}$$

$$\sigma = \sqrt{\sigma_S^2 + \sigma_\varepsilon^2} \tag{4.25}$$

Using the data in Table 4.7 we can demonstrate that Equation 4.25 holds for our standard portfolio and benchmark data from Table 2.1 in Exhibit 4.5.

EXHIBIT 4.5 Specific risk, systematic risk and total risk

$$\text{Specific risk } \sigma_\varepsilon = \sqrt{\frac{\sum\limits_{i=1}^{i=n}(\varepsilon_{Ri} - \bar{\varepsilon})^2}{n}} = \sqrt{\frac{\sum\limits_{i=1}^{i=n}\varepsilon_{Ri}^2}{n}} = \sqrt{\frac{4.22}{36}} = 0.34$$
$$\text{since } \bar{\varepsilon} = 0$$

$$\text{Systematic risk } \sigma_S = \beta_R \times \sigma_b = 0.9814 \times 3.36 = 3.30$$

$$\text{Total risk } \sigma = \sqrt{\sigma_S^2 + \sigma_\varepsilon^2} = \sqrt{3.30^2 + 0.34^2} = 3.32$$

and

$$\text{Specific risk } \sigma_\varepsilon = \sqrt{\sigma^2 - \sigma_S^2} = \sqrt{3.32^2 - 3.30^2} = 0.34$$

[7] $a^2 + b^2 = c^2$. Formally, in a right-angled triangle: the square of the hypotenuse is equal to the sum of the squares of the other sides. Since specific risk and systematic risk are independent, we can assume a right-angled triangle.

TABLE 4.7   Specific risk

Portfolio Monthly Return r_i	Regression Residual or Error Term $\varepsilon_{Ri} = (r_i - \alpha_R - \beta_R \times b_i)$	Residual Squared ε_{Ri}^2
0.3	0.18	0.03
2.6	0.22	0.05
1.1	−0.59	0.35
−0.9	0.26	0.07
1.4	0.10	0.01
2.4	0.22	0.05
1.5	0.20	0.04
6.6	0.30	0.09
−1.4	0.15	0.02
3.9	−0.14	0.02
−0.5	−0.13	0.02
8.1	0.03	0.00
4.0	0.25	0.06
−3.7	0.11	0.01
−6.1	0.06	0.00
1.4	0.01	0.00
−4.9	−0.11	0.01
−2.1	−0.06	0.00
6.2	0.39	0.15
5.8	0.38	0.15
−6.4	0.25	0.06
1.7	−0.09	0.01
−0.4	−0.03	0.00
−0.2	−0.02	0.00
−2.1	0.53	0.28
1.1	0.49	0.24
4.7	0.56	0.31
2.4	−0.37	0.14
3.3	−0.35	0.12
−0.7	−0.43	0.18
4.7	−0.23	0.05
0.6	−0.70	0.48
1.0	−0.20	0.04
−0.2	−0.42	0.17
3.4	0.14	0.02
1.0	−0.98	0.97
Sum	**0.00**	**4.22**

THE GEOMETRY OF RISK

This section is inspired by Handzy[8] (2013). We have seen already in Equation 4.22 that systematic risk and specific risk have a Pythagorean relationship. Because they are uncorrelated the square of specific risk plus the square of systematic risk is equal to the square of total risk. Geometry also explains the relationship of correlated assets.

Suppose that you hold a portfolio of two correlated assets:

- One unit of A, with variability σ_A
- One unit of B, with variability σ_B

Then the variability of the portfolio is:

$$\sigma_{A+B} = \sqrt{\sigma_A^2 + \sigma_B^2 + 2 \times \sigma_A \times \sigma_B \times \rho_{A,B}} \qquad (4.26)$$

This relationship is illustrated in Figure 4.4.
Equation 4.26 can also be rewritten as the law of cosines:

$$\sigma_{A+B} = \sqrt{\sigma_A^2 + \sigma_B^2 - 2 \times \sigma_A \times \sigma_B \times \cos\theta} \qquad (4.27)$$

Where:

θ = the angle between σ_A and σ_B

Note:

$$\rho_{A,B} = -\cos\theta \qquad (4.28)$$

Note when $\theta = 90°$, $\cos\theta = 0$ and the law of cosines reduces to Pythagoras's theorem:

$$\sigma_{A+B} = \sqrt{\sigma_A^2 + \sigma_B^2} \qquad (4.29)$$

To understand better the combination of correlated assets it is helpful to think in terms of the risk compass illustrated in Figure 4.5.

As shown in Figure 4.6 and using the risk compass, adding assets with the same variability but with different correlations with the existing asset (high correlation, zero correlation and negative correlation) illustrates the impact on total variability.

---

[8]D. Handzy (2013) Visual VaR – Intuitive and Effective Risk Communication. *Investor Analytics, Thought Leadership Series*, September.

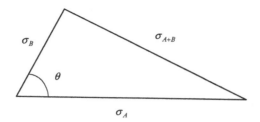

FIGURE 4.4 The geometry of risk

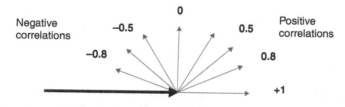

FIGURE 4.5 The risk compass

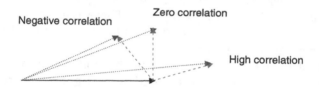

FIGURE 4.6 Risk triangles

The three dashed arrows in Figure 4.6 are the same length, but different correlations result in significantly different total variability. High correlation corresponds with the longest dotted arrow and negative correlation corresponds with the shortest dotted arrow. Note that even introducing an asset with zero correlation, the vertical arrow, increases total variability. This type of presentation is particularly useful for asset owners selecting new asset managers. It provides a visual representation of the total risk resulting from adding particular asset managers. It is not necessarily the best asset manager that should be hired, but rather the asset manager whose style best fits the current portfolio of managers.

This geometric interpretation can also be used to estimate how changes to the portfolio, or to the market, will impact portfolio risk. Suppose one leg of the triangle represents the portfolio's equity book while the other leg represents the fixed-income book. Changes in either variability (volatility) or investment allocation would be modelled as changes to the length of the legs (increasing risk or increasing allocation would lengthen the leg) and the resultant portfolio

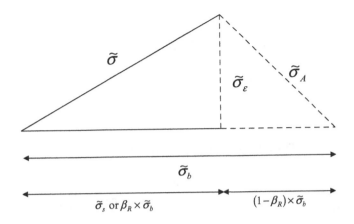

FIGURE 4.7 Visual risk

risk would then be represented by the total (dotted) arrow. Similarly, simulating changes in correlation is done by changing the angle between the legs.

Singer, Kessler, Schwarz, Terhaar and Zerolis[9] (1999) also use geometry to provide the visual risk framework illustrated in Figure 4.7.

From Equation 4.23 $\tilde{\sigma}^2 = \beta_R^2 \times \tilde{\sigma}_b^2 + \tilde{\sigma}_\varepsilon^2$. These risks can also be viewed in visual terms where variabilities correspond to the lengths of the sides of a triangle. Phythagoras tells us the square of the hypotenuse of a right-angled triangle is equal to the sum of squares of the opposite and adjacent sides. Therefore Equation 4.23 can be represented by the right-angled triangle on the left-hand side of Figure 4.7 with a hypotenuse of length $\tilde{\sigma}$ and the other two sides of lengths $\tilde{\sigma}_\varepsilon$ and $\beta_R \times \tilde{\sigma}_b$ (or $\tilde{\sigma}_s$) respectively. The right-angled triangle on the right-hand side of Figure 4.7 has hypotenuse of length $\tilde{\sigma}_A$ and the other two sides of length $\tilde{\sigma}_\varepsilon$ and $(1 - \beta_R) \times \tilde{\sigma}_b$. Note specific risk $\tilde{\sigma}_\varepsilon$ is a common side to both triangles. The hypotenuse of the triangle on the right-hand side represents relative risk or tracking error. Again using Pythagoras we have the relationship:

$$\tilde{\sigma}_A^2 = \tilde{\sigma}_\varepsilon^2 + (1 - \beta_R)^2 \times \tilde{\sigma}_b^2 \tag{4.30}$$

It follows that:

$$\sigma_A^2 = \sigma_\varepsilon^2 + (1 - \beta_R)^2 \times \sigma_b^2 \tag{4.31}$$

$$\sigma_A = \sqrt{\sigma_\varepsilon^2 + (1 - \beta_R)^2 \times \sigma_b^2} \tag{4.32}$$

---

[9]B. Singer, C. Kessler, G. Schwarz, K. Terhaar and J. Zerolis (1999/2000) Improving Risk Measurement, Analysis and Management (with a Little More Help from Euclid). *Journal of Performance Measurement*, Winter, 8–18.

EXHIBIT 4.6   Relative risk and correlation

Relative risk (or tracking error):

$$\sigma_A = \sqrt{\sigma_\varepsilon^2 + (1 - \beta_R)^2 \times \sigma_b^2} = \sqrt{0.34^2 + (1 - 0.9814) \times 3.36^2} = 0.348$$

Correlation:

$$\rho_{r,b} = \frac{(\sigma^2 + \sigma_b^2 - \sigma_A^2)}{2 \times \sigma \times \sigma_b} = \frac{(3.32^2 + 3.36^2 - 0.348^2)}{2 \times 3.32 \times 3.36} = 0.995$$

Also, from the law of cosines the correlation between portfolio and benchmark is:

$$\rho_{r,b} = \frac{(\sigma^2 + \sigma_b^2 - \sigma_A^2)}{2 \times \sigma \times \sigma_b} \tag{4.33}$$

The relationships described in Equation 4.32 and Equation 4.33 are verified with our standard portfolio and benchmark data from Table 2.1 and Table 2.2 in Exhibit 4.6.

TREYNOR RATIO (REWARD TO VOLATILITY)

The Treynor[10] ratio (see Figure 4.8) is similar to but predates the Sharpe ratio by one year; the numerator (or vertical axis graphically speaking) is identical but in the denominator (horizontal axis), instead of total risk we have systematic risk as calculated by *beta*.

$$\text{Treynor ratio } TR = \frac{\tilde{r} - \tilde{r}_F}{\beta} \tag{4.34}$$

Presumably because it is included in most MBA studies, the Treynor ratio is extremely well known but perhaps less frequently used because it ignores specific risk. If a portfolio is fully diversified with no specific risk the Treynor and Sharpe ratios will give the same ranking. Sharpe actually initially favoured the Treynor ratio because he felt any value gained from being not fully diversified was transitory. Unfortunately, the performance analyst does not have the

---

[10]J. L. Treynor (1965) How to Rate Management of Invested Funds. *Harvard Business Review* 44(1), 63–75.

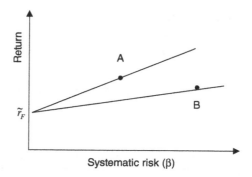

FIGURE 4.8   Treynor ratio

luxury of ignoring specific risk when assessing historic returns, and of course active managers expect to generate alpha from specific risk.

MODIFIED TREYNOR RATIO

A logical alternative form of the Treynor ratio might use systematic risk σ_S in the denominator, which is more consistent with the Sharpe ratio, for convenience called the modified Treynor ratio.

$$MTR = \frac{\tilde{r} - \tilde{r}_F}{\tilde{\sigma}_S} \qquad (4.35)$$

APPRAISAL RATIO (OR TREYNOR–BLACK RATIO)

The appraisal ratio first suggested by Treynor and Black[11] (1973) is similar in concept to the information ratio but using Jensen's *alpha*, excess return adjusted for systematic risk in the numerator, divided by specific risk (standard deviation of the error term) not tracking error.

$$\text{Appraisal ratio} = \frac{\tilde{\alpha}}{\tilde{\sigma}_\varepsilon} \qquad (4.36)$$

The appraisal ratio measures the systematic risk adjusted reward for each unit of specific risk taken. Figure 4.9 demonstrates the consistency of design of all of these composite statistics, a measure of reward in the vertical axis, in this

---

[11]Jack L. Treynor and Fischer Black (1973) How to Use Security Analysis to Improve Portfolio Selection. *Journal of Business*, January, 66–85.

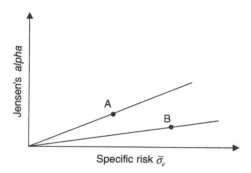

Specific risk $\tilde{\sigma}_\varepsilon$

FIGURE 4.9 Appraisal ratio

case Jensen's *alpha*, and a measure of risk along the horizontal axis, in this case specific risk. The gradient of the line, from the origin in this case, determines which combination of risk and reward is positioned further into the top left of the quadrant. Although seldom used, I must say this statistic appeals to me and perhaps should be given more consideration by more sophisticated investors (assuming of course a stable line of regression).

> ### ⚠ Caution
>
> The appraisal ratio is often described as, and confused with, the informa-
> tion ratio. Assuming the *beta* and *alphas* are of good quality (high R^2) the
> appraisal measure is a good measure of skill removing any return from sys-
> tematic risk in the numerator and also removing systematic risk from the
> denominator.

MODIFIED JENSEN

Smith and Tito[12] (1969) suggested the use of modified Jensen to rank portfolio performance. This measure is similar to the appraisal ratio but Jensen's *alpha* is here divided by systematic risk rather than specific risk.

$$\text{Modified Jensen} = \frac{\tilde{\alpha}}{\beta} \tag{4.37}$$

[12]Keith Smith and Dennis Tito (1969) Risk Return of Ex-Post Portfolio Performance. *Journal of Financial and Quantitative Analysis* 4(4), 449–471.

This measures the systematic risk-adjusted return per unit of systematic risk.

Although not suggested in their paper a logical alternative might be:

$$\text{Alternative modified Jensen } \frac{\tilde{\alpha}}{\tilde{\sigma}_S} \qquad (4.38)$$

FAMA DECOMPOSITION

Fama[13] (1972) extended the concept of Treynor's ratio in his paper "Components of Investment Performance" to further break down the return of a portfolio.

The excess return above the risk-free rate can be expressed as the selectivity (or Jensen's *alpha*) plus the return due to systematic risk as follows:

$$\underbrace{\bar{r} - \bar{r}_F}_{\substack{\text{Excess} \\ \text{return}}} = \underbrace{\bar{r} - \beta \times (\bar{b} - r_F) - \bar{r}_F}_{\text{Selectivity}} + \underbrace{\beta \times (\bar{b} - \bar{r}_F)}_{\substack{\text{Systematic} \\ \text{risk}}} \qquad (4.39)$$

If a portfolio is completely diversified there is no specific risk and the total portfolio risk will equal the systematic risk. Portfolio managers will give up diversification seeking additional return. Selectivity can be broken down into net selectivity and the return required to justify the diversification given up.

SELECTIVITY

Isolating selectivity in Equation 4.39 we notice that it is equivalent to Jensen's *alpha* from Equation 4.8, repeated here:

$$\alpha = \bar{r} - \bar{r}_F - \beta \times (\bar{b} - \bar{r}_F) \qquad (4.8)$$

DIVERSIFICATION

Diversification is the amount of return required to justify moving away from the benchmark and taking on specific risk. It calculates the return that would have been achieved simply by taking the same amount of systematic risk as the total risk of the portfolio. To calculate this return we first have to calculate

---

[13]E. F. Fama (1972) Components of Investment Performance. *Journal of Finance* 27(3), 551–567.

the effective *beta* required so that the systematic risk is equivalent to the total portfolio risk. Call this the Fama *beta,* calculated as follows:

$$\beta_F = \frac{\sigma}{\sigma_b} \tag{4.40}$$

Therefore, the return required to justify not being fully diversified is calculated using the difference in the Fama *beta* from the portfolio *beta* as follows:

$$d = (\beta_F - \beta) \times (\bar{b} - \bar{r}_F) \tag{4.41}$$

Note the Fama *beta* will always be greater than or equal to the portfolio *beta* since total risk is greater than or equal to the systematic risk of the portfolio. If the benchmark return is greater than the risk-free rate, the diversification required will be positive.

NET SELECTIVITY

Net selectivity is the remaining selectivity after deducting the amount of return required to justify not being fully diversified.

$$\text{Net selectivity } S_{\text{Net}} = \alpha - d \tag{4.42}$$

Obviously if net selectivity is negative the portfolio manager has not justified the loss of diversification.

Fama decomposition is useful analysis if we only have access to total fund returns and are unable to perform more detailed analysis on the components of return, the mutual funds of competitors, for example.

Figure 4.10 illustrates Fama's decomposition for portfolio A. A' represents the return from systematic risk plus the risk-free rate and represents the return from the Fama equivalent systematic risk plus risk-free rate.

FAMA–FRENCH THREE-FACTOR MODEL

The CAPM model uses just one factor, *beta* or systematic risk, to describe the relationship of portfolio returns to the benchmark. Eugene Fama and Kenneth French[14] (1993) observed that two classes of stocks tended to do better than the market as a whole: small capitalisation stocks and value stocks. They added two

---

[14]E. F. Fama and K. R. French (1993) Common Risk Factors in the Returns of Stocks and Bonds. *Journal of Financial Economics* 33(1), 3–56.

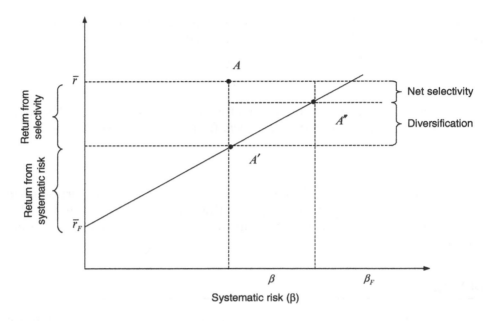

FIGURE 4.10   Fama decomposition

factors to the CAPM model to reflect these exposures, resulting in the following
Fama–French regression equation:

$$r - r_F = \alpha_3 + \beta_3 \times (b - r_F) + \beta_S \times SMB + \beta_v \times HML + \varepsilon_3 \qquad (4.43)$$

Where:

α_3 = three-factor *alpha*
β_3 = three-factor systematic risk
ε_3 = three-factor error term
SMB = small minus big (market capitalisation)
HML = high minus low (book to market ratio)

β_S and β_V are coefficients determined by linear regression. β_S or size *beta*
measures the portfolio's sensitivity to small capitalisation stocks, a coefficient
greater than 1 indicating greater sensitivity to small capitalisation stocks compared to large capitalisation stocks. β_V or value *beta* measures the portfolio's
sensitivity to value stocks, a coefficient greater than 1 indicating greater sensitivity to value stocks rather than growth stocks.

Note

The historical series of returns for Fama and French's factors are publicly available on https://mba .tuck.dartmouth.edu/pages/ faculty/ken.french/data_library .html

THREE-FACTOR *ALPHA* (OR FAMA–FRENCH *ALPHA*)

The resulting *alpha* from the Fama–French regression equation is analogous to the CAPM *alpha* and can be used in exactly the same way. β_3 is similar, but not identical, to CAPM β.

CARHART FOUR-FACTOR MODEL

Carhart[15] (1997) extended the three-factor model to a four-factor model adding a momentum factor resulting in the following Carhart regression equation:

$$r - r_F = \alpha_4 + \beta_4 \times (b - r_F) + \beta_s \times SMB + \beta_v \times HML + \beta_m \times MOM + \varepsilon_4$$

(4.44)

Where:

α_4 = four-factor *alpha*
β_4 = four-factor systematic risk
ε_4 = four-factor error term
MOM = momentum

β_m is a coefficient determined by linear regression. β_m or momentum *beta* measures a portfolio's sensitivity to momentum stocks.

FOUR-FACTOR *ALPHA* (OR CARHART'S *ALPHA*)

Again, the resulting *alpha* from the Carhart regression equation is analogous to the CAPM and three-factor *alpha* and can be used in exactly the same way.

---

[15]M. M. Carhart (1997) On Persistence in Mutual Fund Performance. *Journal of Finance* 52(1), 57–82.

TYPES OF *ALPHA*

Confusingly we now have a number of different definitions of *alpha* – which should we use? Ultimately it depends on the preferences of the asset owner and what exactly they are looking for. *Alpha*, the excess return adjusted for systematic risk, is often described as the holy grail of investment management. Three-factor and four-factor *alphas* could be used in the appraisal ratio to calculate three-factor and four-factor appraisal ratios.

Various definitions of excess return are listed in Table 4.8.

TABLE 4.8 Definitions of excess return

Excess return	Excess return above the risk-free rate. The numerator of the Sharpe ratio.
Arithmetic excess	$(r - b)$ probably the most common. Often confused with *alpha*.
Geometric excess	$\left(\frac{1+r}{1+b}\right) - 1$. The technically correct definition of excess return.
Regression *alpha*	See Equation 4.2.
Jensen's alpha	See Equation 4.8. Excess return adjusted for systematic risk. My preferred definition alpha as opposed to excess return.
Three-factor *alpha*	See Equation 4.43.
Four-factor *alpha*	See Equation 4.44.
M^2 excess	See Equations 11.3 and 11.4 (both arithmetic and geometric versions).
Skew-adjusted M^2 excess	Excess return adjusted for risk and skew preference. See Equation 11.9.
Adjusted M^2 excess	Excess return adjusted for risk and preferences of skew and kurtosis. See Equation 11.8 and Chapter 13; my strong preference for calculating performance fees.
GH1 and GH2	Rarely used.
Omega excess	See Equation 11.11.
Differential return	See Equation 11.6.
Net selectivity	See Equation 4.42.

MULTI-FACTOR MODELS

Further additional systematic risks or factors can be introduced with the objective of explaining the entire return and reducing any *alpha* to zero. Multi-factor models can be divided into three main categories:

  i) Fundamental
 ii) Macroeconomic
iii) Statistical

Fundamental models compare portfolio returns to underlying microeconomic factors such as industry classification, market capitalisation, style and so on.

Macroeconomic models compare portfolio returns to economic factors such as employment, inflation and interest rates.

Statistical models start with no assumption about factors but attempt to determine which factors best explain portfolio returns by using statistical methods such as principal component analysis. Assigning economic interpretation to these factors can be difficult.

> ### ⚠ Caution
>
> Ex-post factor analysis is an additional useful tool to understand better how asset managers are adding (or subtracting) value. Care is required – portfolios change through time, factors change through time, and individual security's sensitivity to factors change through time. If you torture numbers long enough, eventually they will tell you what you want to hear.

CHAPTER 5

Drawdown

"The only thing that makes life possible is permanent, intolerable uncertainty; not knowing what comes next."

Ursula K. LeGuin (1929–2018)

There are a surprisingly large number of appraisal measures based on drawdown and related concepts. Most in my view are fairly redundant with the notable exception of maximum drawdown. Drawdown might be defined as either the peak to valley fall in performance or any continuous, uninterrupted losing return period. The choice of which definition to use will depend on the preferences of the investor, the time period and/or the periodicity of the data. High net worth investors typically using daily data would probably prefer a peak to valley definition, whereas institutional investors using monthly data might be more concerned by periods of continuous negative returns. Other definitions include active drawdown based on relative or active return rather than absolute return.

AVERAGE DRAWDOWN

As its name suggests, the average drawdown is the average continuous negative return (or peak to trough return) over an investment period, three years being a typical period of measurement.

$$\text{Average drawdown } \overline{D} = \left| \sum_{j=1}^{j=d} \frac{D_j}{d} \right| \tag{5.1}$$

Where:

D_j = jth drawdown over entire period
d = total number of drawdowns in entire period

Some investors take the view that only the largest drawdowns in the return series are of any consequence and therefore restrict d to a predetermined maximum limit of say three or five, or even the single largest individual drawdown, thus enabling fair comparison between portfolios.

MAXIMUM DRAWDOWN

The maximum drawdown (D_{Max}), not to be confused with the largest individual drawdown, is the maximum loss over a specific time period, typically three years. Maximum drawdown represents the maximum loss an investor could have suffered in the fund buying at the highest point (the high-water mark) and selling at the lowest (the low-water mark). Like any other statistic it is essential to compare performance over the same time period and of course this measure will be heavily influenced by outliers. Mini-max[1] is an alternative name for maximum drawdown. Maxi-min represents the maximum gain buying at the lowest point and selling at the highest.

LARGEST INDIVIDUAL DRAWDOWN

As its name suggests the largest individual drawdown (D_{Lar}) is the largest individual uninterrupted or peak to valley loss in a return series.

RECOVERY TIME (OR DRAWDOWN DURATION)

The recovery time or drawdown duration is the time taken to recover from an individual or maximum drawdown to the original level.

The recovery time may be measured from the peak or high-water mark or may also be measured from the subsequent valley or low-water mark.

⚠ **Caution**

I'm continually surprised how often drawdown and recovery statistics are requested without any guidance as to the time period in question; always disclose the basis of the analysis.

Individual and maximum drawdowns and recovery time from the high-water mark are illustrated in Figure 5.1 using the continuous interrupted loss definition. The largest individual loss is D_3. D_2 and D_3 would not be classified as separate drawdowns in the peak to trough definition since the

---

[1]Note that the terms mini-max and maxi-min are used differently in decision theory and game theory. Mini-max is a decision rule for minimising the worst-case loss, and maxi-min for maximising the lowest gain.

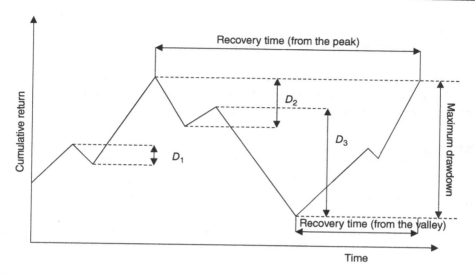

FIGURE 5.1   Drawdown statistics

high-water mark has not been recovered; it is just a small positive bump on the way down to a deeper trough.

DRAWDOWN DEVIATION

Drawdown deviation calculates a standard deviation type statistic using individual drawdowns as follows:

$$\text{Drawdown deviation } DD = \sqrt{\sum_{j=1}^{j=d} \frac{D_j^2}{n}} \qquad (5.2)$$

ULCER INDEX

The Ulcer index developed by Peter G. Martin[2] in 1987 (so called because of the worry suffered by both the portfolio manager and asset owner) is similar to drawdown deviation with the exception that the impact of time "under water" is combined with the depth of drawdown by selecting the negative return for each period below the previous peak or high-water mark. Deeper drawdowns will have a more significant impact because the calculation is squared. Naturally in this index the definition of drawdown is peak to trough.

$$\text{Ulcer index } UI = \sqrt{\sum_{i=1}^{i=n} \frac{D'^2_i}{n}} \qquad (5.3)$$

---

[2]P. G. Martin and B. McCann (1989), *The Investor's Guide to Fidelity Funds: Winning Strategies for Mutual Fund Investors*. John Wiley & Sons.

Where:

D_i' = drawdown since previous peak in period i

This approach is clearly sensitive to the frequency of time period and clearly penalises managers who take time to recover to previous highs considering both the depth and duration of drawdowns.

PAIN INDEX

If the drawdowns are not squared then the resulting Pain index is very similar to the Zephyr Pain index[3] as proposed by Thomas Becker:

$$\text{Pain index } PI = \sum_{i=1}^{i=n} \frac{|D_i'|}{n} \tag{5.4}$$

This statistic combines the depth, duration and frequency of drawdowns in the portfolio manager's return series. Consider the manager's cumulative return series in Figure 5.2. The peaks or high-water marks in the return series act as dams holding back the lakes and increasing the volume of pain

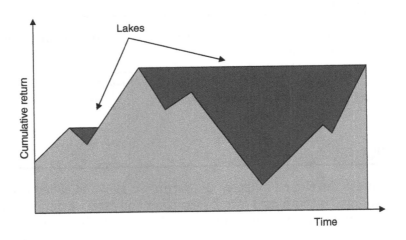

FIGURE 5.2   Pain index

[3]T. Becker (2010) *The Zephyr K-Ratio*, Zephyr Associates.

CALMAR RATIO (OR DRAWDOWN RATIO)

The Calmar ratio proposed by Young[4] in 1991 is a Sharpe-type measure that uses maximum drawdown rather than standard deviation to reflect the investor's risk. In the context of hedge fund performance, it is easy to understand why investors might prefer the maximum possible loss from peak to valley as an appropriate measure of risk. Calmar is an acronym of **Cal**ifornia **M**anaged **A**nnual **R**eports and is always measured over 36 months.

$$\text{Calmar ratio } CR = \frac{\tilde{r} - \tilde{r}_F}{D_{Max}} \tag{5.5}$$

 Note

Early versions of Calmar exclude the risk-free rate in the numerator. Unlike negative Sharpe and negative information ratios I don't see a great deal of value in negative Calmar ratios.

MAR RATIO

The MAR ratio, promoted by a competitor newsletter to California Managed Annual Reports, calculates the Calmar ratio from inception rather than over three years; this makes direct comparisons of portfolios with different inception dates difficult to evaluate.

STERLING RATIO

The Sterling ratio replaces maximum drawdown in the Calmar ratio with the average drawdown over the period of analysis.

There are multiple variations of the Sterling ratio in common usage, perhaps reflecting its use across a range of differing asset categories and outside the field of finance.

---

[4]T. W. Young (1991) Calmar Ratio: A Smoother Tool. *Futures Magazine*, 1 October.

The original definition, attributed to Deane Sterling Jones,[5] a company no longer in existence, appears to be:

$$\text{Original Sterling ratio } OSR = \frac{\tilde{r}}{\overline{D}_{Lar} + 10\%} \tag{5.6}$$

Where:

$\overline{D}_{Lar}$ = average largest drawdown

The denominator is defined as the average largest drawdown plus 10%. The addition of 10% is arbitrary, compensating for the fact that the average largest drawdown is inevitably smaller than the maximum drawdown. Typically, only a fixed number of the largest drawdowns are averaged – for example, the largest three individual drawdowns over three years. Adding additional small drawdowns clearly dilutes the impact of the largest drawdowns. With apologies to Deane Sterling Jones, I suggest the definition is standardised to exclude the 10% (which is redundant in terms of comparison) but in Sharpe form as follows:

$$\text{Sterling ratio } SR_d = \frac{\tilde{r} - \tilde{r}_F}{\overline{D}_{Lar}} = \frac{\tilde{r} - \tilde{r}_F}{\left| \sum_{j=1}^{j=d} \frac{D_j}{d} \right|} \tag{5.7}$$

The number of observations d is fixed to the investor's preference, which could be the largest single drawdown ($d = 1$) or more typically 3 or 5.

STERLING–CALMAR RATIO

Perhaps the most common variation of the Sterling ratio uses the average annual maximum drawdown in the denominator over three years. A combination of both Sterling and Calmar concepts, to avoid confusion and to encourage consistent use across the industry, I suggest the following standardised definition:

$$\text{Sterling–Calmar ratio } SCR = \frac{\tilde{r} - \tilde{r}_F}{\overline{D}_{Max}} \tag{5.8}$$

Where:

$\overline{D}_{Max}$ = average annual maximum drawdown

---

[5]T. McCafferty (2003) *The Market Is Always Right*, McGraw Hill.

Caution

Given the variety of Sterling ratio definitions, great care should be taken to ensure the same definition is used over the same time period using the same frequency of data when ranking portfolio performance.

BURKE RATIO

Burke,[6] in his article "A Sharper Sharpe Ratio", suggested using the familiar concept of the square root of the sum of the squares of each drawdown in order to penalise major drawdowns as opposed to many mild ones.

$$\text{Burke ratio } BR_d = \frac{\bar{r} - \tilde{r}_F}{\sqrt{\sum_{j=1}^{j=d} D_j^2}} \tag{5.9}$$

Just like the Sterling ratio, the number of drawdowns used can be restricted to a set number of the largest drawdowns.

MODIFIED BURKE RATIO

For consistency with other Sharpe-type statistics it might be more appropriate to define the modified Burke ratio using drawdown deviation in the denominator as follows:

$$\text{Modified Burke ratio } MBR_d = \frac{\bar{r} - \tilde{r}_F}{\sqrt{\sum_{j=1}^{j=d} \frac{D_j^2}{n}}} \tag{5.10}$$

Clearly both the modified and standard Burke ratios will generate identical portfolio rankings.

MARTIN RATIO (OR ULCER PERFORMANCE INDEX)

If the duration of drawdowns is a concern for investors the Martin ratio is similar to the modified Burke ratio but using the Ulcer index in the denominator

$$\text{Martin ratio } MR = \frac{\bar{r} - \tilde{r}_F}{\sqrt{\sum_{i=1}^{i=n} \frac{D'^2_i}{n}}} \tag{5.11}$$

---

[6]G. Burke (1994) A Sharper Sharpe Ratio. *The Computerized Trader*, March.

PAIN RATIO

The equivalent to the Martin ratio but using the Pain index is the Pain ratio.

$$\text{Pain ratio } PR = \frac{\bar{r} - \bar{r}_F}{\sum\limits_{i=1}^{i=n} \frac{D'_i}{n}} \tag{5.12}$$

Both the Pain and Martin ratios penalise managers with early high-water marks in their track record, therefore it is far better to peak later rather than earlier when applying these ratios.

Peak to trough drawdown statistics are calculated for our standard portfolio data in Table 5.5 and used to calculate Calmar, Sterling, Burke, Sterling–Calmar, Pain and Ulcer ratios in Exhibit 5.1. Continuous, uninterrupted drawdown statistics are calculated in Exhibit 5.2. Figure 5.3 illustrates the drawdown for our standard portfolio data. This data is dominated by one large drawdown month 14 to month 31 and a few smaller drawdowns. The maximum drawdown occurs through month 14 to month 18 in the manager's return series.

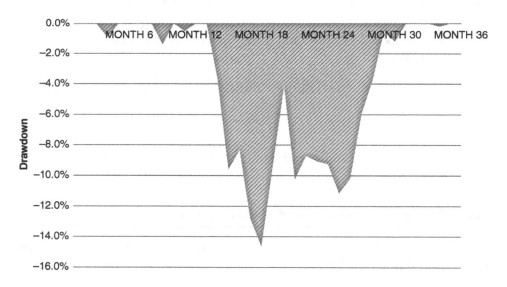

FIGURE 5.3 Drawdown

EXHIBIT 5.1 Drawdown (peak to trough definition)

Calmar ratio $CR = \dfrac{\tilde{r} - \tilde{r}_F}{D_{Max}} = \dfrac{13.29\% - 2.43\%}{14.63\%} = 0.74$

Largest individual drawdowns 14.6%, 1.4% and 0.9%

Average drawdown $\overline{D}_{Lar} = \left| \sum\limits_{j=1}^{j=d} \dfrac{D}{d} \right| = \dfrac{14.6\% + 1.4\% + 0.9\%}{3} = 5.64\%$

Note only the three largest drawdowns have been selected.

Sterling ratio $SR_3 = \dfrac{\tilde{r} - \tilde{r}_F}{\left| \sum\limits_{j=1}^{j=3} \dfrac{D_j}{3} \right|} = \dfrac{13.29\% - 2.43\%}{5.64\%} = 1.92$

Drawdown deviation $DD = \sqrt{\sum\limits_{j=1}^{j=d} \dfrac{D_j^2}{n}} = \sqrt{\dfrac{214.04 + 1.96 + 0.81}{36}} = 2.45$

Modified Burke ratio $MBR_3 = \dfrac{\tilde{r} - \tilde{r}_F}{\sqrt{\sum\limits_{j=1}^{j=3} \dfrac{D_j^2}{n}}} = \dfrac{13.29\% - 2.43\%}{2.45} = 4.43$

Average maximum drawdown $\overline{D}_{Max} = \dfrac{1.4\% + 14.63\% + 2.1\%}{3} = 6.04\%$

Sterling–Calmar ratio $SCR = \dfrac{\tilde{r} - \tilde{r}_F}{\overline{D}_{max}} = \dfrac{13.29\% - 2.43\%}{6.04\%} = 1.80$

Pain index $PI = \sum\limits_{i=1}^{i=n} \dfrac{|D_i'|}{n} = \dfrac{135.33}{36} = 3.76$

Pain ratio $PR = \dfrac{\tilde{r} - \tilde{r}_F}{\sum\limits_{i=1}^{i=n} \dfrac{D_i'}{n}} = \dfrac{13.29\% - 2.43\%}{3.76} = 2.89$

Ulcer index $UI = \sqrt{\sum\limits_{i=1}^{i=n} \dfrac{D_i'^2}{n}} = \sqrt{\dfrac{1285.19}{36}} = 5.97$

Martin ratio $MR = \dfrac{\tilde{r} - \tilde{r}_F}{\sqrt{\sum\limits_{i=1}^{i=n} \dfrac{D_i'^2}{n}}} = \dfrac{13.29\% - 2.43\%}{5.97} = 1.82$

TABLE 5.1　Drawdown statistics

Portfolio Monthly Return (%)	Continuous Drawdown D_j	Continuous Drawdown Squared D_j^2	Drawdown from Peak D'_i	Drawdown from Peak Squared D'^2_i
0.3				
2.6				
1.1				
−0.9	−0.9	0.81	−0.90	0.81
1.4				
2.4				
1.5				
6.6				
−1.4	−1.4	1.96	−1.40	1.96
3.9				
−0.5	−0.5	0.25	−0.50	0.25
8.1				
4.0				
−3.7			−3.70	13.69
−6.1	−9.6	91.67	−9.57	91.67
1.4			−8.31	69.03
−4.9			−12.80	163.87
−2.1	−6.9	47.57	−14.63	214.11
6.2			−9.34	87.23
5.8			−4.08	16.66
−6.4	−6.4	40.96	−10.22	104.45
1.7			−8.69	75.58
−0.4			−9.06	82.07
−0.2			−9.24	85.40
−2.1	−2.7	7.22	−11.15	124.25
1.1			−10.17	103.42
4.7			−5.95	35.37
2.4			−3.69	13.62
3.3			−0.51	0.26
−0.7	−0.7	0.49	−1.21	1.46
4.7				
0.6				
1.0				
−0.2	−0.2	0.04	−0.20	0.04
3.4				
1.0				

Maximum Drawdown 14.63%
(months 14 to 18)
Maximum Drawdown (year 1)
1.4% (month 9)
Maximum Drawdown (year 2)
14.63%
Maximum Drawdown (year 3)
2.1% (month 25)

Total
$$\sum_{i=1}^{i=n} D'_i = -135.33$$

Total
$$\sum_{i=1}^{i=n} D'^2_i = 1285.19$$

EXHIBIT 5.2 Drawdown (continuous uninterrupted definition)

Largest individual drawdowns 9.6%, 6.9% and 6.4%

Average drawdown $\overline{D}_{Lar} = \left| \sum\limits_{j=1}^{j=d} \dfrac{D}{d} \right| = \dfrac{96\% + 6.9\% + 6.4\%}{3} = 7.62\%$

Note all three of these "individual and uninterrupted" drawdowns are part of a much longer peak to trough drawdown. This is best observed in Figure 5.3.

Sterling ratio $SR_3 = \dfrac{\tilde{r} - \tilde{r}_F}{\left| \sum\limits_{j=1}^{j=3} \dfrac{D_j}{3} \right|} = \dfrac{13.29\% - 2.43\%}{7.62\%} = 1.42$

Drawdown deviation $DD = \sqrt{\sum\limits_{j=1}^{j=d} \dfrac{D_j^2}{n}} = \sqrt{\dfrac{91.67 + 47.57 + 40.96}{36}} = 2.24$

Modified Burke ratio $MBR_3 = \dfrac{\tilde{r} - \tilde{r}_F}{\sqrt{\sum\limits_{j=1}^{j=3} \dfrac{D_j^2}{n}}} = \dfrac{13.29\% - 2.43\%}{2.24} = 4.85$

ACTIVE (OR RELATIVE) DRAWDOWN

Drawdown statistics can also be calculated on the basis of active drawdown, relative returns underperforming the benchmark rather than just negative absolute returns. It follows that:

$$\text{Active Pain index } API = \sum\limits_{i=1}^{i=n} \dfrac{|AD'_j|}{n} \tag{5.13}$$

and

$$\text{Active Ulcer index } AUI = \sqrt{\sum\limits_{i=1}^{i=n} \dfrac{AD'^2_j}{n}} \tag{5.14}$$

Where:

AD'_j = active drawdown since previous peak in period j

Bradford and Siliski[7] (2016) suggest the active Calmar ratio based on maximum active drawdown:

$$ACR = \frac{\tilde{g}}{AD'_{Max}}$$ (5.15)

Where:

AD'_{Max} = maximum active drawdown

Active drawdown for the standard portfolio data is shown in Table 5.2 and illustrated in Figure 5.4. Note the disastrous relative performance towards the end of the measurement period, surely bad enough to cause major concern. Active Pain and active Ulcer are calculated in Exhibit 5.3. Note the numerator of the Pain and Ulcer ratios is excess return (arithmetic or geometric). The data in Table 5.2 is based on geometric excess returns. Although calculated, unlike the Sharpe or Information ratio I see no value in negative active Pain, Ulcer and Calmar ratios.

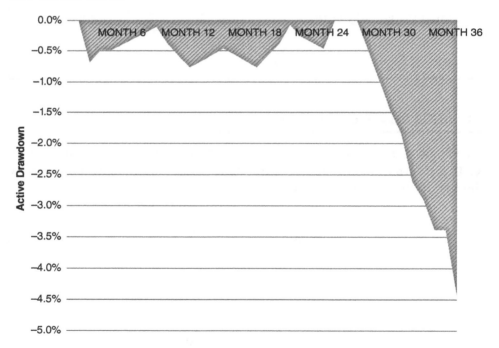

FIGURE 5.4 Active drawdown

[7]D. Bradford and D. Siliski (2016) Performance Drawdowns in Asset Management: Extending Drawdown Analysis to Active Returns. *Journal of Performance Measurement*, Fall, 34–48.

TABLE 5.2   Active drawdown statistics

Portfolio Monthly Return (%)	Active Drawdown AD_j	Active Continuous Drawdown Squared AD_j^2	Active Drawdown from Peak AD_j'	Active Drawdown from Peak Squared $AD_j'^2$
0.1				
0.1				
−0.7	−0.69	0.47	−0.69	0.47
0.2			−0.49	0.24
0.0			−0.49	0.24
0.1			−0.39	0.15
0.1			−0.29	0.08
0.1			−0.20	0.04
0.1			−0.10	0.01
−0.3			−0.38	0.15
−0.2			−0.58	0.34
−0.2	−0.67	0.45	−0.77	0.59
0.1			−0.67	0.45
0.1			−0.57	0.32
0.1			−0.46	0.21
−0.1			−0.56	0.31
−0.1			−0.67	0.44
−0.1	−0.31	0.09	−0.77	0.59
0.2			−0.58	0.34
0.2			−0.39	0.15
0.3			−0.07	0.00
−0.2			−0.27	0.07
−0.1			−0.37	0.13
−0.1	−0.40	0.16	−0.47	0.22
0.5				
0.4				
0.4				
−0.5			−0.49	0.24
−0.5			−0.97	0.93
−0.5			−1.46	2.14
−0.4			−1.84	3.37
−0.8			−2.61	6.82
−0.3			−2.90	8.41
−0.5	−3.01	9.08	−3.38	11.45
0.0			−3.38	11.45
−1.1	−1.08	1.16	−4.42	19.57

Maximum Active Drawdown 4.42%

Maximum Active Drawdown (year 1) 0.77%

Maximum Active Drawdown (year 2) 0.40%

Maximum Active Drawdown (year 3) 4.42%

Total

$$\sum_{i=1}^{i=n} D_i' = -31.66$$

Total

$$\sum_{i=1}^{i=n} D_i'^2 = 69.93$$

EXHIBIT 5.3　Active Pain and active Ulcer

$$\text{Active Pain index } API = \sum_{i=1}^{i=n} \frac{|AD'_j|}{n} = \frac{31.66}{36} = 0.88$$

$$\text{Active Pain ratio } APR = \frac{\tilde{g}}{API} = \frac{-1.16}{0.88} = -1.32$$

$$\text{Active Ulcer index } AUI = \sqrt{\sum_{i=1}^{i=n} \frac{AD'^2_j}{n}} = \sqrt{\frac{69.93}{36}} = 1.39$$

$$\text{Active Ulcer ratio } AUR = \frac{\tilde{g}}{AUI} = \frac{-1.16}{1.39} = -0.83$$

$$\text{Active Calmar ratio } ACR = \frac{\tilde{g}}{AD'_{Max}} = \frac{-1.16}{4.42} = -0.26$$

CHAPTER 6

Partial Moments

"Statistics are like bikinis. What they reveal is suggestive, but what they conceal is vital."

Aaron Levenstein (1910–1986)

"In mathematics you don't understand things. You get used to them."

Johann von Neumann (1903–1957)

S tandard deviation and the symmetrical normal distribution are the foundations of modern Portfolio Theory. Postmodern Portfolio Theory recognises that asset owners prefer upside risk (or if you prefer upside uncertainty) rather than downside risk and utilises semi-standard deviation. Partial or one-sided moment measures allow asset owners to ignore desirable risk and focus on undesirable risk.

DOWNSIDE RISK (OR SEMI-STANDARD DEVIATION)

Semi-standard deviation measures the variability of underperformance below a minimum target rate. The minimum target rate could be the risk-free rate, the benchmark, zero or any other fixed threshold required by the asset owner. All positive returns, above the minimum target rate, are included as zero in the calculation of semi-standard deviation or downside risk as follows:

$$\text{Downside risk } \sigma_D = \sqrt{\sum_{i=1}^{n} \frac{\min[(r_i - r_T), 0]^2}{n}} \qquad (6.1)$$

Where:

r_T = minimum target return

Clearly since positive returns above the minimum target return are excluded there are potentially fewer or in some cases no observations less than the target return. Therefore, great care must be taken to ensure there are sufficient returns to ensure that the calculation is meaningful.

As should be expected, downside variance is the square of downside risk:

$$\text{Downside variance } \sigma_D^2 = \sum_{i=1}^{n} \frac{\min[(r_i - r_T), 0]^2}{n} \tag{6.2}$$

 Note

The downside risk measure is not directly comparable to standard deviation. For a normal distribution with standard deviation of 1.0, the semi-standard deviation will be about 0.6.

DOWNSIDE POTENTIAL

Downside potential is the average sum of returns below target:

$$\text{Downside potential } \mu_D = \sum_{i=1}^{i=n} \frac{\min[(r_i - r_T), 0]}{n} \tag{6.3}$$

By convention the minus sign of downside potential is ignored. Therefore, perhaps a better way of expressing downside potential is as follows:

$$\text{Downside potential } \mu_D = \sum_{i=1}^{i=n} \frac{\max[(r_T - r_i), 0]}{n} \tag{6.4}$$

Note that the term $(r_i - r_T)$ has been reversed and replaced by $(r_T - r_i)$ and that:

$$\sum_{i=1}^{i=n} \max[(r_T - r_i), 0] = -1 \times \sum_{i=1}^{i=n} \min[(r_i - r_T), 0] \tag{6.5}$$

Downside variance is the second lower partial moment of return, and downside potential is the first lower partial moment.

PURE DOWNSIDE RISK

Pure downside risk is the special case of $r_T = 0$; only returns less than zero are included in the calculation.

$$\text{Pure downside risk } \sigma_P = \sqrt{\sum_{i=1}^{i=n} \frac{\min[r_i, 0]^2}{n}} \tag{6.6}$$

HALF VARIANCE (OR SEMI-VARIANCE)

In half variance and half risk calculations only returns lower than the mean are considered, that is, $r_T = \bar{r}$.

$$\text{Half variance } \sigma_H^2 = \sum_{i=1}^{i=n} \frac{\min[(r_i - \bar{r}), 0]^2}{n} \tag{6.7}$$

$$\text{Half risk } \quad \sigma_H = \sqrt{\sum_{i=1}^{i=n} \frac{\min[(r_i - \bar{r}), 0]^2}{n}} \tag{6.8}$$

UPSIDE RISK (OR UPSIDE UNCERTAINTY)

The term "upside risk" may be disconcerting, but it simply refers to the variability of returns that exceed a given target. The equivalent upside statistics are as expected:

$$\text{Upside risk } \sigma_U = \sqrt{\sum_{i=1}^{i=n} \frac{\max[(r_i - r_T), 0]^2}{n}} \tag{6.9}$$

$$\text{Upside variance } \sigma_U^2 = \sum_{i=1}^{i=n} \frac{\max[(r_i - r_T), 0]^2}{n} \tag{6.10}$$

$$\text{Upside potential } \mu_U = \sum_{i=1}^{i=n} \frac{\max[(r_i - r_T), 0]}{n} \tag{6.11}$$

Note in all the above equations the total number of observations n is always used irrespective of the number of observations above or below target.

Loss and gain standard deviation measure the variability of returns above or below target only and are typically not used in performance analysis.

$$\text{Loss standard deviation } \sigma_L = \sqrt{\sum_{i=1}^{i=n} \frac{\min[(r_i - r_T), 0]^2}{n_d}} \qquad (6.12)$$

$$\text{Gain standard deviation } \sigma_G = \sqrt{\sum_{i=1}^{i=n} \frac{\max[(r_i - r_T), 0]^2}{n_U}} \qquad (6.13)$$

Where:

n_d = number of returns less than target
n_U = number of returns greater than target

MEAN ABSOLUTE MOMENT

Similarly, the mean absolute moment calculates the average of downside deviations or the average of upside deviations as follows:

$$\text{Mean downside deviation } MAM_D = \sum_{i=1}^{n} \frac{\min[(r_i - r_t), 0]}{n_d} \qquad (6.14)$$

$$\text{Mean upside deviation } MAM_U = \sum_{i=1}^{n} \frac{\max[(r_i - r_T), 0]}{n_u} \qquad (6.15)$$

OMEGA RATIO (Ω)

In their article "A Universal Performance Measure", Shadwick and Keating[1] (2002) suggest a gain–loss ratio that also captures the information in the higher moments of a return distribution as follows:

$$\text{Omega ratio } \Omega = \frac{\text{Upside potential}}{\text{Downside potential}} = \frac{\frac{1}{n} \times \sum_{i=1}^{i=n} \max(r_i - r_T, 0)}{\frac{1}{n} \times \sum \max(r_T - r_i, 0)} \qquad (6.16)$$

---

[1]W. F. Shadwick and C. Keating (2002) A Universal Performance Measure. *Journal of Performance Measurement*, Spring, 59–84.

When used as a ranking statistic the higher the *Omega* ratio, the better. The *Omega* ratio equals 1 when r_T is the mean return.

Omega ratio implicitly adjusts for both skewness and kurtosis in the return distribution.

BERNARDO AND LEDOIT (OR GAIN–LOSS) RATIO

The Bernardo–Ledoit[2] ratio is a special case of the *Omega* ratio with $r_T = 0$.

$$\text{Bernardo–Ledoit ratio} = \frac{\frac{1}{n} \times \sum_{i=1}^{i=n} \max(r_i, 0)}{\frac{1}{n} \times \sum_{i=1}^{i=n} \max(0 - r_i, 0)} \tag{6.17}$$

d RATIO

The *d* ratio[3] is similar to the Bernardo–Ledoit ratio but inverted and taking into account the frequency of positive and negative returns:

$$d \text{ ratio} = \frac{n'_d \times \sum_{i=1}^{i=n} \max(0 - r_i, 0)}{n'_u \times \sum \max(r_i, 0)} \tag{6.18}$$

Where:

n'_d = number of returns less than zero
n'_u = number of returns greater than zero

The *d* ratio will have values between zero and infinity and can be used to rank the performance of portfolios. The lower the *d* ratio the better the performance, with a value of zero indicating there are no returns less than zero and a value of infinity indicating there are no returns greater than zero. Portfolio managers with positively skewed returns will have lower *d* ratios.

---

[2]A. Bernardo and O. Ledoit (1996) *Gain, Loss and Asset Pricing.* http://www.ledoit.net/gainloss.pdf
[3]S. Lavinio (1999) *The Hedge Fund Handbook.* McGraw-Hill.

OMEGA–SHARPE RATIO

The *Omega* ratio can be converted to a ranking statistic in familiar form to the Sharpe ratio. Clearly the average portfolio return less the target return is equal to the sum of the upside and downside potential:

$$Omega\text{–}Sharpe\ ratio = \frac{\tilde{r} - \tilde{r}_T}{\frac{1}{n} \times \sum_{i=1}^{i=n} \max(r_T - r_i, 0)} \tag{6.19}$$

$$\tilde{r} - \tilde{r}_T \approx \bar{r} - \bar{r}_T = \frac{1}{n} \times \sum_{i=1}^{i=n} r_i - r_T$$

$$= \frac{1}{n} \times \sum_{i=1}^{i=n} \max(r_i - r_T, 0) - \frac{1}{n} \times \sum_{i=1}^{i=n} \max(r_T - r_i, 0) \tag{6.20}$$

Substituting Equation (6.20) into Equation (6.19):

$$= \frac{\frac{1}{n} \times \sum_{i=1}^{i=n} \max(r_i - r_T, 0) - \frac{1}{n} \times \sum_{i=1}^{i=n} \max(r_T - r_i, 0)}{\frac{1}{n} \times \sum_{i=1}^{i=n} \max(r_T - r_i, 0)} \tag{6.21}$$

$$= \frac{\frac{1}{n} \times \sum_{i=1}^{i=n} \max(r_i - r_T, 0)}{\frac{1}{n} \times \sum_{i=1}^{i=n} \max(r_T - r_i, 0)} - \frac{\frac{1}{n} \times \sum_{i=1}^{i=n} \max(r_T - r_i, 0)}{\frac{1}{n} \times \sum_{i=1}^{i=n} \max(r_T - r_i, 0)} = \Omega - 1 \tag{6.22}$$

$$Omega\text{–}Sharpe\ ratio \approx \Omega - 1 \tag{6.23}$$

> **?** **Interpretation**
>
> The *Omega–Sharpe* ratio will rank portfolios in the same order as the *Omega* ratio. Although generating identical rankings the *Omega–Sharpe* ratio is at least in the familiar Sharpe-type format and therefore preferable.

SORTINO RATIO

A natural extension of the Sharpe and *Omega*–Sharpe ratios is the Sortino ratio.[4] It uses downside risk in the denominator as follows:

$$\text{Sortino ratio} = \frac{(\tilde{r} - \tilde{r}_T)}{\tilde{\sigma}_D} \tag{6.24}$$

The Sortino ratio is shown graphically in Figure 6.1.

Clearly investors should be seeking returns greater than the risk-free rate (why take any risk otherwise?), therefore the minimum accepted return in most cases should be greater than the risk-free rate.

REWARD TO HALF-VARIANCE

Reward to half-variance, suggested by Ang and Chua[5] in 1979, is similar to the Sortino ratio, in effect considering only returns less than the mean:

$$\text{Reward to half-variance} = \frac{(\tilde{r} - \tilde{r}_F)}{\tilde{\sigma}_H^2} \tag{6.25}$$

Where:

$\tilde{\sigma}_H^2$ = annualised half variance

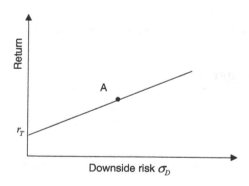

FIGURE 6.1 Sortino ratio

[4]F. Sortino and R. van der Meer (1991) Downside Risk. *Journal of Portfolio Management* 17(4), 27–31.
[5]J. S. Ang and J. H. Chua (1979) Composite Measures for the Evaluation of Investment Performance. *Journal of Financial and Quantitative Analysis* 14(2), 361–384.

DOWNSIDE RISK SHARPE RATIO

Similar to the Sortino ratio but far less common is the Downside risk Sharpe ratio suggested by Ziemba[6] in 2005, which considers only losses less than zero or pure downside risk.

$$\text{Downside risk Sharpe ratio} = \frac{(\tilde{r} - \tilde{r}_F)}{\tilde{\sigma}_P} \tag{6.26}$$

Where:

$\tilde{\sigma}_p$ = annualised pure downside risk

DOWNSIDE INFORMATION RATIO

I'm not aware of any published papers on the topic but certainly for those investors willing to ignore upside tracking error I see no objection to using downside relative risk in the denominator of the information ratio to create a downside information ratio.

$$\text{Downside information ratio (arithmetic)} \ \frac{\tilde{a}}{\sigma_{DA}} \tag{6.27}$$

$$\text{Downside information ratio (geometric)} \ \frac{\tilde{g}}{\sigma_{DG}} \tag{6.28}$$

Where:

$\tilde{\sigma}_{DA}$ = annualised arithmetic downside tracking error
$\tilde{\sigma}_{DG}$ = annualised geometric downside tracking error

SORTINO–SATCHELL RATIO

Rachev, Stoyanov and Fabozzi[7] (2008), Eling, Farinelli, Rossello and Tibiletti[8] (2009), Biglova, Orotobelli, Rachev and Stoyanov[9] (2004) all describe the

---

[6]W. T. Ziemba (2005) The Symmetric Downside-Risk Sharpe Ratio. *Journal of Portfolio Management* 32(1), 108–122.

[7]S. T. Rachev, S. V. Stoyanov and F. J. Fabozzi (2008) *Advanced Stochastic Models, Risk Assessment and Portfolio Optimization*. John Wiley & Sons.

[8]M. Eling, S. Farinelli, D. Rossello and L. Tibiletti (2009) *One-Size or Tailor-Made Performance Ratios for Ranking Hedge Funds*. Fakultat fur Mathematik und Wirtschaftswissenschaften, Universitat Ulm.

[9]A. Biglova, S. Ortobelli, S. T. Rachev and S. Stoyanov (2004) Different Approaches to Risk Estimation in Portfolio Theory. *Journal of Portfolio Management* 31(1), 103–112.

generalised downside risk-adjusted Sortino–Satchell ratio. Kaplan and Knowles[10] in their paper "Kappa: A Generalized Downside Risk-Adjusted Performance Measure" describe the same generalised ratio but name it Kappa. They demonstrate that both the Sortino ratio and the *Omega*–Sharpe ratio are special cases of Kappa:

$$\text{Sortino–Satchell} = K_l = \frac{\tilde{r} - \tilde{r}_T}{\sqrt[l]{\sum_{i=1}^{i=n} \frac{[(r_T - r_i), 0]^l}{n}}} \tag{6.29}$$

❓ Interpretation

For $l = 1$, K_1 is the *Omega*–Sharpe ratio and for $l = 2$, K_2 is the Sortino ratio. l need not be an integer and is set according to investor preference; greater l suggests a higher penalty for more extreme results, suitable for more risk averse investors.

KAPPA RATIO

In particular, K_3 – the third lower partial moment – is known specifically as the Kappa ratio. It perhaps makes most sense to use Sortino–Satchell to name the generalised ratio and Kappa to describe K_3.

$$\text{Kappa ratio} = K_3 = \frac{\tilde{r} - \tilde{r}_T}{\sqrt[3]{\sum_{i=1}^{i=n} \frac{[(r_T - r_i), 0]^3}{n}}} \tag{6.30}$$

UPSIDE POTENTIAL RATIO

The upside potential ratio suggested by Sortino, Van de Meer and Plantinga[11] (1999) can also be used to rank portfolio performance and it combines upside potential with downside risk as follows:

---

[10]P. D. Kaplan and J. A. Knowles (2004) Kappa: A Generalized Downside Risk-adjusted Performance Measure. *Journal of Performance Measurement* 8(1), 42–54.
[11]F. Sortino, R. van de Meer and A. Plantinga (1999) The Dutch Triangle: A Framework to Measure Upside Potential Relative to Downside Risk. *Journal of Portfolio Management* 26, 50–58.

Upside potential ratio

$$UPR = \frac{\text{Upside potential}}{\text{Downside risk}} = \frac{\mu_U}{\tilde{\sigma}_D} = \frac{\sum\limits_{i=1}^{i=n} \dfrac{\max[(r_i - r_T), 0]}{n}}{\tilde{\sigma}_D} \qquad (6.31)$$

 Interpretation

By using the first partial moment on the upside and the second partial moment on the downside investors are expressing a preference – they dislike more the extreme losses on the downside than the extreme gains on the upside.

Note

The Sortino ratio is conceptually more consistent with the Sharpe ratio in design and certainly in more common usage than the upside potential ratio and therefore my preference of the two ratios.

VOLATILITY SKEWNESS

A similar measure to *Omega* but using the second partial moment is volatility skewness,[12] the ratio of the upside variance compared to the downside variance. Values greater than 1 would indicate positive skewness and values less than 1 would indicate negative skewness:

$$\text{Volatility skewness} = \frac{\tilde{\sigma}_U^2}{\tilde{\sigma}_D^2} \qquad (6.32)$$

---

[12]B. M. Rom and K. W. Ferguson (2001) A Software Developer's View: Using Post-Modern Portfolio Theory to Improve Investment Performance Measurement. In F. Sortino and S. Satchell (eds) *Managing Downside Risk in Financial Markets*. Butterworth Heinemann.

> **? Interpretation**
>
> This measure, in particular, rewards extreme positive events and penalises
> extreme negative events. For those like me who are unsure about the merits
> of over rewarding extreme (potentially one-off) positive events, but are still
> concerned by negative extreme events, then perhaps the upside potential
> ratio is more appropriate.

VARIABILITY SKEWNESS

Although the rankings will be identical for consistency with other measures
typically used with asset management, I prefer the square root of volatility
skewness. To differentiate the term, I use the name variability skewness.

$$\text{Variability skewness} = \frac{\text{Upside risk}}{\text{Downside risk}} = \frac{\sigma_U}{\sigma_D} \qquad (6.33)$$

Portfolio downside risk, Sortino ratio, upside and downside potential,
Omega, *Omega*–Sharpe ratio and upside potential ratio and variability skewness
are calculated in Exhibit 6.1 based on data in Table 6.1.

FARINELLI–TIBILETTI RATIO

Farinelli and Tibiletti[13] (2008) suggest a generalised measure similar to
Sortino–Satchell but referencing both the upside and downside:

$$F - T_l^u = \frac{\sqrt[u]{\dfrac{1}{n} \times \sum_{i=1}^{i=n} \max(r_i - r_T, 0)^u}}{\sqrt[l]{\dfrac{1}{n} \times \sum_{i=1}^{i=n} \max(r_T - r_i, 0)^l}} \qquad (6.34)$$

> **? Interpretation**
>
> When u and l are both equal to 1 the Farinelli–Tibiletti ratio is equivalent
> to the *Omega* ratio and when u and l are both equal to two equivalent to
> variability skewness. $l = 2$ and $u = 1$ is the upside potential ratio. u and l
> need not be integers and can be set according to investor preference; $u < 1$
> and $l > 1$ is risk averse and $l < 1$ and $u > 1$ is risk seeking.

---

[13]S. Farinelli and L. Tibiletti (2008) Sharpe Thinking in Asset Ranking with One-Sided
Measures *European Journal of Operational Research* 185(3), 1542–1547.

TABLE 6.1 Portfolio downside risk

Monthly Minimum Target Return = 0.5%, Annual Minimum Target Return = 6.17%

Portfolio Monthly Return (%) r_i	Deviation Against Target (Downside Only) $\min[(r_i - r_T), 0]$	Squared Deviation (Downside Only) $\min[(r_i - r_T), 0]^2$	Upside Only $\max[(r_i - r_T), 0]$	Squared Deviation (Upside Only) $\max[(r_i - r_T), 0]^2$
0.3	−0.2	0.04		
2.6			2.1	4.41
1.1			0.6	0.36
−0.9	−1.4	1.96		
1.4			0.9	0.81
2.4			1.9	3.61
1.5			1.0	1.00
6.6			6.1	37.21
−1.4	−1.9	3.61		
3.9			3.4	11.56
−0.5	−1.0	1.00		
8.1			7.6	57.76
4.0			3.5	12.25
−3.7	−4.2	17.64		
−6.1	−6.6	43.56		
1.4			0.9	0.81
−4.9	−5.4	29.16		
−2.1	−2.6	6.76		
6.2			5.7	32.49
5.8			5.3	28.09
−6.4	−6.9	47.61		
1.7			1.2	1.44
−0.4	−0.9	0.81		
−0.2	−0.7	0.49		
−2.1	−2.6	6.76		
1.1			0.6	0.36
4.7			4.2	17.64
2.4			1.9	3.61
3.3			2.8	7.84
−0.7	−1.2	1.44		
4.7			4.2	17.64
0.6			0.1	0.01
1.0			0.5	0.25
−0.2	−0.7	0.49		
3.4			2.9	8.41
1.0			0.5	0.25
Total	$\sum_{i=1}^{i=n} \min[(r_i - r_T), 0] =$ **−36.3**	$\sum_{i=1}^{i=n} \min[(r_i - r_T), 0]^2 =$ **161.33**	$\sum_{i=1}^{i=n} \max[(r_i - r_T), 0] =$ **57.9**	$\sum_{i=1}^{i=n} \max[(r_i - r_T), 0]^2 =$ **247.81**

EXHIBIT 6.1   Downside and upside partial moments

$$\text{Downside potential } \mu_D = \sum_{i=1}^{n} \frac{\max[(r_T - r_i), 0]}{n} = \frac{36.3\%}{36} = 1.01\%$$

$$\text{Downside risk } \sigma_D = \sqrt{\sum_{i=1}^{n} \frac{\max[(r_T - r_i), 0]^2}{n}} = \sqrt{\frac{161.33}{36}} = 2.12\%$$

$$\text{Annualised downside risk } \tilde{\sigma}_D = \sqrt{t} \times \sigma_D = \sqrt{12} \times 2.12\% = 7.33\%$$

$$\text{Upside potential } \mu_U = \sum_{i=1}^{n} \frac{\max[(r_i - r_T), 0]}{n} = \frac{57.9\%}{36} = 1.61\%$$

$$\text{Upside risk } \sigma_U = \sqrt{\sum_{i=1}^{n} \frac{\max[(r_i - r_T), 0]^2}{n}} = \sqrt{\frac{247.81}{36}} = 2.62\%$$

$$\text{Annualised upside risk } \tilde{\sigma}_U = \sqrt{t} \times \sigma_U = \sqrt{12} \times 2.62\% = 9.09\%$$

$$\textit{Omega} \text{ ratio } \Omega = \frac{\text{Upside potential}}{\text{Downside potential}} = \frac{\frac{1}{n} \times \sum_{i=1}^{i=n} \max(r_i - r_T, 0)}{\frac{1}{n} \times \sum \max(r_T - r_i, 0)}$$

$$= \frac{1.61\%}{1.01\%} = 1.6$$

$$\text{Sortino ratio} = \frac{(\tilde{r} - \tilde{r}_T)}{\tilde{\sigma}_D} = \frac{13.29\% - 6.17\%}{7.33\%} = 0.97$$

$$\text{Upside potential ratio } UPR = \frac{\text{Upside potential}}{\text{Downside risk}} = \frac{\sum_{i=1}^{i=n} \max(r_i - r_T, 0)/n}{\tilde{\sigma}_D}$$

$$= \frac{1.61\%}{7.33\%} = 0.22$$

$$\text{Variability skewness} = \frac{\text{Upside risk}}{\text{Downside risk}} = \frac{\tilde{\sigma}_U}{\tilde{\sigma}_D} = \frac{9.09\%}{7.33\%} = 1.24$$

Both the Farinelli–Tibiletti ratio and Sortino–Satchell offer significant flexibility to investors to design ratios that meet their particular requirements, although it requires considerable investment in time, experience and copious quantities of data to add value.

> ## ⚠ Caution
>
> For asset managers these ratios offer significant opportunities to "data mine"[14] in order to find favourable results. Like all appraisal ratios they are calculated ex post but of course should be implemented ex ante.

GAIN–LOSS SKEWNESS

Gain–loss skewness is a specific version of the Farinelli–Tibiletti ratio representing the 3rd moment for both the upside and downside, in effect giving more weight to more extreme results on both sides of the distribution. $u = 3$ and $l = 3$.

$$\text{Gain–loss skewness} = F - T_3^3 = \frac{\sqrt[3]{\frac{1}{n} \times \sum_{i=1}^{i=n} \max(r_i - r_T, 0)^3}}{\sqrt[3]{\frac{1}{n} \times \sum_{i=1}^{i=n} \max(r_T - r_i, 0)^3}} \tag{6.35}$$

DOWNSIDE SKEWNESS AND KURTOSIS

I'm not convinced of the value of downside skewness or downside kurtosis but they can be found in literature[15] so therefore are included. Just like downside risk, returns above the minimal acceptable return or target return are ignored in the calculation as follows:

$$\text{Downside skewness } \varsigma_D = \sum_{i=1}^{i=n} \left(\frac{\min[r_i - r_T, 0]}{\sigma} \right)^3 \times \frac{1}{n} \tag{6.36}$$

$$\text{Downside kurtosis } \kappa_D = \sum_{i=1}^{i=n} \left(\frac{\min[r_i - r_T.0]}{\sigma} \right)^4 \times \frac{1}{n} \tag{6.37}$$

---

[14]Data mine (or *data dredge*) – the bad practice of analysing data for the exclusive purpose of identifying favourable outcomes.
[15]Y. Watanabe (2014) New Prospect Ratio: Application to Hedge Funds with Higher Order Moments. *Journal of Performance Measurement*, 19(1), 41–53.

SORTINO RATIO WITH HIGHER ORDER MOMENTS

Watanabe[16] (2014) suggests adjusting the Sortino ratio for higher moments, introducing the skew-adjusted Sortino ratio and the adjusted Sortino ratio as follows:

$$\text{Skew-adjusted Sortino ratio} = \frac{r - r_T}{\sqrt{\sigma_D^2 + \varsigma_D^2}} \qquad (6.38)$$

$$\text{Adjusted Sortino ratio} = \frac{r - r_T}{\sqrt{\sigma_D^2 + \varsigma_D^2 + \kappa_D^2}} \qquad (6.39)$$

Whilst these adjustments certainly provide an additional penalty for higher downside skewness and downside kurtosis, whether it is sufficient depends on investor preference. Downside skew and kurtosis are calculated in Exhibit 6.2 using data in Table 6.2.

EXHIBIT 6.2 Downside skew and kurtosis

$$\varsigma_D = \sum_{i=1}^{i=n} \left(\frac{\min[r_i - r_T, 0]}{\sigma} \right)^3 \times \frac{1}{n}$$

$$\varsigma_D = \frac{-896.46}{3.32^3} \times \frac{1}{36} = -0.68$$

$$\kappa_D = \sum_{i=1}^{i=n} \left(\frac{\min[r_i - r_T.0]}{\sigma} \right)^4 \times \frac{1}{n}$$

$$\kappa_D = \frac{3869.44}{3.32^4} \times \frac{1}{36} = 0.89$$

---

[16]Y. Watanabe (2014) New Prospect Ratio: Application to Hedge Funds with Higher Order Moments. *Journal of Performance Measurement*, 19(1), 41–53.

TABLE 6.2   Portfolio downside skew and kurtosis

Monthly Minimum Target Return = 0.5%, Annual Minimum Target Return = 6.17%

Portfolio Monthly Return (%) r_i	Deviation Against Target (Downside Only) $\min[(r_i - r_T), 0]$	Deviation Cubed (Downside Only) $\min[(r_i - r_T), 0]^3$	4th Power Deviation (Downside Only) $\min[(r_i - r_T), 0]^3$
0.3	−0.2	−0.01	0.01
2.6			
1.1			
−0.9	−1.4	−2.74	0.66
1.4			
2.4			
1.5			
6.6			
−1.4	−1.9	−6.86	3.84
3.9			
−0.5	−1.0	−1.00	0.06
8.1			
4.0			
−3.7	−4.2	−74.09	187.42
−6.1	−6.6	−287.50	1384.58
1.4			
−4.9	−5.4	−157.46	576.48
−2.1	−2.6	−17.58	19.45
6.2			
5.8			
−6.4	−6.9	−328.51	1677.72
1.7			
−0.4	−0.9	−0.73	0.03
−0.2	−0.7	−0.34	0.00
−2.1	−2.6	−17.58	19.45
1.1			
4.7			
2.4			
3.3			
−0.7	−1.2	−1.73	0.24
4.7			
0.6			
1.0			
−0.2	−0.7	−0.34	0.00
3.4			
1.0			
Total	$\sum\limits_{i=1}^{i=n} \min[(r_i - r_T), 0] =$ **−36.3**	$\sum\limits_{i=1}^{i=n} \min[(r_i - r_T), 0]^3 =$ **−896.46**	$\sum\limits_{i=1}^{i=n} \min[(r_i - r_T), 0]^4 =$ **3869.44**

CHAPTER 7

Prospect Theory

"Whenever there is a simple error that most laymen fall for, there is always a slightly more sophisticated version of the same problem that experts fall for."

A. Tversky (1937–1996)

PROSPECT RATIO

Watanabe[1] (2014) notes that people tend to feel loss more acutely than the equivalent gain, a well-known phenomenon described by Prospect Theory.[2] Watanabe suggests utilising a Sharpe-type ratio, really an adapted Sortino ratio, which penalises losses more than it rewards gains as shown below.

$$\text{Prospect ratio} = \frac{\frac{1}{n} \times \sum_{i=1}^{i=n} (\max[r_i, 0] + \lambda \times \min[r_i, 0]) - r_T}{\sigma_D} \qquad (7.1)$$

λ reflects investor preference and measures the extent of loss aversion and the greater weight given to losses than gains. If the investor does not exhibit loss aversion $\lambda = 0$. $\lambda < 0$ implies gain seeking behaviour. Based on empirical research Watanabe suggests investors dislike losses two and a quarter times as much as they enjoy gains and sets λ to 2.25. Users might wish to select their own preferences.

---

[1]Y. Watanabe (2014) New Prospect Ratio: Application to Hedge Funds with Higher Order Moments. *Journal of Performance Measurement*, 19(1), 41–53.
[2]D. Kahneman and A. Tversky (1979) Prospect Theory: An Analysis of Decision under Risk. *Econometrica* XLVII, 263–291.

Note

In many ways the Prospect ratio is similar to Kappa but with investor preferences expressed in the numerator of the ratio rather than in the denominator in the form of higher partial moments.

NEW PROSPECT RATIO

Watanabe continues to suggest downside skewness and downside kurtosis adjustments in a Skew-adjusted Prospect ratio and the New Prospect ratio as shown below.

$$\text{Skew-adjusted Prospect ratio} = \frac{\frac{1}{n} \times \sum_{i=1}^{i=n}(\max[r_i, 0] + \lambda \times \min[r_i, 0]) - r_T}{\sqrt{\sigma_D^2 + \varsigma_D^2}}$$

(7.2)

$$\text{New Prospect ratio} = \frac{\frac{1}{n} \times \sum_{i=1}^{i=n}(\max[r_i, 0] + \lambda \times \min[r_i, 0]) - r_T}{\sqrt{\sigma_D^2 + \varsigma_D^2 + \kappa_D^2}}$$

(7.3)

OMEGA–PROSPECT RATIO

Watanabe does not suggest a Prospect ratio using downside potential in the denominator, however an appropriate name for such a ratio would be the *Omega*–Prospect ratio defined as:

$$\textit{Omega}\text{–Prospect ratio} = \frac{\frac{1}{n} \times \sum_{i=1}^{i=n}(\max[r_i, 0] + \lambda \times \min[r_i, 0]) - r_T}{\mu_D}$$

(7.4)

Note

None of these prospect-inspired
ratios are in common usage as far
as I am aware.

The Prospect ratio, Skew-adjusted Prospect ratio, New Prospect ratio and
Omega–Prospect ratio are calculated in Exhibit 7.1 using standard portfolio
data in Table 7.1, Exhibit 6.1 and Exhibit 6.2 using $\lambda = 2.25$.

EXHIBIT 7.1   Prospect ratios

$$\text{Prospect ratio} = \frac{\frac{1}{n} \times \sum_{i=1}^{i=n}(\max[r_i, 0] + \lambda \times \min[r_i, 0]) - r_T}{\sigma_D}$$

$$\text{Prospect ratio} = \frac{\frac{69.2 - 81.23}{36} - 0.5}{2.12} = -0.39$$

$$\text{Skew-adjusted Prospect ratio} = \frac{\frac{1}{n} \times \sum_{i=1}^{i=n}(\max[r_i, 0] + \lambda \times \min[r_i, 0]) - r_T}{\sqrt{\sigma_D^2 + \varsigma_D^2}}$$

$$\text{Skew-adjusted Prospect ratio} = \frac{\frac{69.2 - 81.23}{36} - 0.5}{\sqrt{2.12^2 + -0.68^2}} = -0.37$$

$$\text{New Prospect ratio} = \frac{\frac{1}{n} \times \sum_{i=1}^{i=n}(\max[r_i, 0] + \lambda \times \min[r_i, 0]) - r_T}{\sqrt{\sigma_D^2 + \varsigma_D^2 + \kappa_D^2}}$$

$$\text{New Prospect ratio} = \frac{\frac{69.2 - 81.23}{36} - 0.5}{\sqrt{2.12^2 + -0.68^2 + 0.89^2}} = -0.35$$

$$\text{Omega–Prospect ratio} = \frac{\frac{1}{n} \times \sum_{i=1}^{i=n}(\max[r_i, 0] + \lambda \times \min[r_i, 0]) - r_T}{\mu_D}$$

$$\text{Omega–Prospect ratio} = \frac{\frac{69.2 - 81.23}{36} - 0.5}{1.01} = -0.83$$

TABLE 7.1 Prospect ratios

Portfolio Monthly Return (%) r_i	Downside min$[r_i, 0]$	Loss Aversion $\lambda \times min[r_i, 0]$ $\lambda = 2.25$	Upside max$[r_i, 0]$
0.3			0.3
2.6			2.6
1.1			1.1
−0.9	−1.4	−3.15	
1.4			1.4
2.4			2.4
1.5			1.5
6.6			6.6
−1.4	−1.9	−4.28	
3.9			3.9
−0.5	−1.0	−2.25	
8.1			8.1
4.0			4.0
−3.7	−4.2	−9.45	
−6.1	−6.6	−14.85	
1.4			1.4
−4.9	−5.4	−12.15	
−2.1	−2.6	−5.85	
6.2			6.2
5.8			5.8
−6.4	−6.9	−15.53	
1.7			1.7
−0.4	−0.9	−2.03	
−0.2	−0.7	−1.58	
−2.1	−2.6	−5.85	
1.1			1.1
4.7			4.7
2.4			2.4
3.3			3.3
−0.7	−1.2	−2.70	
4.7			4.7
0.6			0.6
1.0			1.0
−0.2	−0.7	−1.58	
3.4			3.4
1.0			1.0
Total	$\sum_{i=1}^{i=n} min[(r_i - r_T), 0] =$ **−36.3**	$\sum_{i=1}^{i=n} \lambda \times min[r_i, 0] =$ **−81.23**	$\sum_{i=1}^{i=n} max[r_i, 0] =$ **69.20**

CHAPTER 8

Extreme Risk

"Doubt is not a pleasant condition but certainty is absurd."

Voltaire (1694–1778)

"I have hardly ever known a mathematician who was capable of reasoning."

Plato (427 bc–347 bc)

"As far as the laws of mathematics refer to reality, they are not certain; and as far as they are certain, they do not refer to reality."

Albert Einstein (1879–1955)

EXTREME EVENTS

Just like risk itself, extreme events mean different things to different audiences at different times. From the context of this book an extreme event is an event that occurs in the tail of a return distribution however defined, but nevertheless a low probability, high impact event. If these extreme events occur more often than suggested by a normal distribution then the distribution is often described as "fat-tailed" or suffering from leptokurtosis. Clearly asset owners will be most concerned about extreme negative events and are interested in the measurement of extreme risk. The insurance industry in particular is concerned with extreme events such as earthquakes and extreme weather.

EXTREME VALUE THEORY

Extreme value theory concentrates not on the entire shape of the return distribution but rather on the shape of returns in the tail and is outside the scope of this book but well worth investigating.

VALUE AT RISK (VaR)

Value at risk, usually abbreviated as VaR, is an extreme risk measure originally developed in the 1990s by investment banks to manage their daily trading risk.[1] VaR measures the worst expected loss over a given time interval under normal market conditions at a given confidence level. For example, an annual value at risk of £5 million at a 95% confidence level for a portfolio would suggest that only once in 20 years would the annual loss exceed £5 million.

VaR, like tracking error and variability, can be calculated both ex post and ex ante. Typically, VaR is forecast ex ante although again like tracking error it is useful to also calculate ex post to provide a comparison and monitor risk efficiency.[2] Recall that ex-post measures rely on the realised historical total returns of the portfolio, whereas ex-ante measures rely on a snapshot of the current holdings of securities and instruments within a portfolio, and based on their historic relationship with each other forecast the prospective risk.

In the context of portfolio returns, return at risk or performance at risk is perhaps a more appropriate term, although the term VaR is used universally to represent both values and returns at risk.

> **Note**
>
> Although we are concerned with extreme losses and negative returns, VaR by convention is presented as a positive number.

The appealing simplicity of VaR has led to its adoption as the standard risk measure for many trading institutions, retail banks, insurance companies, pension funds and regulators.

---

[1]Sir Dennis Weatherstone, CEO of JP Morgan, requested a 4:15 report that aggregated the firm's risk on one page within 15 minutes of market close at 4 pm. VaR was developed to satisfy his request.
[2]See the Risk efficiency ratio, Equation 16.4.

Caution

Both the time horizon and confidence levels will impact the interpretation of VaR significantly and consistency is essential for comparison.

RELATIVE VaR

VaR can be applied to absolute returns, excess returns above the risk-free rate or excess returns compared to a benchmark, either arithmetic or geometric. The VaR of excess returns is sometimes described as relative VaR. I suspect most asset owners that are concerned about extreme risk are more concerned about absolute risk rather than relative risk.

EX-POST VaR

Ex-post VaR simply reorganises actual historical portfolio returns, putting them in order from best to worst. The value at risk is determined at the 95th percentile when using a 95% confidence level.

POTENTIAL UPSIDE (GAIN AT RISK)

Value at risk measures the downside in the left-hand tail of the return distribution; potential upside measures the equivalent best expected gain in the right-hand side of the tail – not to be confused with the similar partial moment term, upside potential as used in Equation 6.11. You will not find the term "gain at risk" defined elsewhere; I introduce it here as an alternative to potential upside, frankly to make the notation easier, to avoid any confusion between potential upside and upside potential and to emphasise that risk is both positive and negative – asset owners should be interested in both sides of the return distribution.

PERCENTILE RANK

Before going any further, we should focus on the calculation of percentile rank. There are at least five different methods that might be used to calculate percentile rank:

$$\text{Percentile rank method 1} = \frac{n}{N} \tag{8.1}$$

$$\text{Percentile rank method 2} = \frac{n-1}{N} \tag{8.2}$$

$$\text{Percentile rank method 3} = \frac{n-1}{N-1} \tag{8.3}$$

$$\text{Percentile rank method 4} = \frac{n-0.5}{N} \tag{8.4}$$

$$\text{Percentile rank method 5} = \frac{n}{N+1} \tag{8.5}$$

Where:

n = rank of the observation (ranked best to worst)
N = total number of observations

Which percentile rank method to use really depends on the use to which it is put. For small samples the difference between methods can be significant (see Table 8.1) but for large samples the impact will be small. From the performance measurer's perspective, to rank portfolios in a peer group comparison I much prefer method 3 – in effect, whatever the size of the peer group, the percentile rank equates to the equivalent rank as if there were 100 portfolios in the peer group. The top ranked fund would have a percentile rank of 0% and the bottom ranked fund 100%. From a risk perspective I prefer method 2 to determine the 95th percentile for value at risk and method 1 to determine the 5th percentile for the potential upside or gain at risk. Note that method 1 is the mirror image of method 2 when comparing the right-hand tail to the left-hand tail of the return distribution.

Ex-post value at risk and potential upside for the standard portfolio data presented initially in Table 2.1 are shown in Table 8.2. With only 36 monthly

TABLE 8.1 Percentile rank methodologies

Rank	Method 1 $\dfrac{n}{N}$	Method 2 $\dfrac{n-1}{N}$	Method 3 $\dfrac{n-1}{N-1}$	Method 4 $\dfrac{n-0.5}{N}$	Method 5 $\dfrac{n}{N+1}$
1	8.33%	0.00%	0.00%	4.17%	7.69%
2	16.67%	8.33%	9.09%	12.50%	15.38%
3	25.00%	16.67%	18.18%	20.83%	23.08%
4	33.33%	25.00%	27.27%	29.17%	30.77%
5	41.67%	33.33%	36.36%	37.50%	38.46%
6	50.00%	41.67%	45.45%	45.83%	46.15%
7	58.33%	50.00%	54.55%	54.17%	53.85%
8	66.67%	58.33%	63.64%	62.50%	61.54%
9	75.00%	66.67%	72.73%	70.83%	69.23%
10	83.33%	75.00%	81.82%	79.17%	76.92%
11	91.67%	83.33%	90.91%	87.50%	84.62%
12	100.00%	91.67%	100.00%	95.83%	92.31%

TABLE 8.2 Ex-post VaR

Portfolio Monthly Return (%) r_i	Ranked Best to Worst	Percentile	Potential Upside and Value at Risk 5th and 95th Percentile
0.3	8.1	2.78%	
2.6	6.6	5.55%	⟵ 5% $GaR_{95\%}$ Potential Upside
1.1	6.2		$\left(\dfrac{2.22 \times 6.6 + 0.56 \times 8.1}{2.78}\right) = 6.9\%$
−0.9	5.8		
1.4	4.7		
2.4	4.7		
1.5	4.0		
6.6	3.9		
−1.4	3.4	25%	
3.9	3.3		
−0.5	2.6		
8.1	2.4		
4.0	2.4		
−3.7	1.7		
−6.1	1.5		
1.4	1.4		
−4.9	1.4		
−2.1	1.1		
6.2	1.1		
5.8	1.0		
−6.4	1.0		
1.7	0.6		
−0.4	0.3		
−0.2	−0.2		
−2.1	−0.2		
1.1	−0.4		
4.7	−0.5		
2.4	−0.7	75%	
3.3	−0.9		
−0.7	−1.4		
4.7	−2.1		
0.6	−2.1		
1.0	−3.7		
−0.2	−4.9		$\left(\dfrac{2.22 \times -6.1 + 0.56 \times -6.4}{2.78}\right) = -6.16\%$
3.4	−6.1	94.44%	
1.0	−6.4	97.22%	⟵ 95%$VaR_{95\%}$ Value at Risk

observations the 95th percentile falls between the 35th worst return, −6.1%, and the 36th worst return, −6.4%. The VaR is calculated as a weighted average between the 94.44th percentile and the 97.22th percentile. The potential upside is also a weighted average calculation as shown in Table 8.2.

VaR CALCULATION METHODOLOGY

There are three different methods for calculating or forecasting VaR:

  i) Parametric (or analytic)
 ii) Historical simulation (or non-parametric)
iii) Monte Carlo simulation

   VaR is more commonly forecast ex ante but of course it can be calculated ex post in the context of realised total portfolio returns. In effect, therefore, there are six different methodologies for calculating VaR. The language used to describe these methodologies is far from consistent; therefore, in order to establish a standard, I suggest the terms in Table 8.3.

PARAMETRIC VaR

Parametric means that parameters are used to calculate the measure, and the simplest ex-post parametric method for VaR assumes that portfolio returns are normally distributed. This way, only two parameters are required to calculate VaR: the mean return and standard deviation of returns. With 95% confidence, VaR is:

$$VaR_{95\%} = \bar{r} - 1.65 \times \sigma \tag{8.6}$$

With 99% confidence VaR is:

$$VaR_{99\%} = \bar{r} - 2.33 \times \sigma \tag{8.7}$$

TABLE 8.3 VaR methodologies

Methodology	Ex post	Ex ante
Parametric	Parametric	Analytical (or variance–covariance)
Historical	Non-parametric	Historical simulation
Monte Carlo	Ex-post Monte Carlo*	Monte Carlo simulation

*Ex-post Monte Carlo VaR is of course also non-parametric but I prefer to reserve the term for the calculation of ex-post VaR using a historical methodology which is more common.

EXHIBIT 8.1 Parametric VaR

$$VaR_{95\%} = 1.1\% - 1.65 \times 3.32\% = -4.38\%$$

$$VaR_{99\%} = 1.1\% - 2.33 \times 3.32\% = -6.63\%$$

In this example the parametric VaR underestimates the ex-post VaR in Table 8.2 significantly, which – given the extremely small sample in the tail – is not necessarily surprising.

Therefore, using the standard portfolio data from Table 2.1 and portfolio standard deviations from Table 2.2 the following values at risk can be calculated in Exhibit 8.1.

MODIFIED VaR

Alternatively, VaR can be modified[3] parametrically to adjust for the kurtosis and skewness of the return distribution using a Cornish–Fisher expansion as follows:

$$MVaR = \bar{r} + \left[z_c + \frac{z_c^2 - 1}{6} \times \varsigma + \frac{z_c^3 - 3 \times z_c}{24} \times \kappa_E - \frac{2 \times z_c^3 - 5 \times z_c}{36} \times \varsigma^2 \right] \times \sigma$$

$$(8.8)$$

Where:

$z_c = -1.65$ with 95% confidence
$z_c = -1.96$ with 97.5% confidence
$z_c = -2.33$ with 99% confidence

Note if the return distribution is normal, ς and κ_E are zero and Equation 8.8 reduces to the equivalent of Equation 8.6:

$$VaR = \bar{r} + z_c \times \sigma \qquad (8.9)$$

This method works less well for distributions with more extreme skewness and excess kurtosis.

Modified VaRs are calculated in Exhibit 8.2 for the standard portfolio data in Table 2.1 using the descriptive statistics calculated in Exhibit 2.2 and Exhibit 2.4.

---

[3]L. Favre and J. Galeano (2001) Mean-Modified Value at Risk Optimization with Hedge Funds. *The Journal of Alternative Investments* 5, 21–25.

EXHIBIT 8.2 Modified VaR

$$MVaR_{95\%} = \bar{r} + \left[z_c + \frac{z_c^2 - 1}{6} \times \varsigma + \frac{z_c^3 - 3z_c}{24} \times \kappa_E - \frac{2z_c^3 - 5z_c}{36} \times \varsigma^2 \right] \times \sigma$$

$$= 1.1\% + \left[-1.65 + \frac{-1.65^2 - 1}{6} \times -0.24 + \frac{-1.65^3 + 4.95}{24} \right.$$

$$\left. \times -0.02 - \frac{2 \times -1.65^3 + 8.25}{36} \times -0.24^2 \right] \times 3.32\%$$

$$= -4.60\%$$

$$MVaR_{99\%} = \bar{r} + \left[z_c + \frac{z_c^2 - 1}{6} \times \varsigma + \frac{z_c^3 - 3z_c}{24} \times \kappa_E - \frac{2z_c^3 - 5z_c}{36} \times \varsigma^2 \right] \times \sigma$$

$$= 1.1\% + \left[-2.33 + \frac{-2.33^2 - 1}{6} \times -0.24 + \frac{-2.33^3 + 6.99}{24} \right.$$

$$\left. \times -0.02 - \frac{2 \times -2.33^3 + 11.65}{36} \times -0.24^2 \right] \times 3.32\%$$

$$= -7.12\%$$

In this example modifying for the negative skew of the return distribution improves the estimate of VaR a small amount but still remains an underestimate.

HISTORICAL SIMULATION (OR NON-PARAMETRIC)

Historical simulation simply reorganises actual historical returns based on the current portfolio holdings putting them in order from best to worst. The value at risk is determined at the 95th percentile for a 95% confidence level and the gain at risk in effect is the 5th percentile. Ex-post non-parametric VaR is a historical calculation except that there is no element of simulation given that actual portfolio returns are used.

MONTE CARLO SIMULATION

Monte Carlo simulation is similar to historical simulation but rather than use observed changes in market factors a model is chosen for future portfolio returns and a random number generator is used to calculate thousands of hypothetical portfolio returns. The value at risk is then determined at the 95th percentile from this distribution. Ex-post Monte Carlo would use only total portfolio returns to create these hypothetical returns rather than a snapshot of current holdings.

 Note

The Monte Carlo method was coined in the 1940s by Neumann, Ulam and Metropolis,[4] while they were working on a nuclear weapon project. It was named in homage to the Monte Carlo casino (where Ulam's uncle would often gamble away his money) because the roulette wheel was a good source of random numbers.

WHICH METHODOLOGY FOR CALCULATING VaR SHOULD BE USED?

The parametric method is possibly the easiest to implement but it relies on a normal assumption of returns. We know portfolio returns, and hedge fund returns in particular, are not normally distributed.

Historical simulation is perhaps the most straightforward – it is suitable for all asset types and certainly conceptually easier to explain to pension fund trustees but requires the processing of tremendous amounts of historical data.

Monte Carlo simulation is more complex and can suffer from additional model risk, but is considered the gold standard for accurate VaR calculations. This is because Monte Carlo simulations allow the modeller to take into account possible market/portfolio returns that have never happened before (with suitable probability) or that haven't happened during historical windows that would be excluded from historical simulations. Monte Carlo also permits stress-testing VaR by introducing stressed returns or rates, allowing it to simulate portfolio risk during shifting economic regimes.

---

[4]N. Metropolis (1987) The Beginning of the Monte Carlo Method. *Los Alamos Science* (Special Issue dedicated to Stanisław Ulam), 125–130.

VaR INTERPRETATION

People are often confused by the subtleties of VaR and it warrants a few direct comments. Ex-ante VaR is just one point on the distribution of likely returns and it therefore captures only a small portion of the information contained in the entire distribution. The 95% VaR is that point in the tail for which 95% of the distribution is to the right. In other words, 95% of the time the portfolio should do better than the (negative and therefore loss-making) VaR$_{95}$. Within any one month, that means the portfolio should outperform the (negative) VaR$_{95}$ return amount in about 19 out of its 20 trading days. That necessarily means that the portfolio *should do worse* than VaR$_{95}$ about once per month. In fact, if the portfolio does not do worse than VaR$_{95}$ about 5% of the time, then the measure is not accurate. This is an important point and it provides a direct means of testing the VaR calculation in a "back test", ensuring that approximately 5 trading days' profit and loss (P&L) out of every 100 days has a worse P&L than the previous day's VaR number. This is shown graphically in Figure 8.1.

VaR backtesting like the one shown in Figure 8.1 is not an exact accounting and this is why I've written "about 5% of the time" rather than exactly 5% of the time. If, after 100 days only 3 or 4 days have losses greater than the VaR$_{95}$ amount, that does not necessarily mean that the VaR$_{95}$ calculation is wrong.

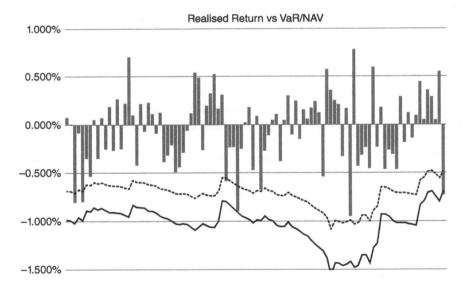

FIGURE 8.1 VaR backtesting

Notes: VaR backtesting for two VaR confidences: 95% in dashed line and 99% in solid line. Note that 5 of the P&L bars are worse than the 95% VaR and exactly 1 P&L is worse than the 99% VaR. (NAV = net asset value)

Because this is a statistical measure, the 5% exceedance is only true in the limit of very many observations and 100 observations may not be enough. There is more "statistical art" to backtesting than engineering.

The backtesting chart highlights another important interpretation point about VaR that often proves confusing: nothing about the VaR methodology says anything about how big the losses may be on the days when the portfolio does break through the VaR limit. Misinterpretation of this fact has resulted in some heated conversations. Imagine a portfolio with a daily VaR_{95} estimate of £10 million. It may be tempting to think that on the days the portfolio exceeds the VaR_{95} amount, it would exceed by an amount "near" the £10 million loss figure: perhaps it loses £12 million or £14 million. But while VaR says something very specific about the *frequency* of exceedances (statistically 5 times in 100), it says *absolutely nothing* about the *sizes* of those exceedances. A loss of £10.1 million counts just as much as a loss of £50 million toward backtesting, much to the surprise of some naïve portfolio managers in the early days of VaR adoption when they mistakenly interpreted it as an estimate of potential large losses.

FREQUENCY AND TIME AGGREGATION

Because we are concerned with only extreme results in the tail of the return distribution, typically VaR is calculated using daily data to ensure statistical significance (and reflecting VaR's history as a risk measure used within investment banks monitoring daily earnings at risk).

In exactly the same way we annualise standard deviation using Equation 2.13 we can annualise VaR.

To annualise daily VaR multiply by $\sqrt{250}$ or $\sqrt{260}$ (practice varies between 250 and 260 days, depending on the assumption of business days within the year – clearly for comparison a consistent policy must be established).

To convert daily VaR to a weekly time horizon, multiply by $\sqrt{5}$.

To convert daily VaR to a fortnightly horizon, multiply by $\sqrt{10}$.

To convert daily VaR to a monthly time horizon, multiply by $\sqrt{20}$ or $\sqrt{21}$ (again practice varies depending on the assumption of business days within the month).

To convert daily VaR to a quarterly horizon, multiply by $\sqrt{60}$.

To annualise monthly calculated VaR, multiply by $\sqrt{12}$.

TIME HORIZON

The time horizon represents the holding period for the VaR calculations, that is, daily, weekly, fortnightly or monthly. Longer holding periods are naturally required for more illiquid assets.

WINDOW LENGTH

The window length is the period of data which is used to calculate or esti-mate VaR – 100, 250 or 500 observations, for example. VaR measures typically become more stable for longer observation periods.

REWARD TO VaR

Reward to VaR suggested by both Dowd[5] (1998) and Alexander and Baptista[6] (2003) is a Sharpe-type measure but with VaR or return at risk replacing stan-dard deviation as the measure of risk in the denominator. This measure is more appropriate for investors concerned with more extreme losses and of course if the non-parametric methods are used it does not rely on a normal assumption of returns.

$$\text{Reward to VaR} = \frac{\tilde{r} - \tilde{r}_F}{VaR_{1-\alpha}} \tag{8.10}$$

Where:

$VaR_{1-\alpha}$ = the absolute of the worst ranked return with $(1 - \alpha)$ confidence

The probability α typically takes a value of 1% or 5% equating to confidence levels of 99% and 95% respectively. VaR is typically calculated using daily or monthly data depending on availability, daily being more common to increase the number of observations.

The general form of the Sharpe-type measure shown in Figure 8.2 should now be very familiar to the reader.

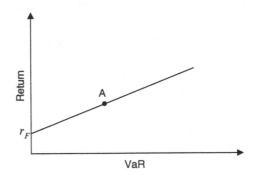

FIGURE 8.2   Reward to VaR

[5]K. Dowd (1998) *Beyond Value at Risk: The New Science of Risk Management.* John Wiley & Sons.

[6]G. J. Alexander and A. M. Baptista (2003) Portfolio Performance Evaluation Using Value at Risk. *Journal of Portfolio Management* 24(4), 93–102.

REWARD TO RELATIVE VaR

Reward to relative VaR is the information ratio equivalent when focusing on the extreme risk of relative returns (see Figure 8.3).

DOUBLE VaR RATIO

Only briefly mentioned in literature[7] but included here for completeness is the double VaR ratio, a gain:loss ratio with potential upside in the numerator and value at risk in the denominator. For a normal or symmetrical distribution, the double VaR ratio should be 1.

$$\text{Double VaR ratio} \qquad DVaR_{\beta,\alpha} = \frac{GaR_{1-\beta}}{VaR_{1-\alpha}} \qquad (8.11)$$

Where:

$GaR_{1-\beta}$ = best ranked return r with $(1 - \beta)$ confidence. Gain at risk or potential upside.

CONDITIONAL VaR (EXPECTED SHORTFALL, TAIL LOSS, TAIL VaR OR AVERAGE VaR)

VaR does not provide any information about the shape of the tail or the expected size of loss beyond the confidence level. In this sense it is a very

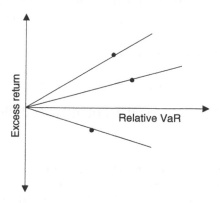

FIGURE 8.3 Reward to relative VaR

---

[7]See V. Zakamouline (2010) On the Consistent Use of VaR in Portfolio Performance Evaluation: A Cautionary Note. *The Journal of Portfolio Management*, Fall, 37(1), 92–104.

unsatisfactory risk measure; of more interest is conditional VaR – otherwise known as expected shortfall, mean expected loss, tail VaR, tail loss or average VaR – which takes into account returns in the remainder of the tail. Conditional VaR is the average return conditional on the return exceeding (more negative than) the value at risk.

$$\text{Conditional VaR} = CVaR_{1-\alpha} = \frac{\left| \sum_{i=1}^{i=n} \langle r_i \,|\, r_i < VaR_{1-\alpha} \rangle \right|}{n_{VaR}} \tag{8.12}$$

Where:

n_{VaR} = number of returns that are more negative than the value at risk

While VaR focuses on the likelihood of extreme events CVaR focuses on both the likelihood and size of losses in the event of extreme losses. Obviously, as the name suggests, expected shortfall is the ex-ante version of conditional VaR but the other labels could be either ex ante or ex post. Conditional VaR is often abbreviated as CVaR, AVaR (average VaR), or TVaR (tail VaR). I prefer to reserve the abbreviation TVaR for the slightly different term tail risk.

VaR is not a coherent risk measure as defined by Artzner, Delbaen, Eber and Heath[8] (1999): it does not satisfy the technical properties of monotonicity, sub-additivity, homogeneity and translational invariance. In particular VaR is not sub-additive; the sum of the value of risks of the underlying securities within the portfolio is typically greater than the total value of risk of the portfolio. CVaR, on the other hand, is a coherent risk measure.

Conditional VaR for a normal distribution can also be calculated parametrically as follows:[9]

$$CVaR_{95\%} = \bar{r} - 2.06 \times \sigma \tag{8.13}$$

Conditional VaR for non-normal distributions is difficult to calculate parametrically.

---

[8]See P. Artzner, F. Delbaen, J. Eber and D. Heath (1999) Coherent Measures of Risk. *Mathematical Finance* 9(3), 203–228.

[9]J. X. Xiong and T. M. Idzorek (2011) The Impact of Skewness and Fat Tails on the Asset Allocation Decision. *Financial Analysts Journal* 67(2), 23–35. W. G. Hallerbach (2002) Decomposing Portfolio Value-at-Risk: A General Analysis. *Journal of Risk* 5(2), 1–18.

> **Caution**
>
> While it is easy to calculate the parametric CVaR, estimating the tail of a financial portfolio distribution with the normal curve deeper than about 95% is known to materially underpredict risk.

UPPER CVaR OR CVaR⁺

Upper CVaR includes only returns in the average calculation that strictly exceed (are more negative than) the value at risk.

LOWER CVaR OR CVaR⁻

Lower CVaR includes returns that weakly exceed (are equal to or more negative than) the value at risk.

If VaR falls between discrete values then $CVaR'$ can be estimated using a weighted average contribution of the two returns straddling VaR. Figure 8.4 shows four returns that strictly exceed VaR. Upper conditional value at risk is the average of these four returns. Modified VaR could be greater or lower than VaR dependent on the skewness and kurtosis of the distribution. Figure 8.5 is a graphical representation of VaR showing the area of interest in the left-hand side of the tail.

Note:

$$VaR \leq CVaR^- \leq CVaR' \leq CVaR^+ \tag{8.14}$$

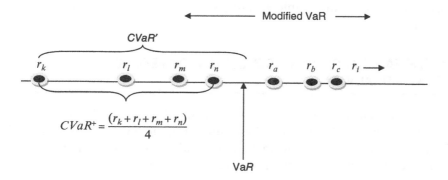

FIGURE 8.4   Calculation of Conditional VaR

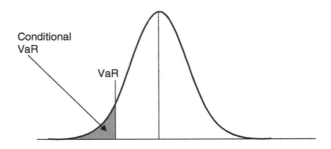

FIGURE 8.5　Conditional VaR

TAIL GAIN (EXPECTED GAIN OR EXPECTED UPSIDE)

Tail gain is the average return conditional on the return exceeding the gain at risk.

$$\text{Tail gain} = CGaR_{1-\beta} = \frac{\left| \sum\limits_{i=1}^{i=n} \langle r_i | r_i > GaR_{1-\beta} \rangle \right|}{n_{GaR}} \tag{8.15}$$

Where:

n_{GaR} = number of returns that are greater in value than the potential upside (or gain at risk)

Value at risk, conditional value at risk, gain at risk and tail gain are calculated in Exhibit 8.3 for the daily portfolio data shown in Table 8.4 and Table 8.5. Table 8.4 shows the worst 40 daily returns in a population of 500 daily returns over 2 years, and Table 8.5 shows the best 40 daily returns in the same population.

CONDITIONAL SHARPE RATIO (STARR RATIO OR REWARD TO CONDITIONAL VaR)

Conditional Sharpe ratio, suggested by Agarwal and Naik[10] (2004), replaces VaR with Conditional VaR in the denominator of the reward to VaR ratio. Since conditional VaR considers the shape of the tail, the conditional Sharpe ratio is demonstrably favourable to the reward to VaR ratio.

$$\text{Conditional Sharpe ratio} = \frac{\bar{r} - \bar{r}_F}{CVaR} \tag{8.16}$$

---

[10]V. Agarwal and N. Y. Naik (2004) Risk and Portfolio Decisions Involving Hedge Funds. *Review of Financial Studies* 17(1), 63–98.

EXHIBIT 8.3   Ex-post VaR and conditional VaR

Ex-post $VaR_{95\%} = 1.65$
Ex-post $VaR_{99\%} = 2.86$

$$\text{Conditional VaR } CVaR_{95\%} = \frac{\left| \sum\limits_{i=1}^{i=n} \langle r_i | r_i < VaR_{95\%} \rangle \right|}{n_{VaR}} = \frac{57.17}{24} = 2.38$$

$$\text{Conditional VaR } CVaR_{99\%} = \frac{\left| \sum\limits_{i=1}^{i=n} \langle r_i | r_i < VaR_{99\%} \rangle \right|}{n_{VaR}} = \frac{12.50}{4} = 3.13$$

Ex-post $GaR_{95\%} = 1.73$
Ex-post $GaR_{99\%} = 2.50$

$$\text{Tail gain } CGaR_{95\%} = \frac{\left| \sum\limits_{i=1}^{i=n} \langle r_i | r_i > GaR_{95\%} \rangle \right|}{n_{GaR}} = \frac{52.5}{24} = 2.19$$

$$\text{Tail gain } CGaR_{99\%} = \frac{\left| \sum\limits_{i=1}^{i=n} \langle r_i | r_i > GaR_{99\%} \rangle \right|}{n_{GaR}} = \frac{11.25}{4} = 2.81$$

The mean, standard deviation, skewness and excess kurtosis of the 500 daily returns shown in Tables 8.4 and 8.5 are 0.08%, 0.992%, −0.35 and 1.14 respectively. Parametric and modified VaRs are calculated in Exhibit 8.4.

This ratio is also known as the stable tail-adjusted return ratio or STARR – see Martin, Rachev and Siboulet[11] (2003).

MODIFIED SHARPE RATIO (REWARD TO MODIFIED VaR)

Similar to the adjusted Sharpe ratio the modified Sharpe ratio uses modified VaR adjusted for skewness and kurtosis.

$$\text{Modified Sharpe ratio} = \frac{\tilde{r} - \tilde{r}_F}{MVaR} \tag{8.17}$$

---

[11]R. D. Martin, S. T. Rachev and F. Siboulet (2003) Phi-alpha Optimal Portfolios and Extreme Risk Management. *Wilmott Magazine* 6, 70–83.

TABLE 8.4 VaR and conditional VaR using daily returns

40 Worst Returns	Ranked Best to Worst	Percentile	$\alpha = 5\%$	$\alpha = 1\%$
461	−1.37			
462	−1.38			
463	−1.39			
464	−1.42			
465	−1.44			
466	−1.46			
467	−1.48			
468	−1.50			
469	−1.52			
470	−1.54			
471	−1.55			
472	−1.56			
473	−1.58			
474	−1.60			
475	−1.62			
476	**−1.65**	**95th Percentile** $VaR_{95\%}$	**−1.65**	
477	−1.69		−1.69	
478	−1.72		−1.72	
479	−1.75		−1.75	
480	−1.79		−1.79	
481	−1.82		−1.82	
482	−1.88		−1.88	
483	−1.92		−1.92	
484	−1.96		−1.96	
485	−1.99		−1.99	
486	−2.02		−2.02	
487	−2.17		−2.17	
488	−2.40		−2.40	
489	−2.54		−2.54	
490	−2.58		−2.58	
491	−2.62		−2.62	
492	−2.66		−2.66	
493	−2.70		−2.70	
494	−2.78		−2.78	
495	−2.82		−2.82	
496	**−2.86**	**99th Percentile** $VaR_{99\%}$	**−2.86**	**−2.86**
497	−2.90		−2.90	−2.90
498	−3.05		−3.05	−3.05
499	−3.24		−3.24	−3.24
500	−3.31		−3.31	−3.31
		Sum	**−57.17**	**−12.50**

TABLE 8.5 GaR and tail gain using daily returns

40 Best Returns	Ranked Best to Worst	Percentile	$\beta = 5\%$	$\beta = 1\%$
1	3.00		3.00	3.00
2	2.90		2.90	2.90
3	2.80		2.80	2.80
4	2.55		2.55	2.55
5	2.50	**1st Percentile** $GaR_{99\%}$	2.50	**2.50**
6	2.40		2.40	
7	2.36		2.36	
8	2.31		2.31	
9	2.30		2.30	
10	2.25		2.25	
11	2.20		2.20	
12	2.15		2.15	
13	2.10		2.10	
14	2.05		2.05	
15	2.00		2.00	
16	1.95		1.95	
17	1.91		1.91	
18	1.89		1.89	
19	1.87		1.87	
20	1.85		1.85	
21	1.83		1.83	
22	1.81		1.81	
23	1.77		1.77	
24	1.75		1.75	
25	1.73	**5th Percentile** $GaR_{95\%}$	**1.73**	
26	1.71			
27	1.69			
28	1.67			
29	1.65			
30	1.63			
31	1.61			
32	1.59			
33	1.57			
34	1.55			
35	1.53			
36	1.50			
37	1.46			
38	1.43			
39	1.41			
40	1.39			
		Sum	52.50	11.25

EXHIBIT 8.4 Parametric and modified VaR

Ex-post $VaR_{95\%} = 1.65$
Ex-post $VaR_{99\%} = 2.86$

Parametric $VaR_{95\%} = 0.08\% - 1.65 \times 0.992\% = -1.55\%$ or 1.55%

Parametric $VaR_{99\%} = 0.08\% - 2.33 \times 0.992\% = -2.23\%$ or 2.23%

Modified $VaR_{95\%}$

$$= \bar{r} + \left[z_c + \frac{z_c^2 - 1}{6} \times \varsigma + \frac{z_c^3 - 3z_c}{24} \times \kappa_E - \frac{2z_c^3 - 5z_c}{36} \times \varsigma^2 \right] \times \sigma$$

$$= 0.08\% + \left[-1.65 + \frac{-1.65^2 - 1}{6} \times -0.35 + \frac{-1.65^3 + 4.95}{24} \times 1.14 \right.$$

$$\left. - \frac{2 \times -1.65^3 + 8.25}{36} \times -0.35^2 \right] \times 0.992\%$$

$$= -1.63\% \text{ or } 1.63\%$$

Modified $VaR_{99\%}$

$$= \bar{r} + \left[z_c + \frac{z_c^2 - 1}{6} \times \varsigma + \frac{z_c^3 - 3z_c}{24} \times \kappa_E - \frac{2z_c^3 - 5z_c}{36} \times \varsigma^2 \right] \times \sigma$$

$$= 0.08\% + \left[-2.33 + \frac{-2.33^2 - 1}{6} \times -0.35 + \frac{-2.33^3 + 4.95}{24} \times 1.14 \right.$$

$$\left. - \frac{2 \times -2.33^3 + 8.25}{36} \times -0.35^2 \right] \times 0.992\%$$

$$= -2.71\% \text{ or } 2.71\%$$

Because of the negative skewness and positive excess kurtosis modified VaR is a much better estimate of the actual ex-post VaR than the parametric VaR based on standard deviation alone.

TAIL RISK

Tail risk, as its name suggests, is a variance type calculation of the returns in the tail of the distribution. It gives greater weight to the more extreme returns in the tail.

$$\text{Tail risk} = TVaR_{1-\alpha} = \sqrt{\frac{\sum\limits_{i=1}^{i=n} \langle r_i | r_i < VaR_{1-\alpha} \rangle^2}{n_{VaR}}} \tag{8.18}$$

> **Note**
>
> In this context tail risk is not the same as tail VaR. Tail risk might also be used to describe a small probability event in general, or more specifically a risk event with probability greater than that expected in a normal distribution three standard deviations away from the mean – a fat tail.

TAIL RATIO

Tail ratio is a familiar Sharpe-type measure using tail risk in the denominator.

$$\text{Tail ratio} = \frac{\tilde{r} - \tilde{r}_F}{TVaR} \tag{8.19}$$

RACHEV RATIO (OR R RATIO)

The Rachev ratio proposed by Biglova, Ortobelli, Rachev and Stoyanov[12] in 2004 is a typical gain:loss ratio with tail gain in the numerator and tail loss or conditional VaR in the denominator.

$$R_{\beta,\alpha} = \frac{\text{Tail gain}}{\text{Tail loss}} = \frac{CGaR_{1-\beta}}{CVaR_{1-\alpha}} \tag{8.20}$$

---

[12]A. Biglova, S. Ortobelli, S. T. Rachev and S. V. Stoyanov (2004) Different Approaches to Risk Estimation in Portfolio Theory. *Journal of Portfolio Management* 3, 103–112.

ⓘ Interpretation

Clearly the higher the Rachev ratio the better, but investors should be reminded that this ratio focuses on the extremes on the return distribution and ignores the greater part of the returns in the middle. The Rachev ratio should not be used in isolation.

Tail risk and Rachev ratios are calculated in Exhibit 8.5 using the data from Table 8.6 (same monthly returns as Table 8.4) and Exhibit 8.4.

GENERALISED RACHEV RATIO

The generalised Rachev ratio[13] allows investors to express their own preferences both in terms of the upside and downside powers u and l but also confidence levels.

$$R_{\beta,\alpha}^{u,l} = \frac{CGaR_{1-\beta}^{u}}{CVaR_{1-\alpha}^{l}} \tag{8.21}$$

EXHIBIT 8.5 Tail risk and Rachev ratio

$$\text{Tail risk} = TVaR_{1-\alpha} = \sqrt{\frac{\sum_{i=1}^{i=n}\langle r_i | r_i < VaR_{1-\alpha}\rangle^2}{n_{VaR}}}$$

$$= TVaR_{95\%} = \sqrt{\frac{142.33}{24}} = 2.44$$

$$= TVaR_{99\%} = \sqrt{\frac{39.17}{4}} = 3.13$$

$$\text{Rachev ratio} = R_{\beta,\alpha} = \frac{\text{Tail gain}}{\text{Tail loss}} = \frac{CGaR_{1-\beta}}{CVaR_{1-\alpha}}$$

$$R_{5\%,5\%} = \frac{2.19}{2.38} = 0.92$$

$$R_{1\%,1\%} = \frac{2.81}{3.13} = 0.90$$

[13]S. Rachev, S. Stoyanov and F. Fabozzi (2008) *Advanced Stochastic Models, Risk Assessment, and Portfolio Optimization* (The Frank J. Fabozzi Series). John Wiley & Sons.

TABLE 8.6   Tail risk

25 Worst Returns	Ranked Best to Worst	Percentile	Squared Return	Squared Return
476	**−1.65**	**95th Percentile** $VaR_{95\%}$		
477	−1.69		2.86	
478	−1.72		2.96	
479	−1.75		3.06	
480	−1.79		3.20	
481	−1.82		3.31	
482	−1.88		3.53	
483	−1.92		3.69	
484	−1.96		3.84	
485	−1.99		3.96	
486	−2.02		4.08	
487	−2.17		4.71	
488	−2.40		5.76	
489	−2.54		6.45	
490	−2.58		6.66	
491	−2.62		6.86	
492	−2.66		7.08	
493	−2.70		7.29	
494	−2.78		7.73	
495	−2.82		7.85	
496	**−2.86**	**99th Percentile** $VaR_{99\%}$	8.18	
497	−2.90		8.41	8.41
498	−3.05		9.30	9.30
499	−3.24		10.50	10.50
500	−3.31		10.96	10.96
		Sum	**142.33**	**39.17**

Where:

$$CGaR_{1-\beta}^{u} = \sqrt[u]{\frac{\sum_{i=1}^{i=n}(\langle r_i | r_i > GaR_{1-\beta}\rangle)^u}{n_{GaR}}}$$

$$CVaR_{1-\alpha}^{l} = \sqrt[l]{\frac{\sum_{i=1}^{i=n}\langle r_i | r_i < VaR_{1-\alpha}\rangle^l}{n_{VaR}}}$$

Note:

$$CVaR_{1-\alpha}^{2} = TVaR_{1-\alpha}$$

DRAWDOWN AT RISK

Drawdown at risk (DaR) is similar to value (or return) at risk except that the drawdowns (continuous negative returns or peak to trough definition) in the return series are ranked best to worst, not each individual return.

 Caution

The variable number of drawdowns in a return series is clearly a potential difficulty for this measure.

CONDITIONAL DRAWDOWN AT RISK

Conditional drawdown at risk is, as expected, the average of drawdowns that exceed the drawdown at risk CDaR.

REWARD TO CONDITIONAL DRAWDOWN

Reward to conditional drawdown is a Sharpe-type ratio with conditional drawdown in the denominator which is very similar to the Sterling ratio in Equation 5.7 except that the drawdowns are determined by the required confidence level, not a specific number of individual drawdowns.

$$\text{Reward to conditional drawdown } \frac{\tilde{r} - \tilde{r}_F}{CDaR} \tag{8.22}$$

 Note

Given the potential variability of the number of drawdowns in a return series, and the consequent impact on the drawdown at risk, I favour the Sterling ratio.

GENERALISED Z RATIO

Zakamouline[14] (2010) hints at without further developing the idea that partial moments and extreme risk measures might be combined in a further

---

[14]V. Zakamouline (2010) On the Consistent Use of VaR in Portfolio Performance Evaluation: A Cautionary Note. *The Journal of Portfolio Management*, Fall, 37(1), 92–104.

generalised ratio (the Z ratio[15] would seem a highly appropriate name). This is another gain:loss type measure, highly adjustable to investor preferences, which might be described as follows:

$$\text{Z ratio} = Z_{0,\alpha}^{u,l} = \frac{\sqrt[u]{\frac{1}{n} \times \sum_{i=1}^{i=n} \max(r_i - r_T, 0)^u}}{\sqrt[l]{\frac{\left|\sum_{i=1}^{i=n} \langle r_i | r_i < VaR_{1-\alpha} \rangle^l\right|}{n_{VaR}}}} \tag{8.23}$$

In this form the Z ratio is expressed as an upper partial moment to downside extreme risk.

$u = 1, l = 1$ generates the upside potential to Tail loss ratio
$u = 1, l = 2$ generates the upside potential to Tail risk ratio

$$\text{Z ratio} = Z_{\beta,0}^{u,l} = \frac{\sqrt[u]{\frac{\sum_{i=1}^{i=n} \langle r_i | r_i > GVaR_{1-\beta} \rangle^u}{n_{GaR}}}}{\sqrt[l]{\frac{1}{n} \times \sum_{i=1}^{i=n} \max(r_T - r_i, 0)^l}} \tag{8.24}$$

In this form the Z ratio is expressed as extreme gain to a downside partial moment.

$u = 1, l = 1$ generates the potential upside to downside potential ratio
$u = 1, l = 2$ generates the potential upside to downside risk ratio

---

[15]Not to be confused with a Z score that quantifies the distance in standard deviations that a data point is from the mean.

CHAPTER 9

Fixed Income Risk

"I used to think if there was reincarnation, I wanted to come back as the president or the Pope or a .400 baseball hitter. But now I want to come back as the bond market. You can intimidate everybody."

James Carville (1944–)

PRICING FIXED INCOME INSTRUMENTS

In many ways it is easier to measure the risk of fixed income instruments or bonds; they consist (for the most part) of predictable future cash flows in the form of coupon payments and a final redemption value.

The price of a bond is the sum of present value of the future cash flows:

$$P = \sum_{i=1}^{n} F_i \times d^{t_i} \tag{9.1}$$

Where:

n = number of future coupon and capital repayments
F_i = ith future coupon and capital repayment(s)
t_i = time in years to the ith coupon or capital repayment
d = discount factor

REDEMPTION YIELD (YIELD TO MATURITY)

The redemption yield of a bond is the internal rate of return (IRR), or the constant rate of return at which the current value of the bond is equal to the sum of discounted values (or present values) of each cash flow.

WEIGHTED AVERAGE CASH FLOW

Clearly the price of a bond is influenced by discount rates, the amount of each cash flow and crucially the time over which these cash flows are discounted. Naturally we are interested in the sensitivity to changes in the future discount rates or yields. Time is crucial because the change in yield will have a greater effect over longer time periods. One such measure is the weighted average cash flow of the bond:

$$\text{Weighted average cash flow } \frac{\sum_{i=1}^{i=n} t_i \times F_i}{\sum_{i=1}^{i=n} F_i} \tag{9.2}$$

DURATION (EFFECTIVE MEAN TERM, DISCOUNTED MEAN TERM OR VOLATILITY)

A more accurate measure of sensitivity replaces the future cash flow with the present value of the cash flow and is called duration.

Duration is defined as the average life of the present values of all future cash flows but it is interpreted as an estimate of the bond's price sensitivity to changes in interest rates. In other words, it expresses the bond's exposure to interest rate risk. For example, a bond with duration of 13 years would be expected to gain approximately 13% in market value if interest rates fall by 1% (100 basis points) and to lose the same amount if interest rates rise by 1%. Duration is thus a systematic risk or volatility measure for bonds. In calculating the present value of the future cash flows, a discount rate equal to the redemption yield is used.

MACAULAY DURATION

Frederick Macaulay[1] was among the first to suggest the use of duration for studying the returns on bonds. Using present values in Equation 9.2 we get:

$$\text{Macaulay duration } D = \frac{\sum_{i=1}^{i=n} t_i \times F_i \times d^{t_i}}{\sum_{i=1}^{i=n} F_i \times d^{t_i}} \tag{9.3}$$

---

[1]Frederick Macaulay (1938) *Some Theoretical Problems Suggested by the Movement of Interest Rates, Bond Yields and Stock Prices in the US since 1856*. National Bureau of Economic Research.

Where:

$$d = \frac{1}{(1+y)} \qquad (9.4)$$

y = yield to maturity or redemption yield

The denominator in Equation 9.3 is equal to the present value of future coupon and capital repayments of the bond or, in other words, the price P.

Substituting Equation 9.1 into Equation 9.3 we have the formula for Macaulay duration:

$$D = \frac{\sum_{i=1}^{n} F_i \times t_i \times d^{t_i}}{P} \qquad (9.5)$$

MACAULAY–WEIL DURATION

There is no reason why the discount rate should be constant for all coupon payments; in fact, interest rates are likely to be different for different time periods. Macaulay–Weil duration uses the appropriate spot rate for each cash flow and is therefore slightly more accurate.

MODIFIED DURATION

Both Macaulay and Macaulay–Weil duration assume coupon payments are re-invested continuously, which is not the case. Duration can be modified for the actual payment frequency as follows:

$$MD = \frac{D}{1 + \frac{y}{k}} \qquad (9.6)$$

Where:
k = number of cash flows or coupons per year

 Note

For $k = \infty$, that is, continuous compounding, modified duration is equal to the Macaulay duration.

For a normal bond the duration will always be between zero and the maturity of the bond. The duration will be equal to the time to maturity for a zero-coupon bond, a bond with a single cash flow. Clearly all normal bonds are simply a series of zero-coupon bonds.

Weighted average cash flow, Macaulay, modified and Macaulay–Weil duration for the simple 20-year bond with a 6% annual coupon payment shown in Table 9.1 is calculated in Exhibit 9.1. Macaulay duration is graphically illustrated in Figure 9.1. The fulcrum marks the balancing point.

EXHIBIT 9.1 Duration

$$\text{Weighted average cash flow} = \frac{3260}{220} = 14.82 \text{ years}$$

$$\text{Macaulay duration} = \frac{1692.7}{128.91} = 13.13 \text{ years}$$

$$\text{Modified duration} = \frac{D}{1 + \frac{y}{k}} = \frac{13.13}{1 + \frac{1.0389}{1}} = 12.64 \text{ years}$$

$$\text{Macaulay–Weil duration} = \frac{1679.67}{128.91} = 13.03 \text{ years}$$

$$\text{Modified Macaulay–Weil duration} = \frac{D}{1 + \frac{y}{k}} = \frac{13.03}{1 + \frac{1.0389}{1}} = 12.54 \text{ years}$$

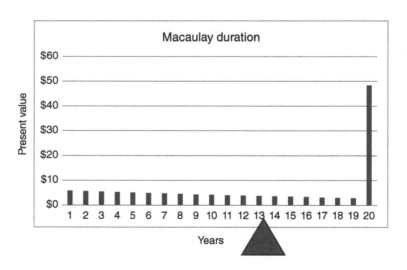

FIGURE 9.1 Macaulay duration

TABLE 9.1 Price, Macaulay, modified and Macaulay–Weil duration

				Macaulay			Macaulay–Weil	
20-year Bond 6% Coupon								
Period	Cash Flow	Time × Cash Flow	Present Value	Time × Present Value	Spot Rate	Present Value	Time × Present Value	
1	6	6	5.78	5.78	3.5%	5.80	5.80
2	6	12	5.56	11.12	3.5%	5.60	11.20
3	6	18	5.35	16.05	3.5%	5.41	16.23
4	6	24	5.15	20.60	3.5%	5.23	20.91
5	6	30	4.96	24.79	3.5%	5.05	25.26
6	6	36	4.77	28.63	3.5%	4.88	29.29
7	6	42	4.59	32.15	3.5%	4.72	33.01
8	6	48	4.42	35.36	3.5%	4.56	36.45
9	6	54	4.25	38.29	3.75%	4.31	38.77
10	6	60	4.1	40.95	3.75%	4.15	41.52
11	6	66	3.94	43.36	3.75%	4.00	44.02
12	6	72	3.79	45.53	3.75%	3.86	46.29
13	6	78	3.65	47.48	3.75%	3.72	48.33
14	6	84	3.52	49.21	3.75%	3.58	50.17
15	6	90	3.38	50.75	3.75%	3.45	51.81
16	6	96	3.26	52.11	3.75%	3.33	53.27
17	6	102	3.13	53.29	4.0%	3.08	52.36
18	6	108	3.02	54.31	4.0%	2.96	53.31
19	6	114	2.9	55.18	4.0%	2.85	54.11
20	106	2120	49.39	987.75	4.0%	48.38	967.54
Total	**220**	**3260**	**128.91**	**1692.70**	**Price**	**128.91**	**1679.67**
	IRR (y)			3.89%	IRR (y)	3.89%	

PORTFOLIO DURATION

Durations in a fixed income portfolio or benchmark are additive. The entire duration of the portfolio can be computed directly from the weighted sum of each bond in the portfolio:

$$\text{Portfolio duration} = \sum_{i=1}^{i=n} w_i \times MD_i \qquad (9.7)$$

EFFECTIVE DURATION (OR OPTION-ADJUSTED DURATION)

Modified duration does not calculate the effective duration of the bond if there is any optionality in future payments.[2] To calculate the effective duration the estimated price must be calculated for both a positive and negative change in interest rates:

$$\text{Effective duration } ED = \frac{P_- - P_+}{2 \times P \times \Delta y} \tag{9.8}$$

Where:

Δy = change in interest rates
P_- = estimated price if interest rate is decreased by Δy
P_+ = estimated price if interest rate is increased by Δy

If there is no optionality in future payments effective duration will be identical to modified duration. Technically, although numerically similar to modified duration, effective duration is a direct measure of sensitivity and not measured in years.

The effective duration of the bond used in Table 9.1 is calculated in Exhibit 9.2 based on a parallel change of 25 basis points using the revised data in Table 9.2. Notice the answer is close to modified Macaulay–Weil duration as expected.

EXHIBIT 9.2 Effective duration

$$\text{Effective duration } ED = \frac{P_- - P_+}{2 \times P \times \Delta y}$$

$$ED = \frac{133.04 - 124.96}{2 \times 128.91 \times 0.25\%} = 12.55$$

DURATION TO WORST

Duration to worst is identical to modified duration except that if there is any optionality (for example, if the bond is callable) the cash flow used in the calculation will be that which results in the worst yield for the investor.

---

[2]Callable bonds, for example.

TABLE 9.2 Effective duration

20-year Bond 6% Coupon	+0.25% Parallel Shift		−0.25% Parallel Shift	
Cash Flow	Spot Rate	Present Value	Spot Rate	Present Value
6	3.75%	5.78	3.25%	5.81
6	3.75%	5.57	3.25%	5.63
6	3.75%	5.37	3.25%	5.45
6	3.75%	5.18	3.25%	5.28
6	3.75%	4.99	3.25%	5.11
6	3.75%	4.81	3.25%	4.95
6	3.75%	4.64	3.25%	4.80
6	3.75%	4.47	3.25%	4.65
6	4.0%	4.22	3.5%	4.40
6	4.0%	4.05	3.5%	4.25
6	4.0%	3.90	3.5%	4.11
6	4.0%	3.75	3.5%	3.97
6	4.0%	3.60	3.5%	3.84
6	4.0%	3.46	3.5%	3.71
6	4.0%	3.33	3.5%	3.58
6	4.0%	3.20	3.5%	3.46
6	4.25%	2.96	3.75%	3.21
6	4.25%	2.84	3.75%	3.09
6	4.25%	2.72	3.75%	2.98
106	4.25%	46.11	3.75%	50.76
Price		124.96	**Price**	133.04

CONVEXITY

Duration is only the 1st order approximation in the change of the bond's price. The approximation is due to the fact that a curved line represents the relationship between bond prices and interest rates – see Figure 9.2. Duration assumes there is a linear relationship. This approximation can be improved by using a second approximation, convexity:

$$C = \frac{\sum_{i=1}^{n} F_i \times t_i \times (t_i + 1) \times d^{t_i}}{P} \tag{9.9}$$

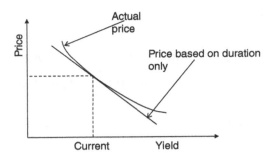

FIGURE 9.2 Convexity

MODIFIED CONVEXITY

Convexity can be modified just like duration for the actual payment frequency of coupons as follows:

$$MC = \left(\frac{1}{1 + \frac{y}{k}} \right)^2 \times \frac{\sum\limits_{i=1}^{n} F_i \times t_i \times (t_i + 1) \times d^{t_i}}{P} \tag{9.10}$$

Modified convexity is often erroneously just called convexity.

EFFECTIVE CONVEXITY

Again, modified convexity does not calculate the effective convexity of the bond if there is any optionality in future payments. Using estimated prices to calculate effective convexity:

$$EC = \frac{P_- + P_+ - 2 \times P}{P \times (\Delta y)^2} \tag{9.11}$$

Convexity, modified convexity and effective convexity based on the same 25 basis points change in yield are shown in Table 9.3 and calculated in Exhibit 9.3.

EXHIBIT 9.3 Convexity

$$\text{Convexity } C = \frac{\displaystyle\sum_{i=1}^{n} F_i \times t_i \times (t_i + 1) \times d^{t_i}}{P}$$

$$C = \frac{29657.64}{128.91} = 230.06 \text{ years}$$

$$\text{Modified convexity } MC = \left(\frac{1}{1 + \frac{y}{k}}\right)^2 \times \frac{\displaystyle\sum_{i=1}^{n} F_i \times t_i \times (t_i + 1) \times d^{t_i}}{P}$$

$$MC = \left(\frac{1}{1 + \frac{3.89\%}{1}}\right)^2 \times 230.06 = 213.14 \text{ years}$$

$$\text{Effective convexity } EC = \frac{P_- + P_+ - 2 \times P}{P \times (\Delta y)^2}$$

$$= \frac{133.04 + 124.96 - 2 \times 128.91}{128.91 \times (0.0025)^2} = 213.00$$

PORTFOLIO CONVEXITY

Just like duration, convexity in a fixed income portfolio or benchmark is additive. The convexity of the portfolio can be computed directly from the weighted sum of each bond in the portfolio:

$$\text{Portfolio convexity} = \sum_{i=1}^{i=n} w_i \times C_i \tag{9.12}$$

TABLE 9.3 Convexity

Period	Cash Flow	Present Value	$t \times (t+1)$	$t \times (t+1) \times$ Present Value
1	6	5.80	2	11.59
2	6	5.60	6	33.61
3	6	5.41	12	64.94
4	6	5.23	20	104.57
5	6	5.05	30	151.56
6	6	4.88	42	205.00
7	6	4.72	56	264.09
8	6	4.56	72	328.07
9	6	4.31	90	387.70
10	6	4.15	110	456.73
11	6	4.00	132	528.27
12	6	3.86	156	601.75
13	6	3.72	182	676.67
14	6	3.58	210	752.55
15	6	3.45	240	828.97
16	6	3.33	272	905.55
17	6	3.08	306	942.55
18	6	2.96	342	1012.92
19	6	2.85	380	1082.18
20	106	48.38	420	20318.35
	Price	**128.91**		**29657.64**

BOND RETURNS

Duration measures the sensitivity of a bond's price to changes in yield. Price changes can be estimated by:

$$\Delta P = -MD \times \Delta y \tag{9.13}$$

A better estimate of the return of a bond would include return from income through time, duration and convexity as follows:

$$r_B = y \times \Delta t - MD \times \Delta y + \frac{C}{2} \times (\Delta y)^2 \tag{9.14}$$

The price return for the bond in Table 9.1 is estimated in Exhibit 9.4 using both modified and effective duration and convexity for both a 25-basis point increase and decrease in yields.

EXHIBIT 9.4 Estimated bond returns

ACTUAL PRICE CHANGE

$$\frac{133.04}{128.91} - 1 = 3.2\% - 0.25\% \text{ change in yield}$$

$$\frac{124.96}{128.91} - 1 = -3.07\% + 0.25\% \text{ change in yield}$$

USING MODIFIED DURATION AND MODIFIED CONVEXITY

For a −0.25% change in yield:

$$r_B = -MD \times \Delta y + \frac{C}{2} \times (\Delta y)^2$$

$$= -12.54 \times (-0.25\%) + \frac{213.14}{2} \times (-0.25\%)^2 = 3.2\%$$

For a 0.25% change in yield:

$$r_B = -MD \times \Delta y + \frac{C}{2} \times (\Delta y)^2$$

$$= -12.54 \times (0.25\%) + \frac{213.14}{2} \times (0.25\%)^2 = -3.07\%$$

USING EFFECTIVE DURATION AND EFFECTIVE CONVEXITY

For a −0.25% change in yield:

$$r_B = -MD \times \Delta y + \frac{C}{2} \times (\Delta y)^2$$

$$= -12.55 \times (-0.25\%) + \frac{213.00}{2} \times (-0.25\%)^2 = 3.2\%$$

For a 0.25% change in yield:

$$r_B = -MD \times \Delta y + \frac{C}{2} \times (\Delta y)^2$$

$$= -12.55 \times (0.25\%) + \frac{213.00}{2} \times (0.25\%)^2 = -3.07\%$$

Both the modified and effective calculations are good estimates of the actual return of the bond.

DURATION *BETA*

The ratio of the portfolio's duration with that of the benchmark duration provides a measure equivalent to a regression *beta*:

$$D_\beta = \frac{D_P}{D_M} \qquad (9.15)$$

REWARD TO DURATION

Reward to duration is the Treynor ratio for fixed income portfolios with modified duration replacing *beta* as the measure of systematic risk.

$$\text{Reward to duration} = \frac{\tilde{r} - \tilde{r}_F}{MD} \qquad (9.16)$$

CHAPTER 10

Miscellaneous Risk Measures

"There are three classes of people: those that see, those who see when they are shown, those who do not see."

"Learning is the only thing the mind never exhausts, never fears, and never regrets."

Leonardo de Vinci (1452–1519). Public Domain

This chapter is really a collection of miscellaneous measures that are difficult to classify or perhaps not properly classified as risk measures at all, but nevertheless used to evaluate the performance of portfolios.

UPSIDE CAPTURE RATIO (OR UP CAPTURE INDICATOR)

Investors and portfolio managers are naturally interested in the relationship between portfolio and benchmark returns and therefore there are a number of additional measures that explore this relationship. The Upside capture ratio (or Up capture indicator) is designed to measure the extent to which the portfolio manager "captures" benchmark returns in positive markets.

$$\text{Upside capture ratio} = \frac{\bar{r}^+}{\bar{b}^+} \qquad (10.1)$$

Where:

$\bar{b}^+$ = average positive benchmark return

$\bar{r}^+$ = average portfolio return for each period in which the benchmark return is positive

The Upside capture ratio divides the average portfolio return by the average benchmark return for each period for which the benchmark return is positive.

 **Interpretation**

Clearly the higher the upside capture ratio the better. Upside capture ratios greater than 100% suggest outperformance and upside capture ratios less than 100% suggest underperformance relative to the benchmark. Note that it is possible for the ratio to be negative if the manager delivers, on average, negative returns in positive months.

DOWNSIDE CAPTURE RATIO (OR DOWN CAPTURE INDICATOR)

The Downside capture ratio (or Down capture indicator) is analogous to the Upside capture ratio (or Up capture indicator) and measures the extent to which the manager "captures" benchmark returns in negative markets.

$$\text{Downside capture ratio} = \frac{\bar{\bar{r}}}{\bar{\bar{b}}} \tag{10.2}$$

Where:

$\bar{\bar{b}}$ = average negative benchmark return
$\bar{\bar{r}}$ = average portfolio return for each period in which the benchmark return is negative

The Downside capture ratio divides the average portfolio return by the average benchmark return for each period for which the benchmark return is negative. Lower values are preferred. Downside capture less than 100% suggests outperformance and downside capture greater than 100% suggests underperformance relative to the benchmark.

 Note

Obviously if the portfolio manager is able to generate positive returns in down markets the ratio will be negative, which of course is a good thing.

UP/DOWN CAPTURE (OR CAPTURE RATIO)

Up/down capture or Capture ratio is simply the Upside capture ratio divided by the Downside capture ratio; it represents another way of measuring the asymmetry of returns.

$$\text{Capture ratio } CR = \frac{UCR}{DCR} = \frac{\bar{r}^{+} \times \bar{b}^{-}}{\bar{b}^{+} \times \bar{r}^{-}} \tag{10.3}$$

A Capture ratio greater that 1 represents positive asymmetry or a convex profile of returns whereas a Capture ratio less than 1 represents negative asymmetry or a concave return profile of returns. For a convex return profile, as benchmark returns increase portfolio returns will increase at a greater rate, and for a concave return profile, returns will increase but at a slower rate.

Upside capture, Downside capture and the Capture ratio are calculated in Exhibit 10.1 from standard portfolio data in Table 10.1 and Table 10.2.

EXHIBIT 10.1 Capture ratios

Upside portfolio average (geometric) $\bar{r}^{+} = (1 + 58.2\%)^{1/24} - 1 = 2.85\%$

Upside benchmark average (geometric) $\bar{b}^{+} = (1 + 58.99\%)^{1/24} - 1 = 3.01\%$

$$\text{Upside capture } \frac{\bar{r}^{+}}{\bar{b}^{+}} = \frac{2.85\%}{3.01\%} = 94.7\%$$

Downside portfolio average (geometric) $\bar{r}^{-} = (1 - 25.97\%)^{1/12} - 1$

$$= -2.47\%$$

Downside benchmark average (geometric) $\bar{b}^{-} = (1 - 26.14\%)^{1/12} - 1$

$$= -2.49\%$$

$$\text{Downside capture } \frac{\bar{r}^{-}}{\bar{b}^{-}} = \frac{-2.47\%}{-2.49\%} = 99.2\%$$

$$\text{Capture ratio} = \frac{UCR}{DCR} = \frac{94.7\%}{99.2\%} = 0.95$$

$$\text{Or Capture ratio } \frac{\bar{r}^{+} \times \bar{b}^{-}}{\bar{b}^{+} \times \bar{r}^{-}} = \frac{2.85\% \times -2.49\%}{3.01\% \times -2.47\%} = 0.95$$

TABLE 10.1   Upside capture

Portfolio Monthly Return r_i	Benchmark Monthly Return b_i	Portfolio Upside Return	Benchmark Upside Return	Cumulative Portfolio Upside	Cumulative Benchmark Upside
0.3	0.2	0.3	0.2	0.30	0.20
2.6	2.5	2.6	2.5	2.91	2.71
1.1	1.8	1.1	1.8	4.04	4.55
−0.9	−1.1			4.04	4.55
1.4	1.4	1.4	1.4	5.50	6.02
2.4	2.3	2.4	2.3	8.03	8.46
1.5	1.4	1.5	1.4	9.65	9.97
6.6	6.5	6.6	6.5	16.89	17.12
−1.4	−1.5			16.89	17.12
3.9	4.2	3.9	4.2	21.44	22.04
−0.5	−0.3			21.44	22.04
8.1	8.3	8.1	8.3	31.28	32.17
4.0	3.9	4.0	3.9	36.53	37.33
−3.7	−3.8			36.53	37.33
−6.1	−6.2			36.53	37.33
1.4	1.5	1.4	1.5	38.44	39.39
−4.9	−4.8			38.44	39.39
−2.1	−2.0			38.44	39.39
6.2	6.0	6.2	6.0	47.03	47.75
5.8	5.6	5.8	5.6	55.55	56.02
−6.4	−6.7			55.55	56.02
1.7	1.9	1.7	1.9	58.20	58.99
−0.4	−0.3			58.20	58.99
−0.2	−0.1			58.20	58.99
−2.1	−2.6			58.20	58.99
1.1	0.7	1.1	0.7	59.94	60.10
4.7	4.3	4.7	4.3	67.46	66.98
2.4	2.9	2.4	2.9	71.48	71.83
3.3	3.8	3.3	3.8	77.13	78.36
−0.7	−0.2			77.13	78.36
4.7	5.1	4.7	5.1	85.46	87.45
0.6	1.4	0.6	1.4	86.57	90.08
1.0	1.3	1.0	1.3	88.44	92.55
−0.2	0.3	−0.2	0.3	88.06	93.13
3.4	3.4	3.4	3.4	94.46	99.69
1.0	2.1	1.0	2.1	96.40	103.89
	Count	**24**	**24**		

TABLE 10.2 Downside capture

Portfolio Monthly Return r_i	Benchmark Monthly Return b_i	Portfolio Upside Return	Benchmark Upside Return	Cumulative Portfolio Upside	Cumulative Benchmark Upside
0.3	0.2			0.00	0.00
2.6	2.5			0.00	0.00
1.1	1.8			0.00	0.00
−0.9	−1.1	−0.9	−1.1	−0.90	−1.10
1.4	1.4			−0.90	−1.10
2.4	2.3			−0.90	−1.10
1.5	1.4			−0.90	−1.10
6.6	6.5			−0.90	−1.10
−1.4	−1.5	−1.4	−1.5	−2.29	−2.58
3.9	4.2			−2.29	−2.58
−0.5	−0.3	−0.5	−0.3	−2.78	−2.88
8.1	8.3			−2.78	−2.88
4.0	3.9			−2.78	−2.88
−3.7	−3.8	−3.7	−3.8	−6.37	−6.57
−6.1	−6.2	−6.1	−6.2	−12.08	−12.36
1.4	1.5			−12.08	−12.36
−4.9	−4.8	−4.9	−4.8	−16.39	−16.57
−2.1	−2.0	−2.1	−2.0	−18.15	−18.23
6.2	6.0			−18.15	−18.23
5.8	5.6			−18.15	−18.23
−6.4	−6.7	−6.4	−6.7	−23.39	−23.71
1.7	1.9			−23.39	−23.71
−0.4	−0.3	−0.4	−0.3	−23.69	−23.94
−0.2	−0.1	−0.2	−0.1	−23.85	−24.02
−2.1	−2.6	−2.1	−2.6	−25.44	−25.99
1.1	0.7			−25.44	−25.99
4.7	4.3			−25.44	−25.99
2.4	2.9			−25.44	−25.99
3.3	3.8			−25.44	−25.99
−0.7	−0.2	−0.7	−0.2	−25.97	−26.14
4.7	5.1			−25.97	−26.14
0.6	1.4			−25.97	−26.14
1.0	1.3			−25.97	−26.14
−0.2	0.3			−25.97	−26.14
3.4	3.4			−25.97	−26.14
1.0	2.1			−25.97	−26.14
	Count	12	12		

UP NUMBER RATIO

The Up number ratio measures the percentage of returns in each measurement period, for which the portfolio returns are greater than zero, when the benchmark returns are greater than zero.

Ideally the ratio should by 100%, the closer to 100% the better.

DOWN NUMBER RATIO

The Down number ratio measures the percentage of returns in each measurement period for which the portfolio returns are less than zero when the benchmark returns are less than zero.

Ideally the ratio should be 0% but it very rarely is. The lower the ratio the better, although for highly correlated returns ratios close to 100% should be expected.

UP PERCENTAGE RATIO

More interestingly the Up percentage ratio measures the percentage of periods in which the excess return of the portfolio against the benchmark is greater than zero in each measurement period when the benchmark return is greater than zero.

In other words, how often does the portfolio manager outperform a rising market?

DOWN PERCENTAGE RATIO

The Down percentage ratio measures the percentage of periods in which the excess return is greater than zero in each measurement period when the benchmark return is less than zero.

Or in other words how often does the portfolio manager outperform a falling market?

PERCENTAGE GAIN RATIO

The Percentage gain ratio is simply the ratio of portfolio returns greater than zero compared to the benchmark returns greater than zero.

$$\text{Percentage gain ratio} = \frac{n_r^+}{n_b^+} \tag{10.4}$$

Where:

n_r^+ = number of portfolio returns greater than zero
n_b^+ = number of benchmark returns greater than zero

Clearly the higher the percentage gain ratio the better, although I find up and down capture indicators of much more value.

BATTING AVERAGE (OR RELATIVE BATTING AVERAGE)

The Relative batting average, or simply Batting average, measures the percentage of positive excess returns divided by the total number of periods.

$$\text{Batting average} = \frac{n_e^+}{n} \tag{10.5}$$

Where:

n_e^+ = number of positive excess returns
n = number of return periods

HURST INDEX (OR HURST EXPONENT)

The Hurst index[1] is a useful statistic for detecting if a portfolio manager's returns are mean reverting (anti-persistent), totally random or persistent. It is estimated as follows:

$$\text{Hurst index } H = \frac{\log(R/S)}{\log(n)} \tag{10.6}$$

Where:

$$\frac{R}{S} = \frac{[\max(k^r) - \min(k^r)]}{\sigma}$$

$$n = \text{number of observations} \tag{10.7}$$

$$_k r = \sum_{i=1}^{i=k}(r_i - \bar{r}) \tag{10.8}$$

---

[1] Robert Clarkson (2001) FARM: A Financial Actuarial Risk Model. In F. Sortino and S. Satchell (eds) *Managing Downside Risk in Financial Markets*, Butterworth Heinemann.

(R/S) is the range of the maximum cumulative deviation from the mean to the minimum cumulative deviation from the mean divided by the standard deviation of portfolio returns, otherwise known as the rescaled range or simply (R/S).

H. E. Hurst originally developed the Hurst Index in 1955 to help in the difficult task of establishing optimal water storage along the Nile. Hurst[2] noted that (R/S) scales by a power law as time increases:

$$\frac{R}{S} = C \times n^{H} \tag{10.9}$$

Taking logarithms, we can obtain an estimate of the Hurst index as follows:

$$\log\left(\frac{R}{s} = \log\ C + H \times \log(n)\right) \tag{10.10}$$

The Hurst index is the gradient of the plot of $\log(R/S)$ against $\log(n)$, the intercept with the vertical axis is the constant log C, which for most time periods shorter than four or five years we can assume is zero, as shown in Figure 10.1.

A Hurst index between 0 and 0.5 would suggest that a portfolio manager's series of returns are mean-reverting (anti-persistent).

A Hurst index of 0.5 would suggest that the series of returns was totally random.

A Hurst index between 0.5 and 1 would suggest that the series of returns are persistent, that is, there is memory in the return series.

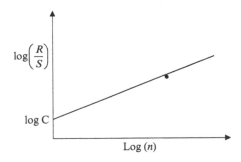

FIGURE 10.1   Hurst index

[2]B. Qian and K. Rasheed (2004) *Hurst Exponent and Financial Market Predictability.* IASTED conference on Financial Engineering and Applications (FEA 2004), 203–209.

> ### ❓ Interpretation
>
> Clearly persistent positive returns or excess returns would be a desirable property for any asset manager; a Hurst index close to 1 would suggest either exceptional performance or fraud. Nile floods are extremely persistent as evidenced by a Hurst index of 0.9; equity markets have a Hurst index of around 0.7.

Hurst indexes for both the standard portfolio and standard benchmark data in Tables 2.1 and 2.2 are calculated in Exhibit 10.2 from data in Tables 10.3 and 10.4.

EXHIBIT 10.2 Hurst index

PORTFOLIO

Maximum cumulative deviation from the mean	14.8%
Minimum cumulative deviation from the mean	−9.2%
Standard deviation σ	3.32%

$$\frac{R}{S} = \frac{[\max(_k r) - \min(_k r)]}{\sigma} = \frac{14.8\% - (-9.2\%)}{3.32\%} = 7.23$$

$$\text{Hurst index} \quad H = \frac{\log(R/S)}{\log(n)} = \frac{\log(7.23)}{\log(36)} = \frac{1.98}{3.58} = 0.55$$

BENCHMARK

Maximum cumulative deviation from the mean	14.0%
Minimum cumulative deviation from the mean	−12.4%
Standard deviation σ	3.36%

$$\frac{R}{S} = \frac{[\max(_k b) - \min(_k b)]}{\sigma_b} = \frac{14.0\% - 12.4\%}{3.36\%} = 7.85$$

$$\text{Hurst index} \quad H = \frac{\log(R/S)}{\log(n)} = \frac{\log(7.85)}{\log(36)} = \frac{2.06}{3.58} = 0.58$$

TABLE 10.3   Portfolio – Hurst index

Monthly Return (%) r_i	Deviation from Average $(r_i - \bar{r})$ $\bar{r} = 1.1\%$	Cumulative Deviation $\sum_{i=1}^{i=k}(r_i - \bar{r})$	
0.3	−0.8	−0.8	
2.6	1.5	0.7	
1.1	0.0	0.7	
−0.9	−2.0	−1.3	
1.4	0.3	−1.0	
2.4	1.3	0.3	
1.5	0.4	0.7	
6.6	5.5	6.2	
−1.4	−2.5	3.7	
3.9	2.8	6.5	
−0.5	−1.6	4.9	
8.1	7.0	11.9	
4.0	2.9	**14.8**	**Maximum**
−3.7	−4.8	10.0	
−6.1	−7.2	2.8	
1.4	0.3	3.1	
−4.9	−6.0	−2.9	
−2.1	−3.2	−6.1	
6.2	5.1	−1.0	
5.8	4.7	3.7	
−6.4	−7.5	−3.8	
1.7	0.6	−3.2	
−0.4	−1.5	−4.7	
−0.2	−1.3	−6.0	
−2.1	−3.2	**−9.2**	**Minimum**
1.1	0.0	**−9.2**	
4.7	3.6	−5.6	
2.4	1.3	−4.3	
3.3	2.2	−2.1	
−0.7	−1.8	−3.9	
4.7	3.6	−0.3	
0.6	−0.5	−0.8	
1.0	−0.1	−0.9	
−0.2	−1.3	−2.2	
3.4	2.3	0.1	
1.0	−0.1	0.0	

TABLE 10.4   Benchmark – Hurst index

Monthly Return (%) b_i	Deviation from Average $(b_i - \bar{b})$ $\bar{b} = 1.2\%$	Cumulative Deviation $\sum_{i=1}^{i=k}(b_i - \bar{b})$	
0.2	−1.0	−1.0	
2.5	1.3	0.3	
1.8	0.6	0.9	
−1.1	−2.3	−1.4	
1.4	0.2	−1.2	
2.3	1.1	−0.1	
1.4	0.2	0.1	
6.5	5.3	5.4	
−1.5	−2.7	2.7	
4.2	3.0	5.7	
−0.3	−1.5	4.2	
8.3	7.1	11.3	
3.9	2.7	**14.0**	**Maximum**
−3.8	−5.0	9.0	
−6.2	−7.4	1.6	
1.5	0.3	1.9	
−4.8	−6.0	−4.1	
−2	−3.2	−7.3	
6	4.8	−2.5	
5.6	4.4	1.9	
−6.7	−7.9	−6.0	
1.9	0.7	−5.3	
−0.3	−1.5	−6.8	
−0.1	−1.3	−8.1	
−2.6	−3.8	−11.9	
0.7	−0.5	**−12.4**	**Minimum**
4.3	3.1	−9.3	
2.9	1.7	−7.6	
3.8	2.6	−5.0	
−0.2	−1.4	−6.4	
5.1	3.9	−2.5	
1.4	0.2	−2.3	
1.3	0.1	−2.2	
0.3	−0.9	−3.1	
3.4	2.2	−0.9	
2.1	0.9	0.0	

RELATIVE HURST INDEX (OR ACTIVE HURST)

Of course, the Hurst index can be applied to excess returns to determine if the portfolio manager's added value is persistent, totally random or mean reverting.

$$\text{Relative Hurst index (arithmetic)} RH_A = \frac{\log(A/S)}{\log(n)} \qquad (10.11)$$

Where:

$$\frac{A}{S} = \frac{[\max(_k a) - \min(_k a)]}{\sigma_A}$$

$$n = \text{number of observations} \qquad (10.12)$$

$$_k a = \sum_{i=1}^{i=k} (a_i - \overline{a}) \qquad (10.13)$$

For geometric excess returns:

$$\text{Relative Hurst index (geometric)} RH_G = \frac{\log(G/s)}{\log(n)} \qquad (10.14)$$

Where:

$$\frac{G}{S} = \frac{[\max(_k g) - \min(_k g)]}{\sigma_G} \qquad (10.15)$$

$$_k g = \sum_{i=1}^{i=k} (g_i - \overline{g}) \qquad (10.16)$$

Relative Hurst indexes arithmetic and geometric for the standard portfolio and benchmark data in Table 2.1 and Table 2.2 are calculated in Exhibit 10.3 from data in Table 10.5 and Table 10.6.

EXHIBIT 10.3 Relative Hurst index

ARITHMETIC EXCESS RETURNS

Maximum cumulative deviation from the mean   3.7%

Minimum cumulative deviation from the mean   −0.2%

Standard deviation (tracking error) σ_A 0.348%

$$\frac{A}{S} = \frac{[\max(_k a) - \min(_k a)]}{\sigma_A} = \frac{3.7\% - (-0.2\%)}{0.348\%} = 11.21$$

Hurst index $RH_A = \dfrac{\log(A/S)}{\log(n)} = \dfrac{\log(11.21)}{\log(36)} = \dfrac{2.42}{3.58} = 0.67$

GEOMETRIC EXCESS RETURNS

Maximum cumulative deviation from the mean   3.64%

Minimum cumulative deviation from the mean   −0.2%

Standard deviation (tracking error) σ_G 0.343%

$$\frac{G}{S} = \frac{[\max(_k g) - \min(_k g)]}{\sigma_G} = \frac{3.64\% - (-0.2\%)}{0.343\%} = 11.19$$

Hurst index $RH_G = \dfrac{\log(G/S)}{\log(n)} = \dfrac{\log(11.9)}{\log(36)} = \dfrac{2.41}{3.58} = 0.67$

It is no surprise that the relative Hurst index is similar for both arithmetic and geometric excess returns and in this particular case somewhat persistent.

TABLE 10.5   Relative Hurst index (arithmetic)

Portfolio Monthly Return (%) r_i	Benchmark Monthly Return (%) b_i	Arithmetic Excess Return $a_i = (r_i - b_i)$	Deviation from Average $(a_i - \bar{a})$	Cumulative Deviation $\sum_{i=1}^{i=k}(a_i - \bar{a})$	
0.3	0.2	0.1	0.2	0.2	
2.6	2.5	0.1	0.2	0.4	
1.1	1.8	−0.7	−0.6	−0.2	**Minimum**
−0.9	−1.1	0.2	0.3	0.1	
1.4	1.4	0.0	0.1	0.2	
2.4	2.3	0.1	0.2	0.4	
1.5	1.4	0.1	0.2	0.6	
6.6	6.5	0.1	0.2	0.8	
−1.4	−1.5	0.1	0.2	1.0	
3.9	4.2	−0.3	−0.2	0.8	
−0.5	−0.3	−0.2	−0.1	0.7	
8.1	8.3	−0.2	−0.1	0.6	
4.0	3.9	0.1	0.2	0.8	
−3.7	−3.8	0.1	0.2	1.0	
−6.1	−6.2	0.1	0.2	1.2	
1.4	1.5	−0.1	0.0	1.2	
−4.9	−4.8	−0.1	0.0	1.2	
−2.1	−2.0	−0.1	0.0	1.2	
6.2	6.0	0.2	0.3	1.5	
5.8	5.6	0.2	0.3	1.8	
−6.4	−6.7	0.3	0.4	2.2	
1.7	1.9	−0.2	−0.1	2.1	
−0.4	−0.3	−0.1	0.0	2.1	
−0.2	−0.1	−0.1	0.0	2.1	
−2.1	−2.6	0.5	0.6	2.7	
1.1	0.7	0.4	0.5	3.2	
4.7	4.3	0.4	0.5	3.7	**Maximum**
2.4	2.9	−0.5	−0.4	3.3	
3.3	3.8	−0.5	−0.4	2.9	
−0.7	−0.2	−0.5	−0.4	2.5	
4.7	5.1	−0.4	−0.3	2.2	
0.6	1.4	−0.8	−0.7	1.5	
1.0	1.3	−0.3	−0.2	1.3	
−0.2	0.3	−0.5	−0.4	0.9	
3.4	3.4	0.0	0.1	1.0	
1.0	2.1	−1.1	−1.0	0.0	

TABLE 10.6 Relative Hurst index (geometric)

Portfolio Monthly Return r_i	Benchmark Monthly Return b_i	Geometric Excess Return $g_i = \frac{(1+r_i)}{(1+b_i)} - 1$	Deviation from Average $(g_i - \bar{g})$	Cumulative Deviation $\sum_{i=1}^{i=k} (g_i - \bar{g})$	
0.3	0.2	0.10	0.2	0.20	
2.6	2.5	0.10	0.19	0.39	
1.1	1.8	−0.69	−0.59	−0.20	**Minimum**
−0.9	−1.1	0.20	0.30	0.10	
1.4	1.4	0.00	0.10	0.20	
2.4	2.3	0.10	0.19	0.39	
1.5	1.4	0.10	0.20	0.59	
6.6	6.5	0.09	0.19	0.78	
−1.4	−1.5	0.10	0.20	0.98	
3.9	4.2	−0.29	−0.19	0.78	
−0.5	−0.3	−0.20	−0.10	0.68	
8.1	8.3	−0.18	−0.09	0.60	
4.0	3.9	0.10	0.19	0.79	
−3.7	−3.8	0.10	0.20	0.99	
−6.1	−6.2	0.11	0.20	1.20	
1.4	1.5	−0.10	0.00	1.20	
−4.9	−4.8	−0.11	−0.01	1.18	
−2.1	−2.0	−0.10	−0.01	1.18	
6.2	6.0	0.19	0.29	1.47	
5.8	5.6	0.19	0.29	1.75	
−6.4	−6.7	0.32	0.42	2.17	
1.7	1.9	−0.20	−0.10	2.07	
−0.4	−0.3	−0.10	0.00	2.07	
−0.2	−0.1	−0.10	0.00	2.06	
−2.1	−2.6	0.51	0.61	2.67	
1.1	0.7	0.40	0.49	3.17	
4.7	4.3	0.38	0.48	3.65	**Maximum**
2.4	2.9	−0.49	−0.39	3.25	
3.3	3.8	−0.48	−0.38	2.87	
−0.7	−0.2	−0.50	−0.40	2.47	
4.7	5.1	−0.38	−0.28	2.18	
0.6	1.4	−0.79	−0.69	1.49	
1.0	1.3	−0.30	−0.20	1.29	
−0.2	0.3	−0.50	−0.40	0.89	
3.4	3.4	0.00	0.10	0.98	
1.0	2.1	−1.08	−0.98	0.00	

BIAS RATIO

The Bias ratio is a simple but ingenious ratio devised by Adil Abdulali[3] of Protégé Partners, published in 2006 to provide some insight into the distribution of returns near zero. It is defined as the number of returns equal to and closely exceeding zero, divided by the number of returns close to but less than zero. The definition of close is set to the investor's preference but typically within one standard deviation.

$$\text{Bias ratio } BR = \frac{\text{Count}\langle r_i | r_i \in [0, \sigma] \rangle}{1 + \text{Count}\langle r_i | r_i \in [-\sigma, 0] \rangle} \tag{10.17}$$

The Bias ratio is a useful indicator of stale prices associated with illiquid assets and perhaps a subjective pricing policy. Hedge fund, real estate and private equity managers are very keen to deliver constant positive returns and may be reluctant to crystallise negative returns, potentially leading to an element of smoothing, avoiding if possible small negative revaluations and only "biting the bullet" if a negative write down is unavoidable. Apart from the obvious impact of hiding volatility, such activity may be an indicator of outright fraud.

A Bias ratio of less than 1 would certainly not be an indicator of fraud but would be undesirable nevertheless. Equity indexes tend to generate Bias ratios between 1 and 1.5; Ponzi schemes would in all likelihood exhibit very high Bias ratios.[4]

 Note

Interestingly the Bias ratio for the Fairfield Sentry Hedge Fund Ltd, a feeder fund for the well-known Bernie Madoff Ponzi scheme,[4] over the period 31 December 1990 to 31 October 2008, I calculate to be 5.2!

---

[3]A. Abdulali (2006) The Bias Ratio™, Measuring the Shape of Fraud. *Protégé Partners – Quarterly Letter 3Q*.
[4]The Madoff Case: A Timeline. *Wall Street Journal*, 6 March 2009

Caution

Bias ratios should not be analysed in isolation or out of context but used as an additional measure by comparison to an appropriate benchmark that reflects the underlying investment strategy. Cash and near cash strategies, in particular, will naturally lead to a large number of small positive returns and few or no negative returns. If genuine, a high bias ratio is desirable.

Bias ratios are calculated in Exhibit 10.4 for the standard portfolio and benchmark data summarised in Tables 10.7 and 10.8.

EXHIBIT 10.4   Bias ratio

PORTFOLIO

$$BR = \frac{\text{Count}\langle r_i | r_i \in [0, \sigma]\rangle}{1 + \text{Count}\langle r_i | r_i \in [-\sigma, 0]\rangle} = \frac{14}{1 + 9} = 1.4$$

Note close returns are within one standard deviation = 3.32%

BENCHMARK

$$BR = \frac{\text{Count}\langle b_i | b_i \in [0, \sigma]\rangle}{1 + \text{Count}\langle b_i | b_i \in [-\sigma, 0]\rangle} = \frac{14}{1 + 8} = 1.56$$

Note close returns are within one standard deviation = 3.36%

ACTIVE SHARE

Active share is a descriptive risk measure suggested by Cremers and Petajisto[5] in 2006 that is perhaps easy to dismiss as being too simple to be of any value

---

[5]K. J. M. Cremers and A. Petajisto (2006) How Active Is Your Fund Manager: A New Measure that Predicts Performance. Yale IFC Working Paper No. 04-14. K. J. M. Cremers and A. Petajisto (2009) How Active Is Your Fund Manager: A New Measure that Predicts Performance. *Review of Financial Studies* 22(9), 3329–3365.

TABLE 10.7 Portfolio bias ratio

Month	Negative Return	Close Return (within one standard deviation)	Positive Return	Close Return
1			0.3	X
2			2.6	X
3			1.1	X
4	−0.9	X		
5			1.4	X
6			2.4	X
7			1.5	X
8			6.6	
9	−1.4	X		
10			3.9	
11	−0.5	X		
12			8.1	
13			4.0	
14	−3.7			
15	−6.1			
16			1.4	X
17	−4.9			
18	−2.1	X		
19			6.2	
20			5.8	
21	−6.4			
22			1.7	X
23	−0.4	X		
24	−0.2	X		
25	−2.1	X		
26			1.1	X
27			4.7	
28			2.4	X
29			3.3	X
30	−0.7	X		
31			4.7	
32			0.6	X
33			1.0	X
34	−0.2	X		
35			3.4	
36			1.0	X
Count		9		14

TABLE 10.8   Benchmark bias ratio

Month	Negative Return	Close Return (within one standard deviation)	Positive Return	Close Return
1			0.2	X
2			2.5	X
3			1.8	X
4	−1.1	X		
5			1.4	X
6			2.3	X
7			1.4	X
8			6.5	
9	−1.5	X		
10			4.2	
11	−0.3	X		
12			8.3	
13			3.9	
14	−3.8			
15	−6.2			
16			1.5	X
17	−4.8			
18	−2.0	X		
19			6	
20			5.6	
21	−6.7			
22			1.9	X
23	−0.3	X		
24	−0.1	X		
25	−2.6	X		
26			0.7	X
27			4.3	
28			2.9	X
29			3.8	
30	−0.2	X		
31			5.1	
32			1.4	X
33			1.3	X
34			0.3	X
35			3.4	
36			2.1	X
Count		8		14

or perhaps should not be described as a risk measure at all. Active share is a measure of the percentage difference of security holdings in the portfolio as opposed to the benchmark defined as:

$$\text{Active share} = \frac{1}{2} \times \sum_{j=1}^{j=n} |PW_j - IW_j| \tag{10.18}$$

Where:

PW_j = weight in portfolio of security j
IW_j = weight in the index (or benchmark) of security j

An active share of 0% represents full replication between the portfolio and index and 100% represents no overlap.

Cremers and Petajisto analysed some 2647 US mutual funds over the period 1980 to 2003 and concluded:

i) Manager active share is persistent
ii) Funds with high active share tend to outperform
iii) Funds with low active share tend to underperform.

Using active share and tracking error they classified managers into four groups as shown in Table 10.9 and illustrated in Figure 10.2.

Not unsurprisingly, portfolios with high active share and low tracking error (stock pickers) – for example, portfolio managers prepared to take big bets yet nevertheless controlling relative risk – were the best performing group. Portfolios with high active share and high tracking error (concentrated portfolios) also performed well, but portfolios with low active share and low tracking error (pejoratively described as closet indexes) tend to underperform and portfolios with low active share and high tracking error (portfolios betting on systematic factors generating high tracking error without taking big individual stock bets against the index, described as factor bet portfolios) also underperform.

TABLE 10.9 Active share

Active Share	Tracking Error	Classification
High	High	Concentrated
High	Low	Stock pickers
Low	High	Factor bets
Low	Low	Closet indexers

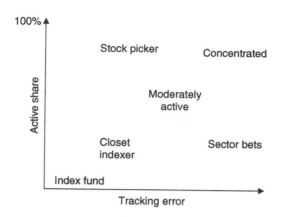

FIGURE 10.2 Active share

> ### ❓ Interpretation
>
> Suggesting that active share is a good predictor of outperformance is perhaps a little optimistic, and as such, has been criticised – see Morrison[6] (2016) and Frazzini, Friedman and Pormorski[7] (2016). However, using active share as a filter rather than a predictor of performance seems reasonable. Regulators are increasingly using active share as a measure to determine if investment strategies are active (and hence justify charging active fees). The Danish Investment Funds Association requires the publication of both active share and tracking error in UCITS annual reports and recommends funds with active share less than 50% and tracking error less than 3% to justify their investment strategies.[8]

K RATIO

In 1996 Lars Kestner[9] introduced a reward to risk measure called the K ratio based on the slope of cumulative portfolio returns through time (see Figure 10.3).

$$\text{K ratio} = \frac{\beta_C}{\sigma_C} \tag{10.19}$$

---

[6]C. Morrison (2016) Key insight or Flawed Measure? *CFA Institute Conference Proceedings Quarterly*, CFA Institute, First Quarter.
[7]A. Frazzini, J. A. Friedman and L. Pomoski (2016), Deactivating Active Share, *Financial Analysts Journal* 72(2), 14–21.
[8]Active/Passive Management in Danish UCITS, 20 April 2016, The Danish FSA.
[9]Lars Kestner (1996) Getting a Handle on True Performance. *Futures* 25(1), 44–46.

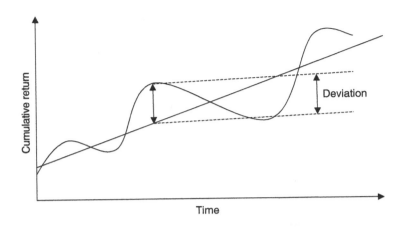

FIGURE 10.3   K ratio

Where:

β_C = the slope of the portfolio's cumulative return through time
σ_C = standard deviation of the resultant regression error term

The "reward" is the slope of the cumulative return – the greater the upward slope the better. The risk is the deviation from the resultant trend line measured by standard deviation, lower standard deviation indicating greater consistency in the delivery of cumulative return. Steady accumulation of the cumulative return is preferred. Other versions of the K ratio use the standard regression error, or the standard error of slope in the denominator. Kestner[10] later modified the K ratio to standardise over different time periods as follows:

$$\text{Modified K ratio} = \frac{\beta_C}{\hat{\sigma}_C \times n} \qquad (10.20)$$

Note the standard regression error (or sample regression error) is linked to the standard deviation of the error term as follows:

$$\text{Standard regression error } \hat{\sigma}_C = \sqrt{\frac{n}{n-2}} \times \sigma_C \qquad (10.21)$$

The Bessel adjustment of $n-2$ indicates the loss of two degrees of freedom.

---

[10]L. N. Kestner (2003) *Quantitative Trading Strategies: Harnessing the Power of Quantitative Techniques to Create a Winning Trading Program* (Traders Edge Series). McGraw-Hill.

Note

All versions of the K ratio will rank portfolios in the same order; therefore, I prefer the conceptually simplest form of the K ratio in Equation (10.19).

The slope of the cumulative return for our standard portfolio is calculated in Exhibit 10.5 using the covariance data calculated in Table 10.10 and the period count variance calculated in Table 10.11.

EXHIBIT 10.5   Slope of cumulative return

$$\text{Cumulative covariance} = \frac{\displaystyle\sum_{i=1}^{i=n}(r_{Ci} - \bar{r}_C) \times (i - \bar{i})}{n} = \frac{3847.14}{36} = 106.86$$

$$\text{Period count variance} = \frac{\displaystyle\sum_{i=1}^{i=n}(i - \bar{i})^2}{n} = \frac{3855.0}{36} = 107.92$$

$$\text{Cumulative slope} = \beta_C = \frac{\displaystyle\sum_{i=1}^{i=n}(r_{Ci} - \bar{r}_c) \times (i - \bar{i})}{\displaystyle\sum_{i=1}^{i=n}(i - \bar{i})^2} = \frac{3847.14}{3885} = 0.99$$

$$\text{Intercept } \alpha_C = \frac{\displaystyle\sum_{i=1}^{i=n} r_{Ci}}{n} - \beta_C \times \frac{\displaystyle\sum_{i=1}^{i=n} i}{n} = 21.73 - 0.99 \times 18.5 = 3.41$$

TABLE 10.10 Portfolio cumulative covariance

Portfolio Monthly Return (%) r_i	Portfolio Cumulative Return (%) r_{Ci}	Portfolio Cumulative Deviation from Average (%)	Period Count i	Period Deviation from Average $(i - \bar{i})$	Portfolio Cumulative Deviation × Period Deviation
0.3	0.30	−21.43	1	−17.5	375.02
2.6	2.91	−18.82	2	−16.5	310.56
1.1	4.04	−17.69	3	−15.5	274.19
−0.9	3.10	−18.63	4	−14.5	270.08
1.4	4.55	−17.18	5	−13.5	231.97
2.4	7.06	−14.67	6	−12.5	183.42
1.5	8.66	−13.07	7	−11.5	150.28
6.6	15.83	−5.90	8	−10.5	61.91
−1.4	14.21	−7.52	9	−9.5	71.42
3.9	18.67	−3.06	10	−8.5	26.04
−0.5	18.07	−3.66	11	−7.5	27.43
8.1	27.64	5.91	12	−6.5	−38.40
4.0	32.74	11.01	13	−5.5	−60.57
−3.7	27.83	6.10	14	−4.5	−27.45
−6.1	20.03	−1.70	15	−3.5	5.94
1.4	21.71	−0.02	16	−2.5	0.04
−4.9	15.75	−5.98	17	−1.5	8.97
−2.1	13.32	−8.41	18	−0.5	4.21
6.2	20.34	−1.39	19	0.5	−0.69
5.8	27.32	5.59	20	1.5	8.39
−6.4	19.18	−2.55	21	2.5	−6.38
1.7	21.20	−0.53	22	3.5	−1.85
−0.4	20.72	−1.01	23	4.5	−4.56
−0.2	20.48	−1.25	24	5.5	−6.90
−2.1	17.95	−3.78	25	6.5	−24.60
1.1	19.24	−2.49	26	7.5	−18.65
4.7	24.85	3.12	27	8.5	26.50
2.4	27.84	6.11	28	9.5	58.08
3.3	32.06	10.33	29	10.5	108.50
−0.7	31.14	9.41	30	11.5	108.20
4.7	37.30	15.57	31	12.5	194.65
0.6	38.13	16.40	32	13.5	221.34
1.0	39.51	17.78	33	14.5	257.77
−0.2	39.23	17.50	34	15.5	271.22
3.4	43.96	22.23	35	16.5	366.82
1.0	45.40	23.67	36	17.5	414.25
	Total		**Total**		**Total**
	$\sum\limits_{i=1}^{i=n} r_{Ci} = 782.27$		$\sum\limits_{i=1}^{i=n} i = 666$		**3847.14**
	Average		**Average**		
	$\bar{r}_c = \dfrac{782.27}{36} = 21.73$		$\bar{i} = \dfrac{\sum\limits_{i=1}^{i=n} i}{36} = \dfrac{666}{36} = 18.5$		

TABLE 10.11   Period count variance

Period Count I	Period Deviation from Average $(i - \bar{i})$	Deviation Squared $(i - \bar{i})^2$
1	−17.5	306.25
2	−16.5	272.25
3	−15.5	240.25
4	−14.5	210.25
5	−13.5	182.25
6	−12.5	156.25
7	−11.5	132.25
8	−10.5	110.25
9	−9.5	90.25
10	−8.5	72.25
11	−7.5	56.25
12	−6.5	42.25
13	−5.5	30.25
14	−4.5	20.25
15	−3.5	12.25
16	−2.5	6.25
17	−1.5	2.25
18	−0.5	0.25
19	0.5	0.25
20	1.5	2.25
21	2.5	6.25
22	3.5	12.25
23	4.5	20.25
24	5.5	30.25
25	6.5	42.25
26	7.5	56.25
27	8.5	72.25
28	9.5	90.25
29	10.5	110.25
30	11.5	132.25
31	12.5	156.25
32	13.5	182.25
33	14.5	210.25
34	15.5	240.25
35	16.5	272.25
36	17.5	306.25

Total

$$\sum_{i=1}^{i=n} (i - \bar{i})^2 = 3885.00$$

TABLE 10.12 K ratio error term

Portfolio Cumulative Return (%) r_{Ci}	Regression Residual or Error Term $\varepsilon_{Ci} = (r_{Ci} - \alpha_c - \beta_c \times i)$	Residual Squared ε_{Ci}^2
0.30	−4.10	16.81
2.91	−2.48	6.16
4.04	−2.34	5.48
3.10	−4.27	18.21
4.55	−3.81	14.55
7.06	−2.30	5.27
8.66	−1.68	2.82
15.83	4.50	20.26
14.21	1.89	3.57
18.67	5.35	28.66
18.07	3.77	14.21
27.64	12.34	152.37
32.74	16.46	270.90
27.83	10.56	111.45
20.03	1.77	3.13
21.71	2.46	6.05
15.75	−4.49	20.20
13.32	−7.92	62.66
20.34	−1.88	3.54
27.32	4.11	16.89
19.18	−5.03	25.30
21.20	−3.99	15.95
20.72	−5.47	29.91
20.48	−6.70	44.90
17.95	−10.22	104.46
19.24	−9.91	98.28
24.85	−5.30	28.08
27.84	−3.29	10.85
32.06	−0.06	0.00
31.14	−1.98	3.92
37.30	3.19	10.20
38.13	3.03	9.16
39.51	3.42	11.68
39.23	2.15	4.62
43.96	5.89	34.72
45.40	6.34	40.22
Sum	**0.00**	**1255.46**

   The K ratio is calculated in Exhibit 10.6 using the K ratio error terms calculated in Table 10.12.

EXHIBIT 10.6   K ratio

$$\text{Standard deviation of K ratio error term } \sigma_C = \sqrt{\frac{(\varepsilon_{Ci} - \bar{\varepsilon}_C)^2}{n}}$$

$$= \sqrt{\frac{1255.46}{36}} = 5.905$$

$$\text{K ratio } \frac{\beta_C}{\sigma_C} = \frac{0.99}{5.905} = 0.168$$

CHAPTER 11

Risk-Adjusted Return

"You can measure opportunity with the same yardstick that measures the risk involved. They go together."

Robert C. Worstell, Earl Nightingale (1921–1989) *How to Completely Change Your Life in 30 Seconds - Part III*, (2017) Lulu.com

The Sharpe ratio is sometimes erroneously described as a risk-adjusted return; the clue is in its name – it's a ratio not a return. We can rank portfolios in order of preference with the Sharpe ratio but it is difficult to judge the size of relative performance. We need a risk-adjusted return measure to gain a better feel of risk-adjusted outperformance. Ratios all suffer the same problem, they allow us to rank portfolios in order of preference but do not inform in terms of the quantity of relative performance. Risk-adjusted returns, on the other hand, convert ratios to a return metric we fully understand and can freely use to make a judgement about relative performance.

M^2

M^2 is perhaps the most commonly used and easiest to calculate risk-adjusted return. M^2 is graphically represented in Figure 11.1. A straight line is drawn vertically through the risk of the benchmark $\tilde{\sigma}_b$; the intercept with the Sharpe ratio line of portfolio B would give the return of the portfolio with the same Sharpe ratio of portfolio B but at the risk of the benchmark. This return is called M^2, a genuinely risk-adjusted return, extremely useful for comparing portfolios with different levels of risk.

In Figure 11.1, M^2 for portfolio B is clearly higher than for portfolio A, even though portfolio A has a higher absolute return. This is an important

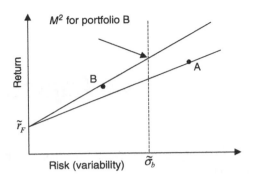

FIGURE 11.1 M^2

point captured by the M^2 measure: it adjusts each portfolio's returns to what it *would have been* had the portfolio managers taken the same amount of risk. In Figure 11.1, portfolio B's return is adjusted up (because it did not take as much risk as the benchmark) while portfolio A's return is adjusted down (because it has taken more risk than the benchmark).

$$M^2 = \tilde{r} + SR \times (\tilde{\sigma}_b - \tilde{\sigma}) \qquad (11.1)$$

Where:

σ_b = market risk (variability, standard deviation of benchmark return)

M^2 is so called not because any element of the calculation is squared, but because it was first proposed by the partnership of Leah Modigliani and her grandfather Professor Franco Modigliani.[1]

Alternatively, you might see the equation for M^2 expressed as:

$$M^2 = (\tilde{r} - \tilde{r}_F) \times \frac{\tilde{\sigma}_b}{\tilde{\sigma}} + \tilde{r}_F \qquad (11.2)$$

Although Equations 11.1 and 11.2 will give the same answer, I prefer the presentation of Equation 11.1, which is directly linked to the geometry of Figure 11.1 and very clearly captures the penalty if portfolio risk is greater than the benchmark risk and the reward if portfolio risk is less than benchmark risk (assuming of course the Sharpe ratio is positive).

Using the data from Table 3.1 M^2 is calculated in Table 11.1.

---

[1]Leah Modigliani (1997) Risk-Adjusted Performance, Part 1: The Time for Risk Measurement Is Now. *Morgan Stanley's Investment Perspectives*, February.

TABLE 11.1 M^2

	Portfolio A	Portfolio B
Annualised return	7.9%	6.9%
Annualised risk	5.5%	3.2%
Sharpe ratio	1.07	1.53
Risk-free rate	2.0%	2.0%
$M^2 = \tilde{r} + SR \times (\tilde{\sigma}_b - \tilde{\sigma})$	$7.9\% + 1.07 \times (4.5\% - 5.5\%)$	$6.9\% + 1.53\% \times (4.5\% - 3.2\%)$
	$= 6.83\%$	$= 8.89\%$
$M^2 = (\tilde{r} - \tilde{r}_F) \times \dfrac{\tilde{\sigma}_b}{\tilde{\sigma}} + r_F$	$(7.9\% - 2.0\%) \times \dfrac{4.5\%}{5.5\%} + 2.0\%$	$(6.9\% - 2.0\%) \times \dfrac{4.5\%}{3.2\%} + 2.0\%$
	$= 6.83\%$	$= 8.89\%$

M^2 EXCESS RETURN

Exactly the same arguments apply to geometric or arithmetic M^2 excess returns as they do to normal excess returns. Simple geometry from Figure 11.1 might suggest arithmetic excess return would be more appropriate; however, it is easy to argue that continuously compounded returns should be used. For consistency I prefer the geometric definition.

$$M^2 \text{ excess return} = \frac{(1 + M^2)}{(1 + \tilde{b})} - 1 \tag{11.3}$$

or, arithmetically

$$M^2 \text{ excess return} = M^2 - \tilde{b} \tag{11.4}$$

DIFFERENTIAL RETURN

The differential return is similar in concept to M^2 excess return except that the benchmark return is adjusted to the risk of the portfolio. The differential return is the difference between the portfolio return and the adjusted benchmark return. For the same portfolio the M^2 excess return and the differential return will differ because the Sharpe ratio lines of the portfolio and benchmark will diverge over time.

The adjusted benchmark return $\tilde{b}'$ is calculated as follows:

$$\tilde{b}' = \tilde{r}_F + \left(\frac{\tilde{b} - \tilde{r}_F}{\tilde{\sigma}_b}\right) \times \tilde{\sigma} \tag{11.5}$$

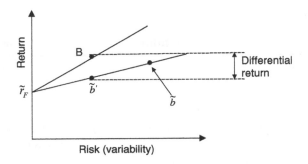

FIGURE 11.2　Differential return

Therefore, subtracting the adjusted benchmark return from the portfolio return we derive the differential return (see Figure 11.2):

$$\text{Differential return } DR = \tilde{r} - \tilde{r}_F - \left(\frac{\tilde{b} - \tilde{r}_F}{\tilde{\sigma}_b} \right) \times \tilde{\sigma} \qquad (11.6)$$

Differential returns are calculated in Table 11.2 based on the data from Table 11.1.

Differential return is less useful for comparing multiple portfolios because multiple risk-adjusted benchmark returns are required to be calculated; for M^2 the benchmark returns are consistent for all portfolios. M^2 is a demonstrably better measure than either Sharpe ratio from which it is derived or differential return. It is possible to calculate differential return geometrically.

TABLE 11.2　Differential return

	Portfolio A	Portfolio B
Annualised return	7.9%	6.9%
Annualised risk	5.5%	3.2%
M^2	6.83%	8.89%
M^2 excess return (arithmetic)		
$M^2 - \tilde{b}$	6.83% − 7.5% = −0.67%	8.89% − 7.5% = 1.39%
Differential return $\tilde{r} - \tilde{r}_F - \left(\dfrac{\tilde{b} - \tilde{r}_F}{\tilde{\sigma}_b} \right) \times \tilde{\sigma}$	7.9% − 2.0% − $\dfrac{7.5\% - 2.0\%}{4.5\%}$ × 5.5% = −0.82%	6.9% − 2.0% − $\dfrac{7.5\% - 2.0\%}{4.5\%}$ × 3.2% = +0.99%

GH1 (GRAHAM AND HARVEY 1)

GH1, suggested by John Graham and Campbell Harvey[2] (1997), is similar to the differential return but utilises an efficient frontier created by combining various weights of the benchmark and risk-free rate (noting the variability of the risk-free rate is not necessarily zero). The difference between the return of the portfolio and the combined benchmark and risk-free rate notional portfolio with identical risk (or variability) is GH1, as shown in Figure 11.3.

GH2 (GRAHAM AND HARVEY 2)

GH2 is similar to M^2 – instead of combining the benchmark and risk-free rate, increasing weights of actual portfolio returns are combined with reducing weights of the risk-free rate. GH2 is calculated at the risk of the benchmark as shown in Figure 11.4.

CORRELATION AND RISK-ADJUSTED RETURN M^3

Muralidhar[3] proposed an extension to M^2, M^3, in which returns are adjusted for correlation to achieve a target tracking error as well as adjusting the portfolio variability to that of the benchmark. Tracking error and absolute return targets are normally viewed as being inconsistent. It is unreasonable, I think, to require

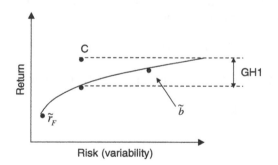

FIGURE 11.3 GH1

[2]J. R. Graham and C. R. Harvey (1997) Grading the Performance of Market-Timing Newsletters. *Financial Analysts Journal* 53(6), 54–66.
[3]A. Muralidhar (2000) Risk-adjusted Performance – The Correlation Correction. *Financial Analysts Journal* 56(5), 63–71.

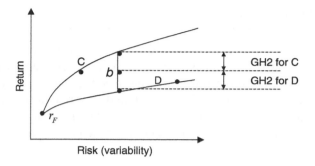

FIGURE 11.4 GH2

a portfolio manager to both generate absolute return and minimise tracking error against a benchmark.

RETURN ADJUSTED FOR DOWNSIDE RISK

Like all ranking statistics it is easy to rank portfolios in order of preference using the Sortino ratio but it is rather more difficult to answer the question of exactly how much better one portfolio is than the other.

M^2 can be calculated for downside risk in the same way as it is calculated for total risk.

In Figure 11.5 a straight line is drawn vertically through the downside risk of the benchmark; the intercept with the Sortino ratio line of portfolio A would give the return of the portfolio with the same Sortino ratio of portfolio A, but at the same downside risk of the benchmark.

$$M_S^2 = \tilde{r} + \text{Sortino ratio} \times (\tilde{\sigma}_{Db} - \tilde{\sigma}_D) \qquad (11.7)$$

M_S^2 is calculated in Exhibit 11.1 using data from Exhibit 6.1 and Table 11.3.

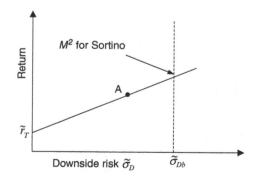

FIGURE 11.5 M^2 for downside risk

EXHIBIT 11.1 M_S^2

Benchmark downside risk

$$\sigma_{Db} = \sqrt{\sum_{i=1}^{i=n} \frac{\min[(b_i - r_T), 0]^2}{n}} = \sqrt{\frac{167.99\%}{36}} = 2.16\%$$

Annualised downside risk $\tilde{\sigma}_{Db} = \sqrt{t} \times \sigma_{Db} = \sqrt{12} \times 2.16\% = 7.48\%$

$M_S^2 = \tilde{r} + \text{Sortino ratio} \times (\tilde{\sigma}_{Db} - \sigma_D) = 13.29\% + 0.97 \times (7.48\% - 7.33\%)$

$\quad = 13.43\%$

 Note

Of course, M^2 can be calculated using a variety of different measures of risk, simply relabelling the horizontal axis. Return adjusted for both systematic and extreme risks are obvious examples, although variability is certainly the most common.

ADJUSTED M^2

Assuming benchmark returns are normally distributed the Sharpe ratio can be replaced with a line of different gradient using the adjusted Sharpe ratio and a risk-adjusted return that also incorporates the third and fourth moments of the return distribution, as shown in Figure 11.6. In this example the portfolio manager is penalised with a shallower gradient, represented by an adjusted Sharpe ratio reflecting less desirable skewness and kurtosis. Therefore, the intercept with the variability of the benchmark is that bit lower, producing a lower risk-adjusted return.

$$\text{Adjusted } M^2 = \tilde{r} + ASR \times (\tilde{\sigma}_b - \sigma) \tag{11.8}$$

TABLE 11.3   Benchmark downside risk

Monthly Minimum Target Return = 0.5%, Annual Minimum Target Return = 6.17%		
Benchmark Monthly Return (%) b_i	Deviation Against Target (Downside Only) $(b_i - r_T)$	Squared Deviation $(b_i - r_T)^2$
0.2	−0.30	0.09
2.5		
1.8		
−1.1	−1.60	2.56
1.4		
2.3		
1.4		
6.5		
−1.5	−2.00	4.00
4.2		
−0.3	−0.80	0.64
8.3		
3.9		
−3.8	−4.30	18.49
−6.2	−6.70	44.89
1.5		
−4.8	−5.30	28.09
−2.0	−2.50	6.25
6.0		
5.6		
−6.7	−7.20	51.84
1.9		
−0.3	−0.80	0.64
−0.1	−0.60	0.36
−2.6	−3.10	9.61
0.7		
4.3		
2.9		
3.8		
−0.2	−0.70	0.49
5.1		
1.4		
1.3		
0.3	−0.20	0.04
3.4		
2.1		

$$\text{Total} = \sum_{i=1}^{i=n} \min[(b_i - r_T), 0]^2 = 167.99$$

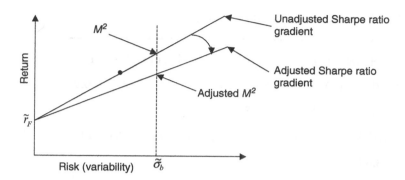

FIGURE 11.6   Adjusted M^2

> **❓ Interpretation**
>
> Adjusted M^2 is a very appealing statistic that incorporates all four moments of the return distribution and converts to a readily understood single return metric.

SKEW-ADJUSTED M^2

Skew-adjusted M^2, as its name suggests, incorporates just the third moment (skewness) and not the fourth moment (kurtosis).

$$\text{Skew-adjusted } M^2 = \tilde{r} + SASR \times (\tilde{\sigma}_b - \sigma) \tag{11.9}$$

M^2, adjusted M^2 and skew-adjusted M^2 for the standard portfolio are calculated in Exhibit 11.2 using data from Exhibit 3.1.

OMEGA EXCESS RETURN

Another form of downside risk-adjusted return is *omega* excess return[4] (not related to the *Omega* ratio). Similar to differential return, the downside risk-adjusted benchmark return is calculated by multiplying the downside variance of the style benchmark by 3 times the style *beta*.

---

[4]F. Sortino, G. Miller and J. Messina (1997), Short Term Risk-adjusted Performance: A Style-based Analysis. *Journal of Investing* 6(2), 19–27.

EXHIBIT 11.2 M^2, skew-adjusted M^2 and adjusted M^2

$M^2 = \tilde{r} + SR \times (\tilde{\sigma}_b - \tilde{\sigma}) = 13.29\% + 0.94 \times (11.65\% - 11.49\%) = 13.44\%$

Skew-adjusted $M^2 = \tilde{r} + SASR \times (\tilde{\sigma}_b - \tilde{\sigma}) = 13.29\% + 0.91$

$\times\ (11.65\% - 11.49\%) = 13.43\%$

Adjusted $M^2 = \tilde{r} + ASR \times (\tilde{\sigma}_b - \tilde{\sigma}) = 13.29\% + 0.91 \times (11.65\% - 11.49\%)$

$= 13.43\%$

There is only a tiny difference, lost in rounding, in this example because the distribution is close to normal.

The 3 is arbitrary and assumes the investor requires 3 units of return for one unit of variance ($3 \times \sigma_{MD}^2$ effectively take the place of the benchmark excess return above the risk-free rate in the differential return calculation). The style *beta* adjusts for the downside risk taken by the portfolio manager by taking the ratio of the downside risk of the portfolio divided by the downside risk of the style benchmark.

$$\text{Downside risk-adjusted style benchmark } 3 \times \beta_S \times \sigma_{MD}^2 \qquad (11.10)$$

$$\textit{Omega} \text{ excess return } \omega = \tilde{r} - 3 \times \beta_S \times \sigma_{MD}^2 \qquad (11.11)$$

Where:

$$\text{style } \textit{beta } \beta_S = \frac{\sigma_D}{\sigma_{MD}} \qquad (11.12)$$

σ_{MD}^2 = style benchmark variance

CHAPTER 12

A Periodic Table of Risk Measures

"For the first time I saw a medley of haphazard facts fall into line and order. All the jumbles and recipes and hotchpotch of the inorganic chemistry of my boyhood seemed to fit into the scheme before my eyes – as though one were standing in a jungle and it suddenly transformed itself into a Dutch garden."

C. P. Snow (1905–1980), *The Search, House of Stratus*, 2000.

Dimitri Mendeleev first published his periodic table of chemical elements in 1869.[1] This extremely useful table, familiar to all students of science, orders chemical elements according to atomic number, electron configuration and chemical properties. Mendeleev wasn't the first to publish such a table but his table received recognition because it left gaps in the table and predicted the properties of then undiscovered elements that would eventually fill those gaps.

A periodic table for risk measures is such a good idea I wish I'd thought of it first, but sadly I can't claim credit as the initial inspiration resulted from a rare invasion of my son's bedroom in which I found and studied a wallchart detailing a periodic table of cocktail drinks. This basic idea, applying the concept of the periodic table to anything other than chemical elements was further reinforced in a presentation by Bruce Feibel in a CFA conference in 2012.[2] As already discussed in the previous chapters of this book there are so many different risk measures available to performance analysts that to fully appreciate the relative merits of each measure and their relationship with each other, it makes sense to attempt to categorise them into some sort of logical structure. To be fair,

---

[1] D. Mendeleev (1869) Uber die Beziehungen der Eigenschaften zu den Atomgewichten der Elemente. *Zeitschrift für Chemie* (in German), 405–406.
[2] CFA GIPS Conference, Boston, September 2012.

Cogneau and Hubner[3] (2009) attempt with some success to do this, classifying over 100 performance appraisal measures based on their objectives, properties and degree of generalisation. The periodic table shown in Table 12.1 is my attempt to build on Bruce's idea. This is the third version of a periodic table of risk measures that I have attempted, the first was developed soon after the first edition of this book was published and the second was published in the *Journal of Performance Measurement*.[4] I used the initial attempt to clarify my own ideas, organise the first edition of this book into logical chapters and, just like the original Mendeleev periodic table, identify new measures and gaps in my own knowledge worthy of further research. I filled some of those gaps myself, other gaps were closed by finding measures as a result of targeted research and finally an article by Watanabe on the New Prospect Ratio published in the Fall 2014 edition of the *Journal of Performance Measurement*[5] filled many more.

PERIODIC TABLE DESIGN

The main body of the table contains most, but not all, of the performance appraisal measures or composite ratios used to assess the performance of asset managers and described in earlier chapters of this book. They are either in typical Sharpe form, the acknowledged grandfather of all appraisal measures, Reward–Risk or in a Gain–Loss format.

Vertically the main body of the table is split into six columns based on different types of appraisal measures:

1. Absolute – measures based on the absolute return of the portfolio
2. Relative – measures based on the relative return against a benchmark
3. Downside – using partial moments, measures based on downside risk
4. Gain–loss – measures reflecting upside in the numerator and downside in the denominator
5. Prospect – measures based on Prospect Theory (or other investor preference measures)
6. Drawdown – measures based on drawdown

---

[3]P. Cogneau and G. Hubner (2009a) The (More Than) 100 Ways to Measure Portfolio Performance Part 1: Standardized Risk-adjusted Measures. *The Journal of Performance Measurement,* Summer, 56–71. P. Cogneau and G. Hubner (2009b) The (More Than) 100 Ways to Measure Portfolio Performance Part 2: Special Measures and Comparison. *The Journal of Performance Measurement,* Fall, 56–69.

[4]C. R. Bacon (2015) A Periodic Table of Risk Measures – Version 2. *The Journal of Performance Measurement,* Spring, 25–58.

[5]Y. Watanabe (2014) New Prospect Ratio: Application to Hedge Funds with Higher Order Moments. *The Journal of Performance Measurement,* 19(1), 41–53.

TABLE 12.1 Periodic table of risk measures

Descriptive Statistics		Absolute	Relative	Partial Moments			Drawdown	Risk-Adjusted Returns
				Downside	Gain-Loss	Prospect		
1st moment	Average	MAD Ratio	Relative Batting Average	Omega-Sharpe Ratio	Omega	Omega–Prospect Ratio	Sterling Ratio	Excess Return
2nd moment	Variability	Sharpe Ratio	Information Ratio	Sortino Ratio	Variability skewness	Prospect Ratio	Burke Ratio	M^2
3rd moment	Skewness	Skew-adjusted Sharpe Ratio	Skew-adjusted Information Ratio	Kappa	Gain-Loss Skewness	Skew-adjusted Prospect Ratio	Calmar Ratio	Skew-adjusted M^2
4th moment	Kurtosis	Adjusted Sharpe ratio	Adjusted Information Ratio	Sortino–Satchell Ratio	Farnelli–Tibiletti Ratio	New Prospect Ratio	Pain Ratio	Adjusted M^2
Systematic risk	Beta	Treynor Ratio	Appraisal Ratio	Return to Duration	Timing Ratio	Generalised Z Ratio	Ulcer Ratio	Alpha
Extreme risk	VaR	Reward to VaR	Reward to Relative VaR	Conditional Sharpe Ratio	Rachev Ratio	Generalised Rachev Ratio	Reward to Conditional Drawdown	M^2 for VaR
Miscellaneous Risk measures		K Ratio	Upside Capture	Downside Capture	Capture Ratio	R^2	Bias Ratio	Factor Alpha
		Absolute Batting Average	Risk Efficiency Ratio	Tail Ratio	Convexity	Bera–Jarque Statistic	Active Share	Omega Excess

To the left of the table, I've listed the key descriptive statistics in six rows, the four moments of the return distribution in descending order of importance:

The 1st moment or average return

The 2nd moment, variability or standard deviation

The 3rd moment, skewness

The 4th moment, kurtosis

Systematic risk

And finally risk measures focusing on the tail of the return distribution (extreme risk)

In earlier versions I included extreme risk measures as an additional column, which to be honest always felt a little uncomfortable. I've concluded in this third attempt to construct a table that extreme risk measures can be catered for in an additional row of the table, not a column.

FILLING THE PERIODIC TABLE

Appraisal measures based on absolute return are listed in the first column of the main table corresponding to the descriptive statistics on the left. The Sharpe ratio (Equation 3.1) and Treynor ratio (Equation 4.34) are well known but the MAD ratio (Equation 3.13) based on mean absolute deviation is less well known. In effect the Sharpe ratio gives greater weight to more extreme results than the MAD ratio. Critics of the Sharpe ratio point out that there is an implicit assumption of a normal distribution of returns. These criticisms can be addressed by adjusting for skewness in the skew-adjusted Sharpe ratio (Equation 3.6), reflecting the investor's preference for positive skew and dislike of negative skew or even more completely adjusting for both skew and kurtosis in the adjusted Sharpe ratio (Equation 3.5), which in addition reflects the investor's preference for kurtosis less than 3. These measures are shown in the appropriate rows. The Treynor ratio includes systematic risk in the denominator and the Reward to VaR ratio (Equation 8.10) clearly includes VaR, an extreme risk measure, in the denominator.

In the relative column we find the very popular Information ratio (Equations 3.21 and 3.22), a direct descendant of the Sharpe ratio but comparing excess or relative return to tracking error or relative risk. The excellent, but seldom used, Appraisal ratio (Equation 4.36) strips out any return due to systematic risk in the numerator and excludes systematic risk in the denominator focusing only on specific risk. It's a bit of a stretch but Batting average (Equation 10.5) is a simplistic relative return measure that can head the relative column. The Information ratio can be adjusted for the skew and kurtosis of excess returns in a similar way as the Sharpe ratio (Equations 3.27 to 3.30). Reward to relative VaR is clearly appropriate in the final row.

Other critics of the Sharpe ratio may suggest that asset managers are equally penalised for upside risk and downside risk and in reality, shouldn't be penalised for upside risk. The downside risk column caters for these critics. The *Omega*–Sharpe ratio (Equation 6.19) is very similar to the Sharpe ratio except that in the numerator the minimum acceptable return replaces the risk-free rate and the denominator is replaced by downside potential, the simple average of returns that are worse than the minimum acceptable return. The Sortino ratio (Equation 6.24) is similar to the *Omega*–Sharpe ratio, replacing downside potential with downside risk (a variance type calculation equivalent to the 2nd moment on the second row). The third row is naturally filled by the Kappa ratio (Equation 6.30) or potentially by the skew-adjusted Sortino ratio (Equation 6.38). I'm not sure I like this ratio, but that is not the point. Investors must determine their own preferences. The fourth row could be completed by the adjusted Sortino ratio (Equation 6.39) which adjusts for kurtosis as well as skewness but I prefer the Sortino–Satchell ratio (Equation 6.29), which is a generalised ratio; in effect the investor can chose the moment by preference. Reward to duration (Equation 9.16) and conditional Sharpe ratio (Equation 8.16) do not fit well in the downside column. Duration, of course, is a systematic risk measure for fixed income so the row is appropriate. Reward to duration is equivalent to the Treynor ratio and I wanted to make sure it was included in the table somewhere. The denominator of the conditional Sharpe ratio (Equation 8.16) is conditional VaR which clearly belongs in the extreme risk row.

The Gain–loss column also relies on partial moments separating the upside in the numerator and downside in the denominator. Omega (Equation 6.16) is in the first row because the measures of upside potential and downside potential are simple averages. Skewness variability (Equation 6.33) despite its name is in the second row because the 2nd moment is calculated in both the numerator and in the denominator. The third row is now occupied by Gain–loss skewness (Equation 6.35) and the fourth row is completed by the Farnelli–Tibiletti ratio (Equation 6.34), which is another generalised ratio. The Timing ratio (Equation 4.14) separates upside systematic risk from downside systematic risk with the bull beta in the numerator and bear beta in the denominator. The Rachev ratio (Equation 8.20) rightly belongs in this column with extreme gains in the numerator and extreme losses in the denominator.

Watanabe not only provides the inspiration to fill gaps but also provides the inspiration to add an additional column not found in my original drafts of the periodic table, based on Prospect Theory. This column is headed by the *Omega*–Prospect Ratio (Equation 7.4) in the first row, followed by the Prospect ratio (Equation 7.1) in the 2nd row, the skew-adjusted Prospect ratio (Equation 7.2) in the third row and the New Prospect ratio (Equation 7.3) as defined by Watanabe in the fourth row. The generalised Rachev ratio (Equation 8.21) and generalised Z ratio (Equations 8.23 and 8.24) don't relate exactly to Prospect Theory. More appropriately they are generalised gain–loss ratios that include extreme risk elements but they are based on investor preferences and should be included somewhere. For the time being I've included them in this column.

The drawdown column only includes appraisal measures which utilise drawdown. The first and second rows are obvious as the Sterling ratio (Equation 5.7) is an average and the Burke ratio (Equation 5.9) uses a variance type calculation in the denominator. I chose to put the remaining four drawdown measures, which should be included in the table, in this column even though they don't necessarily correspond to the 3rd and 4th moments and systematic risk. The most well-known drawdown ratio, Calmar (Equation 5.5), I've shown in the third row since it will most likely be impacted by skewed returns. Reward to conditional drawdown (Equation 8.22) is probably correctly classified in the final, extreme risk row.

The final column separated from the main body of the table on the extreme right lists risk-adjusted returns, starting naturally enough comparing portfolio return against a benchmark in the excess return through the various definitions of M^2 (Equations 11.1, 11.2, 11.8 and 11.9), which convert the Sharpe ratio, skew-adjusted Sharpe ratio and adjusted Sharpe ratio to return metrics that are easily understood and interpreted, and finishing with alpha (Equation 4.10), the added value adjusted for systematic risk.

The bottom two rows detached from the main body of risk measures provide a list of miscellaneous descriptive statistics and measures from Chapter 10 that don't fit naturally within the periodic structure but nevertheless deserve to be shown.

The box on the bottom far right represents miscellaneous risk-adjusted returns such as Fama–French three-factor alpha (Equation 4.43), Cahart four-factor alpha (Equation 4.44) and Omega excess (Equation 11.11).

NOTATION

Notation for these risk measures is not really required but in the spirit of the original periodic table I suggest the following notation in Figures 12.1 to 12.5 and Table 12.2.

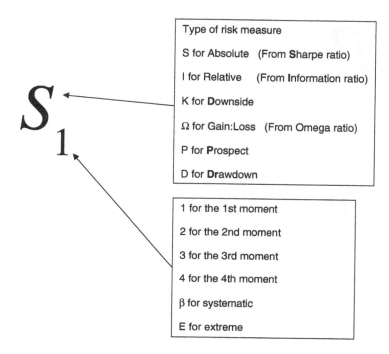

FIGURE 12.1   Notation – type of risk measure

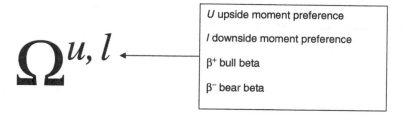

FIGURE 12.2   Notation – gain:loss moment preference

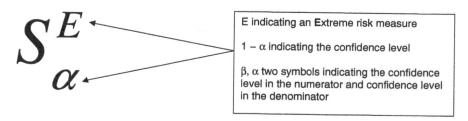

FIGURE 12.3   Notation – extreme risk measures

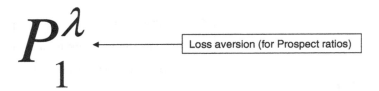

FIGURE 12.4 Notation – investor preference

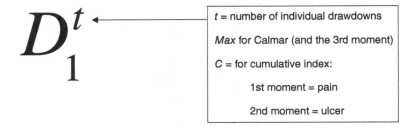

FIGURE 12.5 Notation – drawdown

TABLE 12.2 Periodic table – notation

				Partial Moments			
Descriptive Statistics		**Absolute**	**Relative**	**Downside**	**Gain–Loss**	**Prospect**	**Drawdown**
1st moment	Average	S_1	I_1	K_1	$\Omega^{1,1}$	P_1^λ	D_1^t
2nd moment	Variability	S_2	I_2	K_2	$\Omega^{2,2}$	P_2^λ	D_2^t
3rd moment	Skewness	S_3	I_3	K_3	$\Omega^{3,3}$	P_3^λ	D_3^{Max}
4th moment	Kurtosis	S_4	I_4	K_l	$\Omega^{u,l}$	P_4^λ	D_1^C
Systematic risk	Beta	S_β	I_β	S_D	Ω^{β^+,β^-}	$\Omega_{\beta,\alpha}^{u,l}$	D_2^C
Extreme risk	VaR	S_α^E	I_α^E	$S_\alpha^{E,1}$	$\Omega_{\beta,\alpha}^{E,1,1}$	$\Omega_{\beta,\alpha}^{E,u,l}$	D_α^E

CHAPTER 13

Risk-Adjusted Performance Fees

"If all the rich people in the world divided up their money among themselves there wouldn't be enough to go around."

Chrstina Stead (1902–1983), *House of all Nations,*
Simon and Schuster, (1938) "Credo"

PERFORMANCE FEES

A performance fee is a variable fee based on the performance of the portfolio.

Supporters[1] of performance fees would suggest that they are desirable because they align the interests of the asset manager with that of the asset owner. If the asset manager performs well then the owner's assets rise in value and for the most part asset owners appear happy to pay performance fees for good performance. If the asset manager performs poorly, only a smaller base fee and no incentive fee is paid.

Those not in favour[2] claim that rather than aligning interests, performance fees create a conflict of interest, and for the most part performance fees are biased when designed, in favour of the asset manager. Without doubt, performance fees have had a beneficial impact on asset management revenues. In my early career the pressure on fees was always down while later average fees increased across the entire industry responding to incentive fees for alternative strategies. More recently low fee passive strategies have again exerted downward pressure. Hedge funds demonstrated to the entire industry that asset owners, including institutions like endowments, pension funds and sovereign

---

[1]L. E. Davanzo and S. I. Nesbitt (1987) Performance Fees for Investment Managers. *Financial Analysts Journal*, 43(1), 14–20.

[2]W. N. Goetzmann, J. E. Ingersoll and S. A. Ross (2003) High-water Marks and Hedge Fund Management Contracts. *The Journal of Finance* 58(4), 1685–1718.

wealth funds, are prepared to accept high management fees if they are "dressed up" in the form of a performance or incentive fee.

ASYMMETRIC OR SYMMETRIC

Whether, or not, performance fees are beneficial for asset owners depends on how the performance fees are structured. There are many flavours but essentially there are two main types: asymmetric and symmetric. Asymmetric fees shown in Figure 13.1 are by far the most common and are very seductive to asset owners.

Typically, asset managers will present this type of fee to clients at a base fee rate considerably lower (perhaps less than half) than their normal management fee with an incentive fee for performance greater than an agreed hurdle rate.[3] This is extremely attractive to asset owners; they pay a lower fee, and will only pay higher fees if the asset manager performs well. There is considerable opportunity to negotiate the hurdle rate, angle of the participation rate, time period, excess or absolute return, caps and collars and perhaps a high-water mark,[4] but the basic structure is the same.

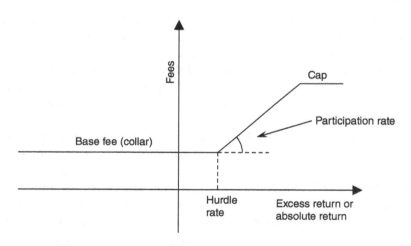

FIGURE 13.1 Asymmetric performance fees

---

[3]The minimum absolute return (risk-free rate or target return perhaps) or relative return against an agreed benchmark that has to be reached before a performance fee is earned.

[4]The highest peak in value. In subsequent periods asset managers must exceed the high-water mark before receiving performance incentives.

A rare alternative would be a symmetric structure.[5] In this type of structure, the base fee would probably not be lower and may even be higher than the normal management fee. Incentive fees are paid for outperformance, but crucially fees are rebated for underperformance to the extent that the asset manager may ultimately make a net payment to the client if performance is sufficiently bad. Though unpopular with asset managers these types of fee genuinely align the interest of both parties.[6]

Some critics of performance fees make the claim that asymmetric fees in particular encourage asset managers to take more risk if performance is poor because they have little further downside and considerable upside. This is not my personal experience; I've observed that often when in a hole portfolio managers in effect stop digging and take less risk when performing badly. On the flip side I have observed portfolio managers "lock in" outperformance when they have achieved the cap and take much less risk. This obviously reduces the business risk of the asset manager but presumably the asset owner would prefer the asset manager to continue taking risk if they are obtaining good rewards. Risk-adjusted returns such as M^2 – or even better, adjusted M^2 – would help alleviate this problem. Muralidhar[7] (2009) reviews the available literature on performance fees and in conclusion supports the use of risk-adjusted returns such as M^2.

Schliemann and Stanzel[8] (2008), among other issues, emphasise the option-like character of performance fees. Chevalier and Ellison[9] (1997) demonstrate that asymmetrical performance fees create call option-like components in the incentives of the asset manager. The price of the call option is implicitly borne by the asset owner but the asset manager receives the benefits. The higher the risk, the more valuable the call option, thus incentivising the asset manager to take more risk particularly when close to hurdle rate boundaries.

---

[5]In the USA, under the Investment Advisers Act (1940) any performance fee charged to a mutual fund can only utilise symmetrical performance fee structures. Consequentially, performance fees are rare in US mutual funds; asset managers do not like rebating fees to clients. In the USA symmetrical fee structures are often called fulcrum fees.
[6]L. T. Starks (1987) Performance Incentive Fees: An Agency Theoretic Approach. *Journal of Financial and Quantitative Analysis* 22(1), 17–32.
[7]A. Muralidhar (2009) Risk and Skill-adjusted Investment Compensation. *Journal of Performance Measurement*, Summer, 40–55.
[8]M. Schliemann and M. Stanzel (2008) Performance-based Compensation Contracts in the Asset Management Industry. *Journal of Performance Measurement*, Spring, 61–70.
[9]J. Chevalier and G. Ellison (1997) Risk Taking by Mutual Funds as a Response to Incentives. *Journal of Political Economy* 105(6), 1167–1200.

Sadly, performance fee arrangements often end in acrimony. For long-term agreements the original authors on both sides may have moved on, and if badly written, at the point when both partners should be celebrating good performance, relationships can be damaged by a dispute about the size of fees to be paid. Performance fee agreements should be clear, concise and as simple as possible. I would always recommend including a few worked examples to ensure both parties fully understand the agreement. There is a tendency to complicate performance fees with high-water marks and variable hurdle rates; frankly the more complex the agreement the more likely interests will be misaligned. Investor interests are best protected by structuring performance fees over longer time periods, three or even five years.

Endowments, pension funds and sovereign wealth funds typically select a portfolio of asset managers to diversify their selection risk. Asset owners should think through the implications before establishing a performance fee structure for their asset managers. Theoretically, the existence of a performance fee should not alter the actual performance enjoyed.

A portfolio manager is either skilled or unskilled – those extra hours staying behind in the office will not necessarily add to performance. Sufficient constraints and incentives already exist such that managers are always encouraged to deliver good performance with or without performance fees. The evidence on the impact of performance fees is mixed; in a recent study of Dutch pension funds by Broeders, van Oord and Rijsbergen[10] they find no statistical evidence that the returns of pension funds that pay performance fees to asset managers for active investing are significantly higher or lower than the returns of pension funds that do not pay performance fees. They found this is true for most asset classes and more robust if corrected for risk. In order to attract new investors, asset managers must demonstrate a superior, consistent track record. The portfolio manager cannot favour performance fee clients over and above other clients without a performance fee; they have a fiduciary duty to treat all clients equally. Why pay a performance fee for performance you might expect to receive anyway?

Obviously, the asset owner chooses the asset manager. Is it then not rather perverse that the asset owner is rewarded by a lower fee (i.e. no performance fee) for choosing an underperforming asset manager and penalised (by paying a performing fee) for choosing an outperforming asset manager? Consider for a moment that the asset owner is an average selector of asset managers; the overperformance of the good performing asset managers will offset the

---

[10]D. W. G. A. Broeders, A. van Oord and D. R. Rijsbergen (2019) Does it Pay to Pay Performance Fees? Empirical Evidence from Dutch Pension Funds. *Journal of International Money and Finance* 93, 299–312.

underperformance of the poor performing asset managers leading to average performance overall. However, if the performance fee arrangement is asymmetric the performance fees paid will more than exceed the advantage gained from the lower base fees of the poor performing asset managers, leading to above average fees paid for average performance overall! Asset owners should treat performance fees as a necessarily evil, only accepting performance fees to access demonstrably superior asset managers where a simple base fee is not available.

PERFORMANCE FEES IN PRACTICE

If used, performance fees should be:

1. **Unambiguous and fair to both parties**

   The performance fee structure should be fair and equitable to both asset owners and asset managers. The performance fee structure should be consistent with the portfolio's objective and should provide reward commensurate with the skill exercised in achieving the performance.

   The agreement should be clear and unambiguous, preferably including a worked example. Calculation methodologies should be agreed, mechanisms for adjusting for cash flows, changing benchmarks and arbitration processes should be approved at the start of the relationship. The performance fee calculation should be verifiable. A worked example of the performance fee calculation should be included in the performance fee agreement.

2. **Symmetrical**

   Symmetrical fees are more likely to align the interests of the asset owner and asset manager on both the upside and the downside.

3. **Simple**

   The more complex the performance fee structure the more likely the interests of the asset manager and asset owner will be misaligned.

4. **Risk-adjusted**

   The performance fee structure should not influence the risk strategy of the asset manager. Ideally, performance calculations should be risk-adjusted.

Unfortunately, many performance fee structures are unfair and ambiguous, asymmetrical rather than symmetrical, frequently complex and rarely risk-adjusted. There is no barrier to risk-adjusted performance fees: in fact, for absolute returns M^2 and adjusted M^2 are ideal risk-adjusted return measures. Likewise, information ratio and adjusted information ratio are suitable for relative performance targets. *Alpha* and the appraisal ratio should also be considered. There is no excuse for giving an asset manager a free ride on risk.

🗊 Note

In terms of my own preference if asked to rank fee arrangements, of any type, from an asset owner's perspective, I would simply prefer a fixed fee, a simple fixed amount, for example $100,000 per annum. Clearly, asset managers need to cover costs, reward staff as appropriate and deliver a return on capital (mostly human capital). The ideal structure is an annual fee (paid quarterly) over a fixed period, say three or five years (immediately cancellable if the investment mandate is breached) with or without an inflation uplift. Reward, based on good performance would be renewing the mandate for an extended period at perhaps an increased cost. Admittedly, this type of arrangement is rare in the asset management industry. More common is my second preference – an "ad valorem" fee, a fee rate based on the assets under management, for example 40 basis points per annum. Some would say the asset manager is automatically rewarded with a higher fee for growing the asset base. My third preference is a symmetrical performance fee – for example, a 50 basis points base fee, with 10% profit participation above, say, 1% outperformance and a 10% performance rebate below 1% underperformance. Least favoured, but common, an asymmetrical performance fee – for example, 2% base fee plus 20% profit participation above a 5% hurdle rate.

> ### ⚠ Caution
>
> The parameters of a performance fee structure should clearly specify:
>
> 1. The return calculation methodology
> 2. The agreed benchmark (one only)
> 3. Hurdle rate (soft or hard)
> 4. High-water mark
> 5. Resetting arrangements[11]
> 6. Profit participation rate and rebate rate
> 7. Time period (one, three or five years, for example)
> 8. Fee accrual and payment schedule
> 9. Capital basis for determination of base performance fee (a key area of ambiguity in practice)
> 10. Clawback arrangements
> 11. Arbitration procedures

---

[11] The periodic resetting of contractually defined high-water marks. If high-water marks are not reset, asset managers may find they are unable to generate performance fees and are thus dis-incentivised; alternatively, if high-water marks are reset too early, asset managers may be rewarded for partially recovered performance below the previous high-water mark.

CHAPTER 14

Performance Dashboards

"Though it's cold and lonely in the deep dark night, I can see paradise by the dashboard light."

Jim Steinman (1947–present), *Paradise By The Dashboard Light*, 1977.

Performance analysts and risk controllers are required to process large volumes of data. They must analyse quickly and communicate effectively. Excellent data visualisation skills are essential. Data visualisation illuminates complex relationships within masses of data. Most people are more comfortable with visual representation and process information quicker if it is presented in graphical format. Well-designed performance dashboards facilitate quick analysis and communicate at a glance what has happened to, and in, the portfolio of assets. Within a dashboard, utilising size, colour, font, positioning and graphical tools, complex relationships can be identified, explained and presented.

La Grouw[1] defines a dashboard as:

A means to provide "at a glance" visibility into key performance using simple visual elements displayed within a single digital screen.

EFFECTIVE DASHBOARDS

Effective dashboards should:

1. *Focus on the key measures.* It is all too easy to drown in information. The key skill set of any performance analyst or risk controller is not, surprisingly, the accurate calculation and distribution of numbers. Too much data

---

[1]G. La Grouw (2012) *Effective Dashboard Design: Design Secrets to Getting More Value from Performance Dashboards.* Electrosmart.

is nearly as bad as inaccurate data. The key skillset is to determine with the end user what is relevant and make sure that information is communicated efficiently and effectively. The goal of dashboards is to alert the user to potential issues and allow action to be taken.

2. *Be available.* Dashboards should be available to multiple stakeholders (portfolio managers, senior management, risk controllers, marketing and sales, compliance and, not least, asset owners) through multiple devices in and out the office. Different stakeholders, no doubt, will require different views and some access may well need to be restricted.

3. *Be interactive.* Dashboards should be interactive to allow users the ability to drill down to root causes of issues.

DATA VISUALISATION TOOLS

The humble table of numbers can still be effective in communicating data but may be enhanced if accompanied with appropriate graphical presentation. Remember, simpler is better. All dashboards should be to the point, uncluttered, focused on the key information, internally consistent, accurate, available to relevant stakeholders, labelled coherently and should not mislead the user. All too often analysts are seduced to present the "cool" graphic that looks good but frankly fails in its primary role of communicating information. Effective data visualisation graphical tools include:

1. *Scatter graphs.* Great for demonstrating correlations and relationships between variables (portfolio and benchmark returns for example)

2. *Line graphs.* Great to show the trends of a variable over a period of time (ex-ante and ex-post tracking error against limits for example.)

3. *Histograms.* As discussed in Chapter 2, a histogram is an excellent tool for demonstrating the distribution of returns – an essential visual tool for performance analysts.

4. *Pie charts.* The familiar pie chart is a circular graph which is divided into slices to illustrate numerical proportion. Pie charts, bar charts and line graphs were all invented by William Playfair.[2]

5. *Heat maps.* Essentially heat maps use colour and size to illustrate complex and large data relationships. They can be useful to identify and focus on particular issues. They look great but need to be used with great care; they are sometimes difficult to interpret – looking good is not sufficient, they need to meet a purpose.

---

[2] Bar charts and line charts in his *Commercial and Political Atlas* published in 1786 and pie charts in *Statistical Breviary* published in 1801.

6. *Speed dials.* A speed dial uses the metaphor of a speedometer to visually compare risk levels and limits, often colour coded. **Green** = good, **red**= bad. Keep in mind that about 8% of males of Northern European decent are colour-blind[3] (only 0.5% of females are afflicted) and that there is a higher occurrence of colour-blindness in quantitative people than in the general population. Good design avoids using colour contrast alone to express information.

7. *Risk triangles.* Risk triangles can be used to represent the expected total risk of a portfolio should an additional asset or portfolio be added to an existing portfolio or asset manager mix.

8. *Snail trail diagrams.* Snail trails are useful for showing the progression of an appraisal ratio consisting of two variables through time (reward in the vertical access, risk in the horizontal). Normally more recent time periods are shown by a thicker, darker line (or *trail*).

9. *Spider chart (radar, web or star chart).* A spider chart consists of a number of equi-angular spokes, each spoke representing a variable. The length of each spoke is proportional to the size of each variable. A line can be drawn connecting all points. It is used to identify outliers.

10. *Floating bar charts.* Floating bar charts (or box plots) are useful for showing the distribution of a variable (return, risk measure or appraisal ratio) over a number of portfolios and time periods. Showing the relationship between the median, various percentiles (quartiles, quintiles or deciles) and outliers.

---

[3]National Eye Institute (2015) Facts about Colour Blindness, February.

CHAPTER 15

Manager Selection

"If you can't describe what you're doing as a process, you don't know what you are doing."

W. E. Deming (1900–1993)

To do it justice, asset manager selection deserves a whole book in its own right, such as *Manager Selection* by Stewart.[1] In this chapter I can only scratch the surface, and only from the perspective of an asset manager and not of an asset owner. Performance appraisal measures are often used in the context of asset manager selection and ongoing monitoring and reporting, so it must be worth a chapter considering the process of manager selection.

ASSET MANAGER SELECTION

Asset management is a negative sum game. Before costs, the average of all asset managers, in the broadest definition, can only at best match the total market. Even before management fees, but after transaction costs, asset managers as a group must underperform the market. However, for some asset managers to outperform others must underperform. Most academic research concludes that the average manager will underperform: that's clearly true. But do superior (skilled) managers exist? If they do, can you identify them? And if you can identify them can you build a portfolio of asset managers that meets the objectives of the asset owner? My experience would suggest that skilled managers do exist but they are far outnumbered by managers that lack skill. I would suggest that persistence in skilled managers also exists but is difficult to find and

---

[1] S. D. Stewart (2013) *Manager Selection*, The Research Foundation of the CFA Institute.

statistically the period required to be certain that skill exists is probably shorter than changes in asset manager firms, investment conditions and cycles.[2]

Waring, Whitney, Pirone and Castille[3] (2000) and Waring and Siegel[4] (2003) suggest that selecting a portfolio of asset managers is equivalent to selecting a portfolio of assets or securities – it is a portfolio optimisation issue. The inputs are expected *alpha*, expected relative risk and the expected correlation of *alpha*.

Risk management in the context of asset manager selection is really a three-step process:

1. *Manager evaluation*. Quantitative and qualitative analysis of individual asset managers, including appropriate due diligence.
2. *Portfolio evaluation*. The "best" asset manager in isolation need not be the best fit with the existing portfolio of asset managers. Selection diversification is a key part of the process. Asset owners should choose the asset manager that best fits the existing portfolio.
3. *Monitoring and control*. Continuous monitoring is essential.

MANAGER EVALUATION

Manager evaluation processes will vary from asset owner to asset owner but due diligence is essential.

Manager due diligence is commonly described as a consideration of "Four Ps": People, Process, Performance and Potential:

1. *People*. Asset management is a people business. The asset owner should examine the ethics, experience and availability of the key people managing the account. Is senior management accessible not just in the sales process but ongoing? What have been the past mistakes (a good manager has nothing to hide)?
2. *Process*. The asset owner needs to understand the asset manager's investment process. Is it well articulated? Is it supported by appropriate documentation? Is it repeatable and sustainable? What are the asset manager's internal risk controls? Is the risk control function independent? Has the strategy been stress tested?

---

[2]L. Harris (2002) *Trading and Exchanges*, Oxford University Press (Chapter 22 "Performance Evaluation and Prediction", 442–481).

[3]B. M. Waring, D. M. Whitney, J. Pirone and C. Castille (2000) Optimizing Manager Structure and Budgeting Manager Risk. *Journal of Portfolio Management* 26(3), 90–104.

[4]B. M. Waring and L. B. Siegel (2003) The Dimensions of Active Management. *Journal of Portfolio Management* 29(3), 35–51.

3. *Performance.* Quantitative and qualitative analysis of the asset manager's track record is essential.
   - Have the returns been ethically produced?
   - Are they GIPS compliant?
   - Are they consistent?
   - Are the returns and associated attribution analysis in line with the investment process?
   - What do the appraisal measures say about the risk-adjusted performance of the asset manager?
   - Why have specific appraisal measures been chosen?
   - Has the appraisal measure been data-mined?
   - Do the appraisal measures tie in with the investment process – is there more than one? More than one appraisal measure is a red flag!
   - Is the investment process designed to maximise a particular performance measure?
   - Are performance returns based on model calculations or based on actual managed assets? Back-tested and model calculations might be of value to verify internal processes, but are of little value for external use. No-one will publish back-test numbers if the result is negative.
4. *Potential.* Most asset managers have some sort of capacity limit – a size beyond which the strategy does not similarly perform. Does this strategy continue to work in the future, and will the alpha be diluted? What is the asset manager's assessment of their own capacity? What is the total market capacity for this type of strategy?

PORTFOLIO EVALUATION

Asset managers should not be selected in isolation: a good fit within the existing portfolio of asset managers is essential.

Grinold's[5] "Fundamental Law of Active Management" provides for an estimate of the information ratio as follows:

$$IR = IC \times \sqrt{Br} \qquad (15.1)$$

Where:

IC = information coefficient, defined as the correlation of ex-ante forecasts with ex-post return

Br = breadth or the number of independent bets

---

[5] R. C. Grinold (1989) The Fundamental Law of Active Management. *Journal of Portfolio Management* 15(3), 30–38.

Applied to a portfolio of asset managers Grinold's fundamental law implies that increasing the number of asset managers, hence increasing breadth should be beneficial; however, the transfer costs of firing one asset manager and hiring another, together with the ongoing costs of monitoring should be considered. Risk triangles are particularly useful for assessing the added value of introducing a new asset manager to the existing portfolio of asset managers. A good manager in isolation might add value but not reduce risk if highly correlated with existing asset managers – we should seek asset managers with investment styles that are negatively correlated with existing asset managers. A slightly inferior manager might add a little less value but could well reduce risk, significantly resulting in an improved information ratio overall.

MONITORING AND CONTROL

Asset managers that have been appointed should be reviewed on a regular basis and a judgement made about the continuing appropriateness within the asset owner's wider portfolio. A variety of issues might provoke a decision to terminate, such as:

1. Underperformance below benchmark
2. Style drift
3. Identification of more skilled asset managers
4. Reputational damage
5. Operational issues
6. Changes in asset and risk allocations
7. Changes in personnel, confidence in individuals
8. Increased correlations with other asset manager styles

Appropriate actions will range from discussing problems with asset managers, putting asset managers on alert or on a watchlist and of course terminating the relationship. Care should be taken though; Goyal and Wahal[6] (2008) demonstrated that asset owners often overreact to near term underperformance by "selling low", terminating existing asset managers, and "buying high", hiring asset managers with good near-term outperformance. Also, Stewart, Heisler, Knittel and Neumann[7] (2009) estimated that more than

---

[6] A. Goyal and S. Wahal (2008) The Selection and Termination of Investment Management Firms by Plan Sponsors. *Journal of Finance* 63(4), 1805–1847.
[7] S. Stewart, J. Heisler, C. Knittel and J. Neumann (2009) Absence of Value: An Analysis of Investment Allocation Decisions by Institutional Plan Sponsors. *Financial Analysts Journal*, 65(6), 34–51.

$170 billion was lost during the period 1984–2007 by asset owners making rebalancing or reallocation decisions. In their study investment products receiving contributions (hired asset managers) subsequently underperform products experiencing withdrawals (fired asset managers) over one-, three- and five-year periods.

⚠ Caution

The transaction cost of switching asset managers is not trivial, in terms of actual cost of rebalancing the portfolio (bid/offer spread, commission and taxes), the physical cost of search and due diligence and of course the risk of hiring a subsequently underperforming manager and firing a subsequently outperforming manager. My rule of thumb over the years has been that this cost might be as great as 3% – that's a lot of relative return to deliver.

CHAPTER 16

The Four Dimensions of Performance

"Design in art, is a recognition of the relationship between various things, various elements in the creative flux. You can't invent a design. You recognise it, in the fourth dimension. This is, with your blood, your bones as well as your eyes."

D. H. Lawrence (1885–1930)

This book focuses, almost exclusively, on just one of the four dimensions of performance measurement – ex-post risk. As illustrated in Figure 16.1, it is helpful to view performance measurement or performance analytics in four dimensions:

1st dimension	Ex-post return
2nd dimension	Ex-post risk
3rd dimension	Ex-ante return
4th dimension	Ex-ante risk

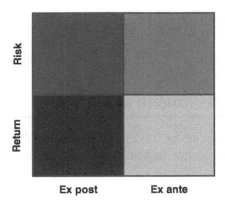

FIGURE 16.1 The four dimensions of performance

Asset managers should manage, analyse and communicate in all four dimensions.

EX-POST RETURN (THE TRADITIONAL DIMENSION)

Ex-post return is clearly the most well-established dimension and the starting point of any analysis; fundamentally all asset owners are looking for positive ex-post returns – the traditional or foundation dimension. Ex-post returns have been calculated for decades – standard policies and methodologies are well understood, codified and globally consistent. There might be a debate about whether, or not, to use time-weighted or money-weighted returns, but in general the issues are well known. Policies for timing of external cash flow, income accrual and valuation of assets are universally followed. Most asset owners fully understand ex-post return, and expect consistent reporting of both absolute and relative return. Global Investment Performance Standards (GIPS®)[1] are primarily focused on the consistent calculation and fair representation of these ex-post returns.

EX-POST RISK (THE NEGLECTED DIMENSION)

Ex-post risk is also well established and reasonably well understood, but perhaps a little neglected. Most investment professionals understand that risk must be taken into account, but frequently they choose just to report ex-post return in isolation, particularly in relation to performance fees. Ever since Sharpe's[2] seminal work in 1966 (and perhaps before), it has been accepted that performance is at least two dimensional. Ex-post return and ex-post risk are most commonly linked in the reward to risk ratios extensively covered in this book – performance appraisal:

$$\text{Performance appraisal} = \frac{\text{Reward}}{\text{Risk}} \qquad (16.1)$$

EX-ANTE RETURN (THE UNKNOWN DIMENSION)

I describe ex-ante return as the unknown dimension, but that's not strictly true. Ex-ante returns are of course unknown but they can, and should, be forecast.

---

[1]Global Investment Performance Standards (GIPS®) for Firms, CFA Institute, June 2019.
[2]W. F. Sharpe (1966) Mutual Fund Performance. *Journal of Business* 39, 119–138.

Asset managers should have an *alpha* thesis, they should be able to describe how they expect to add value and by how much. They should be able to demonstrate that *alpha* is sustainable and they should make specific returns forecasts. These ex-ante return forecasts should be reviewed and compared directly to the realised ex-post returns once available. How close to the realised return is the forecast return? Do realised returns exceed the forecast? This comparison is described as return efficiency.

$$\text{Return efficiency} = \frac{\text{Ex-post return}}{\text{Ex-ante return}} \qquad (16.2)$$

Asset managers should publish a range of return scenarios.

EX-ANTE RISK (THE "SEXY" DIMENSION)

I've described ex-ante risk as the "sexy" dimension because it attracts the most heat and attention. Professional risk managers are a curious combination of artist, scientist and practitioner, simultaneously employing intuition, complex mathematical analysis and hard-earned experience. It's no wonder, then, that the field of financial risk management attracts the best and brightest, luring some from the most challenging fields in academia. Forecasting risk and protecting the portfolio from future risk is much more interesting and rewarding than reporting on risk ex post and determining whether the reward was worth the risk taken after the fact. Ex-ante return should be compared to ex-ante risk to ensure the forecast is reasonable and achievable. Why forecast an information ratio of greater than one when past experience would suggest that it is very difficult to achieve?

$$\text{Performance forecast} = \frac{\text{Ex-ante return}}{\text{Ex-ante risk}} \qquad (16.3)$$

RISK EFFICIENCY RATIO

Ex-post risk measures are lagging indicators that typically do not change dramatically through time. However, for effective risk control it is essential to compare the predictive ex-ante risk calculated by internal systems with the actual realised ex-post risk of portfolios.

It is important to monitor changes over time in both the ex-ante and ex-post risk measures. It is also important to compare forecast risk with realised risk to gauge how close the forecast is to reality.

The risk efficiency ratio compares realised risk with forecast risk; ideally, we would like this ratio to be one, indicating that our forecasting tools were efficient. If the ratio is much greater than one then we are aware that our forecasting tool is underestimating risk. Similarly, if the ratio is much less than one, then we are aware that our forecasting tool is overpredicting risk. Either situation is undesirable.

$$\text{Risk efficiency} = \frac{\text{Ex-post risk}}{\text{Ex-ante risk}} = \frac{\text{Realised risk}}{\text{Forecast risk}} \qquad (16.4)$$

Risk efficiency is most often calculated using tracking error but could just as easily be used with variability, VaR, or conditional VaR.

Clearly this measure compares the prospective risk of a current snapshot of the portfolio with the historic ex-post risk of the portfolio after-the-fact, including transactional history over an extended period of typically three years. There will be differences reflecting past transactions and potential window dressing (the process of reducing bets immediately before measurement, which will of course reduce prospective risk) but the real value of this statistic is the simple comparison of ex-post with ex-ante risk statistics and the questions this will raise. All too often ex-post statistics are calculated by performance measurers and ex-ante statistics forecast by risk managers with very little communication between the two.

PERFORMANCE EFFICIENCY

Finally, asset managers should compare their chosen realised performance appraisal measure to the forecast appraisal measure.

$$\text{Performance efficiency} = \frac{\text{Performance appraisal}}{\text{Performance forecast}} \qquad (16.5)$$

EX-ANTE RISK STANDARDS

Ex-post return methodologies, and to a lesser degree ex-post risk standard, are well established. Ex-ante risk standards are not. Risk management is awash in many creative and innovative approaches to both measuring and managing different types of ex-ante risk.

Medicine is an apt analogy for ex-ante risk: both are complex fields requiring years of training and experience to master. Both are combinations of art and science. In both fields, skilled experts are held in high regard and egos are plentiful: a combination of attributes that resists standardisations. Yet both fields benefit from standardisation: costs are lowered, transparency is increased and quality is increased. Consider the historical example of surgeons resisting checklists in the operating theatre because it was *"beneath their level of expertise*". Today, operating theatres rely both on the expertise of the surgeon and on the safety net of checklists, just as airplane passengers rely on the expertise of the pilot and on the pre-flight checklists. Similarly, risk managers can be highly regarded experts while adhering to standards that benefit the industry, their employer and their investors.

CONSISTENCY IN CALCULATIONS AND COMPARISON

The most obvious benefit to all parties is a consistency of methodology behind the calculations so that the ex-ante risk measures can be compared. Some measures, like volatility (using the far more common term for variability), have largely achieved that standard as there is only one universally accepted way to calculate volatility. Still, we find nuanced differences like *exponentially weighted volatility* and *fat tail adjusted volatility*. At the other extreme is VaR, a risk measure with seemingly as many varieties of calculation as there are stakeholders calculating it. I don't suggest that asset managers should stop using proprietary formulae for their own purposes, but a standardisation of formulae, methodology and vocabulary is required if ex-ante risk is to be universally adopted.

DISCLOSURE

Just as accounting standards and performance standards allow us to compare numerical results across a wide range of firms and asset managers, risk disclosure will allow a more robust comparison across investment portfolios. Full disclosure of important details on presented risk analyses, such as non-linearities, calculation methodologies, modelling assumptions and estimations can demonstrate to investors and prospective investors that the asset manager takes its risk management responsibilities seriously and has the expertise to analyse its own assets. Unfortunately, such transparency is often seen at odds with an asset manager's own financial interests. As the industry matures, this conflict should dissipate away.

RECOGNITION OF ADHERENCE TO BEST PRACTICE

Those asset managers who adopt such ex-ante risk standards would easily be recognised by the industry as adherents to best practice. We've already seen this phenomenon take hold without formal standards as the industry has matured: increased transparency and willingness to share risk information, albeit without formal (or forced) standards, differentiate leading asset managers. This recognition would only grow with standardisation.

MORE ROBUST INTERNAL PROCESS AND CONTROL

There is no doubt that people are more careful about their work when they know others are watching. An asset manager choosing to adopt standardised ex-ante risk measures would boost its own internal processes and controls simply because another set of eyes will be on the results. This will have an added effect in promoting the practice of risk management, as more people will be aware and responsible for its accurate reporting.

Establishing a bona fide and wide-reaching standard for ex-ante risk measures will permit more accurate comparisons. The impact such standardisation had on performance measurement is now well known – the industry grew significantly, partially because investors could trust the numbers more. In today's risk sensitive investing environment, increasing the trust in risk reporting across the investment landscape will help asset owners and asset managers alike. Standards will improve communication through a more consistent vocabulary. Labels and names are notoriously confusing if they aren't specific enough to define precisely what they mean because everyone hearing the word tends to interpret it according to their own biases. The insidiousness of this error is that no one realises that everyone has a different understanding unless painstaking efforts are made to clarify the discussion. Standards reduce the uncertainty and add clarity to the conversation. This is especially important in technical conversations between experts and laymen. Again, consider the analogy with medicine and how difficult decision making would be if each lab had a different methodology of measuring, say, cholesterol level, for different patients.

Once standards are established, trust is increased through heightened credibility. The past several years has seen an increasing awareness of risk measurement and of the complexities and pitfalls in interpretation of risk numbers, partially because of a lack of standardisation. Standards will improve this but will not solve this issue alone.

Those firms that adhere to the standards can expect a significant boost to their marketing efforts as they can claim the high ground in their risk transparency efforts.

Adopting such standards will not be a rapid or easy process. Standards are most likely to be successful if crafted by a consortium of asset managers, asset owners and industry associations representing the various complexities of the industry and then promoted by an established industry standards board – GIPS provide the ideal template. GIPS is a huge success, the standards are endorsed by 41 countries and over 1700 asset management firms claim compliance, including 87[3] of the largest global asset managers[4] representing approximately 61% of global assets. Many asset owners require traditional asset managers to be compliant (to date the standards are not as successful for alternative asset managers, although GIPS 2020 attempts to address this). Compliance with the standards has raised the quality of investment presentations throughout the industry, establishing a global level playing field and facilitating comparability. I would anticipate similar benefits would be gained by an ex-ante risk standard, hopefully far outweighing the costs of implementing such a standard, but the effort will be significant. It will require persistence, stamina and patience and its success is hardly guaranteed. But in the end, standardised risk measures would benefit all participants – asset managers and asset owners alike.

---

[3]Compliant for the whole firm or including a GIPS compliant defined firm that is compliant. Not all the assets of the firm are necessarily compliant.
[4]Source: Cerulli Associates Global, November 2015.

CHAPTER 17

Which Risk Measure to Use?

"The theory of probabilities is at the bottom nothing but common sense reduced to calculus."

Laplace (1749–1827) *Theorie analytique des probabilities,* V. Courcier, 1820.
Public Domain

WHY MEASURE EX-POST RISK?

Many commentators would argue that there is little value and obviously no uncertainty when measuring ex-post or historic risk, so why bother? I maintain there are good reasons to measure risk ex post:

i) Ex-post portfolio performance is two dimensional; it is simply not acceptable to focus only on return; risk must also be assessed. If an asset manager achieved a reasonable but unexciting return, but took very high risk to achieve this return, then the asset owner should be very disappointed. The return achieved should justify the risk taken. Virtually all performance fee arrangements are based on return only; theoretically they should be calculated using risk-adjusted return.

ii) Asset owners must articulate their risk preferences in advance: they should determine which risk measure they want their portfolio manager to maximise and then they should monitor performance against that chosen risk measure ex post.

iii) Both asset owners and asset managers should compare realised or ex-post risk, against the forecast or ex-ante risk. It is essential that forecasts of risk are consistently compared against actual realised risk. Risk controllers, in particular, need to be grounded in reality; it is essential that they compare realised risk with their previous forecasts of risk.

WHICH RISK MEASURES TO USE?

Risk, like beauty, is very much in the eye of the beholder. The objectives and preferences of the investor should determine which risk measure to use. Although most ex-post risk measures are easy to calculate, they are not all easy to interpret and are often contradictory.

There is little value in monitoring multiple risk measures. The ideal measure is determined in advance, consistent with investment objectives and easily understood by all parties. Additional descriptive statistics can be useful but asset managers should be allowed to focus and maximise a single reward to risk appraisal measure.

Most appraisal measures are fundamentally the same structure: a ratio, the numerator of which is a measure of reward desired by the asset owner corresponding to the vertical axis of a two-dimensional graph; and the denominator of which is a measure of risk that most concerns the asset owner corresponding to the horizontal axis. The reward to risk ratio corresponds to the slope of the line from a starting point on the vertical axis to the combined reward and risk of the portfolio. Reward to risk ratios are logically categorised in the periodic table (Table 12.1) shown in Chapter 12 and also listed with comments in Table 17.1.

Reward to risk ratios are most suitable for ranking portfolio performance. The most appropriate ratios take account of asset owners' risk tolerances. For downside risk measures, the minimum acceptable or target return should be consistent with the asset manager's investment objectives and strategy. There is relatively little value in using a range of minimum target returns to analyse portfolio performance if the asset manager is targeting relative return.

Ratios all suffer the same problem: they allow us to rank portfolios in order of preference but do not inform in terms of the quantity of relative performance. Risk-adjusted returns, on the other hand, convert ratios to a return metric we do understand. A summary of risk-adjusted returns available are shown in Table 17.2. Although M^2 is shown for total risk and downside risk, in theory M^2 can be calculated for any measure of risk.

HEDGE FUNDS

The more complex risk measures tend to be reserved for alternative investment strategies such as hedge funds that expect non-normal return distributions.

There are numerous definitions of hedge funds. My favourite is from Ineichen[1] (2003):

> *A hedge fund constitutes an investment program whereby the managers or partners seek absolute returns by exploiting investment opportunities while protecting principal from potential financial loss.*

---

[1] Alexander M. Ineichen (2003) *Absolute Returns: The Risk and Opportunities of Hedge Fund Investing*. John Wiley & Sons.

TABLE 17.1 Reward to risk ratios

Ratio	Reward (or Return) Vertical Axis Numerator	Risk Measure Horizontal Axis Denominator	Comment
Traditional			
Sharpe	Return above risk-free rate	Variability Standard deviation	Reward to variability. The grandfather of all reward to risk ratios
Treynor	Return above risk-free rate	Systematic risk β or volatility	Reward to volatility. Actually, defined before the Sharpe ratio but rarely used in practice
Information	Excess return	Tracking error Relative risk	Frequently used. Favoured by institutional asset managers
Appraisal	Jensen's *alpha*	Specific risk	Often confused with the Information ratio
Modified Jensen	Jensen's *alpha*	Systematic risk β or Volatility	Rarely used
Drawdown			
Calmar	Return above risk-free rate	Maximum drawdown	Quite common for commodity, future and hedge funds
Burke	Return above risk-free rate	Drawdown deviation	Penalises deep drawdowns in particular
Sterling–Calmar	Return above risk-free rate	Average annual maximum drawdown	Most common form of Sterling ratio
Sterling	Return above risk-free rate	Average drawdown	Similar to *Omega*–Sharpe ratio. Multiple definitions of average drawdown used
Martin	Return above risk-free rate	Ulcer index	Similar to Burke, penalises both depth and duration of drawdowns
Pain	Return above risk-free rate	Pain index	Similar to Martin index but not squared

(*continued overleaf*)

TABLE 17.1   *(Continued)*

Ratio	Reward (or Return) Vertical Axis Numerator	Risk Measure Horizontal Axis Denominator	Comment
Downside			
Sortino	Return above risk-free rate	Downside risk	The most appropriate downside risk statistic
Upside potential	Upside potential	Downside risk	Combines upside potential with downside risk
Omega	Upside potential	Downside potential	Similar to upside potential but extreme losses are less harshly penalised
Omega– Sharpe	Return above risk-free rate	Downside potential	Identical ranking statistic to *Omega*
Prospect	Utility adjusted return	Downside risk	Gives greater weight to negative returns
Variability skewness	Upside risk	Downside risk	Similar to *Omega* but extreme returns more significant on both the upside and downside
VaR			
Reward on VaR	Return above risk-free rate	VaR	Unconcerned with shape of tail
Conditional Sharpe or STARR ratio	Return above risk-free rate	Conditional VaR Tail loss or Tail VaR Expected shortfall Average VaR	Takes account of tail shape
Double VaR ratio	Potential upside (VaR)	VaR	Not really used
Modified Sharpe	Return above risk-free rate	Modified VaR	Adjusts for skewness and kurtosis
Tail ratio	Return above risk-free rate	Tail risk	Takes account of tail shape and penalises more extreme returns
Rachev ratio	Tail gain	Tail loss	Takes account of both right-hand and left-hand tail shape

TABLE 17.1 *(Continued)*

Ratio	Reward (or Return) Vertical Axis Numerator	Risk Measure Horizontal Axis Denominator	Comment
Other			
Adjusted Sharpe	Return above risk-free rate	Risk, skewness and kurtosis	For those concerned takes account of higher moments. Surprisingly easy to calculate
Reward to duration	Return above risk-free rate	Duration Systematic risk Volatility	For fixed income only. Equivalent to Treynor ratio
Gini	Return above risk-free rate	Mean difference	Pair wise dispersion, suitable for non-normal distributions. Not well known
K ratio	Slope of cumulative portfolio returns through time	Variability of error term	A reward to risk measure related to cumulative returns
Generalised			
Kappa or Sortino– Satchell	Return above risk-free rate	*l*th Lower moment	Generalised downside measure. For *l* = 1 equivalent to *Omega*–Sharpe ratio, for *l* = 2 equivalent to Sortino ratio
Farinelli and Tibiletti	*u*th upper partial moment	*l*th lower partial moment	Generalised gain:loss partial moment ratio
Generalised Rachev ratio	Extreme *u*th upper power	Extreme *l*th lower power	Generalised extreme gain: extreme loss ratio
Z ratio	Extreme *u*th upper power or *u*th upper partial moment	Extreme *l*th lower power or *l*th lower partial moment	Gain:loss ratio combining partial moments with extreme gains or losses

TABLE 17.2 Risk-adjusted return measures

Measure	Risk-adjusted for	Comment
Total Return		
M^2	Total risk variability	The original and my preferred measure. Underused throughout the asset management industry
M^2 for downside risk	Downside risk	Rarely used although demonstrably better than Sortino ratio
Skew-adjusted M^2	Variability and skewness	Theoretically better than M^2
Adjusted M^2	Variability, skewness and kurtosis	Theoretically better than both M^2 and Skew-adjusted M^2 although in practice the impact of kurtosis is relatively small
Excess Return		
Jensen's *alpha*	Systematic risk	By far the most common. Term often confused with simple excess return. Jensen's *alpha* is more accurately excess return adjusted for systematic risk
Regression *alpha*	Systematic risk	Similar to Jensen's *alpha* ignoring risk-free rate
Three-factor *alpha*	Systematic risk, market capitalisation and value	Uses Fama–French three-factor model
Carhart's *alpha* or four-factor *alpha*	Systematic risk, market capitalisation, value and momentum	Uses Carhart's four-factor model
M^2 excess	Depends on the M^2 measure used	Most often expressed arithmetically but geometric is more appropriate
Net selectivity	Systematic risk and diversification	Good measure for mutual funds. Early version of attribution
Differential return	Total risk	Benchmark return adjusted to risk of portfolio. Less effective than M^2 excess
GH1	Total risk	Efficient frontier equivalent of differential return
GH2	Total risk	Efficient frontier equivalent of M^2
Omega excess	Downside style variance	Rarely used

Predominately hedge fund management styles are designed to be asymmetric in their return patterns. If successful, this leads to variability of returns on the upside but not on the downside. Investors are less concerned with variability on the upside but of course are extremely concerned about variability on the downside. This leads to an extended family of risk-adjusted measures reflecting the downside risk tolerances of investors seeking absolute, not relative, returns. Investors should prefer high average returns, lower variance or standard deviation, positive skewness and lower kurtosis.

Hedge funds can be further differentiated by:

i) More flexible investment strategies and the ability to employ leverage
ii) Substantial personal holding by the portfolio manager and performance fees
iii) Lighter regulation
iv) Restricted liquidity – investors are typically subject to a lock-up period.

SMOOTHING

All of these return measures assume accurate valuations of portfolios. Of course, if valuations are inaccurate then the risk calculations will be incorrect; in particular, if there is any smoothing employed in the valuation process then volatility will be hidden and lower than it should be. This is an obvious issue for real estate and private equity investment strategies but also for some less liquid hedge fund strategies. Investors should be cognisant of this issue and in particular should take care not to compare liquid and illiquid investment strategies. Care should also be taken when using measures that attempt to adjust for smoothing. Smoothing is one issue when comparing illiquid and liquid investment strategies; there are others. Adjusting for smoothing offers yet another opportunity for asset managers to self-select favourable measures.

⚠ **Caution**

Avoid comparing performance appraisal measures of liquid and illiquid strategies. Always compare like with like.

A number of statistics summarised in Table 17.3 are descriptive only and cannot be used for ranking portfolios but do provide additional information about the nature of portfolio returns.

TABLE 17.3 Descriptive statistics

Statistic	Comment
Regression Statistics	
Covariance	Tendency of the portfolio and benchmark returns to move together
Correlation	Standardised covariance
Autocorrelation	Correlation of a lagged return with itself
R^2	Square of correlation. Shows how much of the portfolio risk relates to the variance of the benchmark
Beta	Systematic risk or volatility
Specific risk	Standard deviation of the error term
Other	
Tracking error	Standard deviation of excess returns. The dominating
Tracking risk	measure of risk for long only institutional asset managers.
Relative risk	Not to be confused with tracking error as used in the ETF
Active risk	industry. Relative risk is perhaps the best term to use.
Total risk	Standard deviation of portfolio returns
Standard deviation	
Variability	
Volatility	
Downside risk	Semi-standard deviation of returns below target
Kurtosis	A measure of the weight of returns in the tails of the distribution
Relative kurtosis	A measure of the weight of excess returns against the benchmark in the tails of the distribution
Skewness	A measure of asymmetry
Relative skewness	A measure of asymmetry of excess returns against the benchmark
Hurst index	Persistency
Up capture indicator	Measure of performance capture in positive markets
Down capture indicator	Measure of performance capture in negative markets
Up number ratio	Percentage of portfolio returns greater than zero when benchmark return is greater than zero
Down number ratio	Percentage of portfolio returns less than zero when benchmark return is less than zero
Up percentage ratio	How often does the portfolio manager outperform in rising markets
Down percentage ratio	How often does the portfolio manager outperform in falling markets
Percentage gain ratio	Ratio of portfolio return greater than zero compared to benchmark returns greater than zero

TABLE 17.3 (*Continued*)

Statistic	Comment
Bias ratio	Stale prices
Largest drawdown	Largest single drawdown. Popular with hedge funds
Average drawdown	Average of largest drawdowns
Drawdown deviation	Standard deviation of largest drawdowns
Maximum drawdown	Maximum loss over any investment period. Buy at the top, sell at the bottom. Popular with hedge funds
Fixed Income Measures	
Modified duration	Systematic risk for bonds
Volatility	
Convexity	Rate of change of duration
Value at Risk Statistics	
VaR	Expected maximum loss with certain level of confidence.
Conditional VaR	Average return conditional on exceeding the value at risk
Expected shortfall	
Tail loss	
Modified VaR	VaR modified for kurtosis and skewness
Potential upside	Positive (right-hand) equivalent of value at risk
Tail risk	Variance type calculation in the left-hand tail

OUTLIERS

In engineering or agriculture, it may be appropriate to ignore extreme results assuming they are measurement errors and not real returns. This is almost never appropriate for finance: extreme results represent real extreme losses. It may represent an unlikely event, such as Porsche building an undisclosed stake in VW using options and literally catching many short sellers desperately short of stock,[2] but this extreme event resulted in real losses.

 Caution

Outliers should never be excluded in portfolio risk calculations.

---

[2]W. Boston (2008) Hedge Funds Shorting VW Stung by Porsche. *Time Magazine*, 29 October.

DATA MINING

Clearly with such a large number of risk measures available it is extremely tempting to data mine after the fact and find the appraisal measure that favours the asset manager in the best possible way. This of course is not useful; appraisal measures will generate different rankings according to asset owner preferences. These preferences must be established in advance and articulately expressed and documented. The asset manager's role is to maximise the chosen appraisal measure. Normally one measure, expressed over time, will suffice; multiple measures will lead to potential conflicts of objectives.

 Caution

Avoid the temptation to present multiple appraisal measures.

RISK MEASURES AND THE GLOBAL INVESTMENT PERFORMANCE STANDARDS (GIPS®)

To date, the Global Investment Performance Standards, or GIPS, have taken only a small step in terms of requiring appraisal measures in GIPS Reports. GIPS are a set of voluntary, ethical standards for calculating and presenting investment performance to prospective clients. The relevant clauses regarding risk measures are as follows:

> **2.A.18** *When calculating additional risk measures:*
>   **a.** *The periodicity of the composite or pooled fund returns and the benchmark must be the same.*
>   **b.** *The risk measure calculation methodology of the composite or pooled fund and the benchmark must be the same.*
> **4.A.1.** *The firm must present in each GIPS Report:*
>   **j.** *For composites for which monthly composite returns are available, the three-year annualized ex-post standard deviation (using monthly returns) of the composite and the benchmark as of each annual period end.*
>   **4.B.3** *For all periods for which an annualized ex-post standard deviation of the composite and the benchmark are presented, the firm should present the corresponding annualized return of the composite and the benchmark.*

4.B.4 *For all periods greater than three years for which an annualized return of the composite and the benchmark are presented, the firm should present the corresponding annualized ex-post standard deviation (using monthly returns) of the composite and the benchmark.*

4.B.5 *The firm should present relevant ex-post additional risk measures for the composite and benchmark.*

4.C.36 *For composites with at least three annual periods of performance, the firm must disclose if the three-year annualized ex-post standard deviation of the composite and/or benchmark is not presented because 36 monthly returns are not available.*

4.C.43 *If the firm presents additional risk measures, the firm must:*
　a. *Describe any additional risk measure*
　b. *Disclose the name of the risk-free rate if a risk-free rate is used in the calculation of the additional risk measure.*

4.C.44 *The firm must disclose if gross-of-fees or net-of-fees returns are used to calculate presented risk measures.*

5.B.5 *The firm should present an appropriate ex-post risk measure for the composite and the benchmark. The same ex-post risk measure should be presented for the composite and the benchmark*

5.C.41 *If the firm presents additional risk measures, the firm must:*
　a. *Describe any additional risk measure*
　b. *Disclose the name of the risk-free rate if a risk-free rate is used in the calculation of the additional risk measure.*

5.C.42 *The firm must disclose if gross-of-fees or net-of-fees returns are used to calculate presented risk measures.*

6.B.3 *For all periods for which an annualized ex-post standard deviation of the pooled fund and the benchmark are presented, the firm should present the corresponding annualized return of the pooled fund and the benchmark.*

6.B.4 *For all periods greater than three years for which an annualized return of the pooled fund and the benchmark are presented, the firm should present the corresponding annualized ex-post standard deviation (using monthly returns) of the pooled fund and the benchmark.*

6.B.5 *The firm should present relevant ex-post additional risk measures for the pooled fund and the benchmark.*

6.C.29 *For pooled funds with at least three annual periods of performance, the firm must disclose if the three-year annualized ex-post standard deviation of the pooled fund and/or benchmark is not presented because 36 monthly returns are not available.*

6.C.35 *The firm must disclose if pooled fund gross-of-fees or pooled fund net-of-fees returns are used to calculate presented risk measures.*

7.B.4 *The firm should present an appropriate ex-post risk measure for the pooled fund and the benchmark. The same ex-post risk measure should be presented for the pooled fund and the benchmark.*

7.C.36 *If the firm presents additional risk measures, the firm must:*
   a. *Describe any additional risk measure*
   b. *Disclose the name of the risk-free rate if a risk-free rate is used in the calculation of the additional risk measure*

7.C.37 *The firm must disclose if pooled fund gross-of-fees or pooled fund net-of-fees returns are used to calculate presented risk measures.*

In GIPS terminology, *must* is a requirement and *should* is a recommendation. This small step by GIPS is entirely sensible, although not without controversy. Some users of the standards make the claim that GIPS are performance, not risk, standards and should remain silent on risk issues. Fortunately, the GIPS Executive Committee also takes my view that performance is a combination of risk and return and have required that standard deviations of both the portfolio and benchmark are presented. Standard deviation is widely used, easy to calculate, simple to understand and adds value in that the variability of a strategy's return is relevant to clients and directly comparable across various strategies and liquid asset types. Comparison with benchmark variability is particularly useful. Of course, the return distribution may not be normally distributed, but the asset manager is allowed to provide additional measures if appropriate. Care should be taken to compare risk calculations of assets with similar liquidity. Illiquid asset types, for example private equity (but also to a lesser degree real estate and hedge funds), typically suffer smoothed valuations that hide volatility, which ultimately leads to reward to risk measures that look better on comparison with more liquid asset types.

Composite returns that include many portfolios are inevitably more diversified than isolated portfolios and therefore the variability of composite returns will tend to be less than the variability of individual portfolios within the composite. An alternative approach might have been a weighted or equal average of the variability of the constituent portfolios, perhaps a high/low range of variability or even the variability of the representative account. Of course, the choice of representative account should be consistent through time if one were allowed to use this measure for the disclosure. On balance the GIPS decision to use the variability of composite returns avoids any gaming of results and is consistent with the presentation of composite returns.

The GIPS standards also draw a distinction between external and internal risk. External risk measures are applied to the returns of composite through time whilst internal risk measures apply to the dispersion of annual portfolio returns within the composite. Internal measures of dispersion within the composite are not portfolio risk measures within the context of this book; nevertheless, a description of various internal risk measures can be found in Appendix A.

FUND RATING SYSTEMS

Noel Amenc and Veronique Le Sourd[3] wrote a very interesting article on fund rating systems critiquing the methods of Standard & Poor's Micropal, Morningstar and Lipper – essential reading for any portfolio manager benchmarked against one of these peer group providers. Good ratings from these organisations will influence retail investors and drive sales, therefore it is essential that portfolio managers understand how the ratings are calculated. In effect, these organisations select the most appropriate risk measures on behalf of the retail investor.

The Standard & Poor's Micropal star rating is based on the information ratio relative to the sector average (or median) performance of the funds belonging to the same peer group over a 36-month period. Stars are attributed as follows:

Fund Percentile	Rating
Top 10%	*****
10% to 30%	****
30% to 50%	***
50% to 75%	**
Bottom 25%	*

Morningstar created their own risk-adjusted performance measure $MRAR(\gamma)$:

$$MRAR(\gamma) = \left[\frac{1}{T} \times \sum_{t=1}^{t=T} \left(\frac{1 + r_t}{1 + r_{Ft}} \right)^{-\gamma} \right]^{-\frac{12}{\gamma}} - 1 \qquad (17.1)$$

Where:

γ = a parameter reflecting the investor's degree of risk aversion.

This measure is subtracted from the annualised excess return relative to the risk-free rate over 36 months. Morningstar set $\gamma = 2$, thus more variable

---

[3]N. Amenc and V. Le Sourd (2007) A Critical Analysis of Fund Rating Systems. *Journal of Performance Measurement*, Summer, 42–57.

excess returns relative to the risk-free rate are penalised. Stars are attributed as follows:

Fund Percentile	Rating
Top 10%	*****
10% to 32.5%	****
32.5% to 67.5%	***
67.5% to 90%	**
Bottom 10%	*

Lipper Micropal provides several different rankings using total return, persistence, capital preservation and expense ratios. For persistence the Hurst index is used, for capital preservation the sum of negative returns over the cumulative period. Lipper Micropal scores are attributed as follows:

Fund Percentile	Score
Top 20%	Lipper Leaders
20% to 40%	2
40% to 60%	3
60% to 80%	4
Bottom 20%	5

Scores are allocated for 3, 5, 10 years and overall. The overall calculation uses an equal weighted average percentile for each period thus giving greater weight to recent performance.

The usefulness of these rankings will very much depend on the quality and monitoring of each sector to ensure consistency by the peer group provider and the relevance of the risk measure to the investor.

WHICH MEASURES ARE ACTUALLY USED?

Two recent industry surveys, the Risk Survey[4] (2011) from the Spaulding Group and an article by Amnec, Goltz and Lioui[5] (2011), support my own experience that, in practice, managers are only using the simplest of reward to

---

[4]Risk Survey, The Spaulding Group, 2011.
[5]N. Amnec, F. Goltz and A. Lioui (2011) Practitioner Portfolio Construction and Performance Measurement: Evidence from Europe. *Financial Analysts Journal* 67(3), 39–50.

risk ratios. The Amnec, Goltz and Lioui article was based on an online questionnaire that generated responses from 229 institutions based in Europe. The Risk Survey represents a broader response of close to 140 firms with a bias towards North America. Table 17.4 identifies that for absolute returns the Sharpe ratio is extremely popular, with a good showing for the Sortino ratio, and a surprisingly high rating for VaR based measures.

Table 17.5 demonstrates that the information ratio dominates (quite rightly) for relative performance.

The Spaulding Group make the interesting observations that over half of the firms responding to their survey indicated that they use value at risk and that less than half the firms indicated that they used downside deviation despite the poor performance of markets in recent years. It is no surprise, as evidenced in Table 17.6, that standard deviation and tracking error are extremely popular.

The Spaulding Group also noted the dominance of the Sharpe ratio and information ratio in Table 17.7.

TABLE 17.4 What measures do managers use to measure absolute performance?

Choice	Observations	Percentage
Sharpe ratio	177	77%
Treynor ratio	23	11%
Sortino ratio	63	28%
VaR-based measure	66	29%
Average excess return	95	41%
Other	11	5%

Source: Amenc, N., Goltz, F., & Lioui, A. (2011). Practitioner Portfolio Construction and Performance Measurement: Evidence from Europe. *Financial Analysts Journal*, 67(3), 39–50.

TABLE 17.5 What measures do managers use to measure relative performance?

Choice	Observations	Percentage
M^2	7	3%
Graham–Harvey (GH1)	3	1%
Jensen's *alpha*	78	34%
Information ratio	149	65%
VaR-based measure	15	7%
Average excess return	75	31%
Other	7	3%

Source: Amenc, N., Goltz, F., & Lioui, A. (2011). Practitioner Portfolio Construction and Performance Measurement: Evidence from Europe. *Financial Analysts Journal*, 67(3), 39–50.

TABLE 17.6 Which of the following risk measures do you currently use?

Measure	Number of Responses	Response Ratio
Standard deviation	104	92.8%
Downside deviation	45	40.1%
Tracking error	93	83%
Beta	88	78.5%
VaR	60	53.5%
Other	17	15.1%

Source: Risk Survey, The Spaulding Group 2011.

TABLE 17.7 Which of the following risk-adjusted return measures do you currently use?

Measure	Number of Responses	Response Ratio
Jensen's *alpha*	51	48.1%
Sharpe ratio	99	93.3%
Treynor ratio	37	34.9%
Sortino ratio	37	34.9%
Information ratio	90	84.9%
M^2	18	16.9%
Other	4	3.7%

Source: Risk Survey, The Spaulding Group 2011.

With regard to hedge funds it is interesting to note the prevalence of very simple measures such as drawdown and its variants in Table 17.8. Hedge fund managers may prefer drawdown measures because, unlike standard deviation and related measures, they do not make any inherent assumption about the shape of the return distribution.

WHICH RISK MEASURES SHOULD REALLY BE USED?

Basic risk calculations are actually very straightforward and relatively simple to compute. It is perhaps unfortunate that risk is considered a complex subject that requires an understanding of advanced mathematics. It is the role of both the performance analyst and the risk controller to ensure the broadest understanding of the statistics presented.

Eling and Schumacher[6] in 2007 and Eling[7] again in 2008 suggest that most of the appraisal measures catalogued in this book are all highly correlated, that

---

[6]M. Eling and F. Schuhmacher (2007) Does the Choice of Performance Measure Influence the Evaluation of Hedge Funds? *Journal of Banking and Finance* 31(9), 2632–2647.
[7]M. Eling (2008) Performance Measurement in the Investment Industry: Does the Measure Matter? University of St. Gallen, Working Paper Series in Finance No. 73.

TABLE 17.8 Hedge funds: which of the following risk-adjusted return measures do you currently use?

Measure	Number of Responses	Response Ratio
Drawdown	38	59.3%
Average drawdown	22	34.3%
Maximum drawdown	50	78.1%
Largest individual drawdown	17	26.5%
Drawdown duration	22	34.3%
Drawdown deviation	15	13.4%
Calmar ratio	14	21.8%
Sterling ratio	14	21.8%
Ulcer index	4	6.2%
Pain index	7	10.9%
Burke ratio	6	9.3%
Martin ratio	4	6.2%
Pain ratio	6	9.3%
Lake ratio	4	6.2%
Peak ratio	3	4.6%
Other	5	7.8%

Source: Risk Survey, The Spaulding Group 2011

is to say an asset manager exhibiting a good combination of risk and reward will tend to score highly using all of these measures. They conclude, therefore, that the Sharpe ratio, easy to calculate, easily understood and widely calculated, should be used exclusively and that there is little value using more complex risk measures. This neither coincides with my experience nor my intuition. I suspect that it may hold true for certain time periods but I would expect to see different ranking from time to time. Thankfully, an article published by Zakamouline[8] (2011) concurs with this view. Zakamouline concludes that the choice of appraisal measure will influence the evaluation of hedge funds and that both skewness and kurtosis play significant roles in performance evaluation.

It's when these appraisal measures generate different rankings that asset managers really should be interested in understanding why and understanding the impact on asset owner investment objectives.

There is value in simplicity and many of these risk measures are too nuanced to be of real use. *Asset owners*, and I emphasise *asset owners*, must choose for themselves their preferred appraisal measure.

For absolute return strategies, for simplicity, ease of calculation, familiarity and effectiveness, I would use the grandfather of risk measures, the Sharpe ratio. Yes, I am concerned about the 3rd and 4th moments of the return

[8]V. Zakamouline (2011) The Performance Measure You Choose Influences the Evaluation of Hedge Funds. *Journal of Performance Measurement*, Spring, 48–63.

distribution and would be happy to use the adjusted Sharpe ratio as an improvement (at a small cost in terms of familiarity and ease of calculation). I would also be happy to convert this ratio into a return metric such as M^2 or adjusted M^2. I'm perhaps too old fashioned and out of date to distinguish between upside and downside risk; I appreciate that return profiles are not symmetric and that many investment strategies are asymmetric in nature but I'm reluctant to lose the information contained in upside risk. However, if downside risk is a concern the Sortino ratio is available.

If extreme risk is a concern, then maximum drawdown and value at risk are relevant. For simplicity, the Calmar ratio is an option but the conditional Sharpe ratio is perhaps the most appropriate using conditional VaR, a more coherent risk measure than value at risk on its own.

For benchmark driven investment strategies, I strongly favour the Information ratio; it is very well known, a simple extension of the Sharpe ratio, just as easy to calculate and easy to explain. There is no harm adjusting for relative skewness and kurtosis but it is probably unnecessary and perhaps not worth the additional complication.

COMMON ERRORS TO AVOID

1. Ensure the same risk-free rate is used in all appraisal measures when making a comparison.
2. Use simple or continuously compounded returns consistently.
3. Use the same periodicity of data (monthly, weekly, daily).
4. Do not compare liquid strategies with illiquid strategies.
5. Do not data mine – focus on the risk measure that best reflects the asset owner's preference. Document the target risk measure and apply it consistently.
6. Avoid calculating appraisal measure over short time periods (use 36 months or 20 quarters).

CHAPTER 18

Risk Control

"I don't give a damn if we get a little bureaucracy as long as we get results. If it bothers you, yell at it. Kick it. Scream at it. Break it!"

Jack Welch (1935–2020)

"You can do everything with bayonets, but you are not able to sit on them."

Otto von Bismarck (1815–1898)

"For the night is dark and full of terrors."

George R. R. Martin (1948–?) *A Clash of Kings* (A Song of Ice and Fire, Book 2), 2011

REGULATIONS IN THE INVESTMENT RISK AREA

Investment risk management has been the focus of interest of regulators not only in the case of investment banks but also increasingly in the area of retail products, such as mutual funds. Already back in 2002 as part of the UCITS III framework in Europe, dedicated guidelines were issued by the EU regulators with respect to financial risk management for investment funds that use derivatives.

In the course of the revision of the UCITS framework (UCITS IV, effective from 1 July 2011), these guidelines have been reinforced and enhanced. In particular, the new Guidelines on Risk Measurement and Calculation of Global Risk Exposure and Counterparty Risk for UCITS (CESR/10-788) issued in 2010 by the Committee of European Securities Regulators (now renamed the European Securities and Markets Authority (ESMA)) include very detailed provisions on measurement of market and credit risks in the UCITS funds, including methodology and formulae.

Complex investment funds are required to use a VaR approach where:

- a UCITS engages in complex investment strategies which represent more than a negligible part of the UCITS' investment policy;
- a UCITS has more than a negligible exposure to exotic derivatives; or
- the commitment approach does not adequately capture the market risk of the portfolio, for example option strategies, interest rate and convertible bond arbitrage, long/short and market neutral strategies.

Both relative and absolute VaR can be used but the chosen approach must be used consistently. When using a relative approach, the reference benchmark portfolio should have a risk profile very close to that of the UCITS. If the definition of the reference portfolio is not possible, the absolute VaR approach should be used. The absolute VaR limit cannot be more than 20% of the fund's net asset value.

UCITS funds are free to select an appropriate VaR model. However, for UCITS largely employing derivatives with nonlinear risk features, the parametric VaR model is not considered appropriate and such UCITS should use a historical simulation model or a Monte Carlo model. VaR models should take into account the general market risk and the idiosyncratic risk of securities. Event risk should be captured within stress-testing. VaR models should accommodate appropriate risk factors, such as:

- Interest rate risk: maturity segments of the yield curve
- Credit risk: credit spreads over government bonds
- Equities: market and/or sector indices.

In addition, stress tests must be carried out at least on a monthly basis and should cover all risks which significantly affect the UCITS, in particular those risks that are not fully captured by the VaR model. Stress scenarios should be selected to reflect extreme changes in markets and other environmental factors.

UCITS with instruments where the risk profile cannot be adequately captured by the computation of VaR should use additional risk management methods to ensure that both the maximum loss and the sensitivity to market movements in adverse conditions are adequately captured and limited. UCITS with complex strategies subject to the fat-tail risk should use conditional VaR or other methods capable of quantifying the potential impact of low-probability market events.

In addition, back-testing observations must be conducted on at least a monthly basis to test the accuracy of the VaR model.

> ⚠ **Caution**
>
> The problem with a regulatory model like this is that if the majority of market participants measure risk the same way, then it increases the likelihood that everyone overlooks the same risk.

RISK CONTROL STRUCTURE

Risk control is of course about controlling future risk, not historical risk; however, historical ex-post risk does play a significant role in the total risk control environment of any firm.

Control of risk is a matter of common sense, good competent management, appropriate incentives, robust structures, connected systems, simplicity, transparency and awareness.

Whichever appraisal measure you decide to focus on, it is important to monitor the change in that measure over time. Risk controllers can never assume the measure is accurate; far better to analyse the change over time and investigate any sudden changes.

The change may result from data errors, system or model errors, change in model assumptions, or an intentional or unintentional change in actual portfolio risk. Whatever the reason for the change, it should be discussed with the asset manager and fully understood.

Performance analysts have a key role to play in the risk control environment of asset managers. In the ideal asset management organisation I would have performance measurement, risk control, the legal department and the internal audit function reporting to the head of middle office as shown in Figure 18.1. Performance measurers should never report to the front office or the marketing department.

RISK MANAGEMENT

For effective risk management in an asset management firm the following should be in place:

i) *Documented risk management process.* To provide a framework for the risk control environment every asset management firm should have a risk management process policy document that clearly articulates the firm's attitude, management and reporting of risk. Risk controllers cannot establish a risk framework in the absence of a risk policy. The entire board must take ownership and articulate clearly the firm's policy for risk

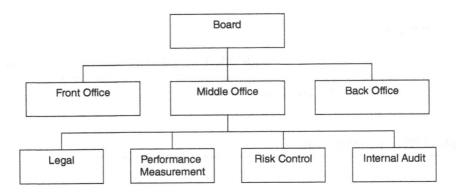

FIGURE 18.1   Middle office infrastructure

and their risk appetite. The availability of a written risk policy is a regulatory requirement in many instances, for example for managers of mutual funds.

ii) *Independence.* For effective risk control it is essential there are appropriate checks and balances within the firm with a clear front, middle and back office structure with clear areas of responsibility and reporting lines. The middle office, which neither takes investment decisions nor processes transactions, should be independent of both the front and back office.

iii) *Risk awareness.* Risk awareness should be embedded within the firm. Every employee will own some aspect of risk; it is essential they understand the risks they own and are constantly self-assessing their own risks. Risk literacy, at all levels, in all functions, should be encouraged. Once identified there are four possible responses to risk:

   a. *Accept.* A risk, although identified, may be accepted if the cost (including opportunity cost) of controlling is greater than the potential cost of risk failure.

   b. *Mitigate or transfer.* Arranging appropriate insurance cover or hedging may mitigate the cost of risk failure or transfer risk to another party.

   c. *Control.* Risk may be controlled by establishing risk limits and establishing monitoring procedures.

   d. *Eliminate.* It may be appropriate to eliminate an identified risk by ceasing that type of activity.

iv) *Clear risk limits.* Risk limits should be clear, unambiguous, quantifiable and agreed by the asset owner and asset manager in the investment management agreement.

v) *Risk and performance attribution.* The sources of risk and return should be identified and monitored independently using return attribution and other techniques. Accurate return and risk attribution can be used to identify the consistency of added value across the firm and consistency with the agreed investment objectives.

vi) *Appropriate risk-adjusted measures.* Risk and reward should be combined in risk-adjusted performance measures appropriate to the investment management strategy.

vii) *Stress and scenario tests.* Portfolios should be stressed under extreme scenarios to understand vulnerabilities in turbulent, abnormal markets

viii) *Review process for new products, instruments and strategies.* All new products, instruments and strategies should be rigorously reviewed. For example, a new derivative instrument may meet the needs of the portfolio manager but could generate significant operational and counterparty risks that must be assessed and approved.

ix) *Monitoring of risk efficiency.* Ex-ante and ex-post risk measures should be monitored through time and consistently compared to ensure that the forecast of risk is close to the realised risk or, if different, that there is a good understanding of the possible reasons that explain the difference.

An appropriate risk control infrastructure for an asset management firm would include:

i) *Risk Management Committee.* Reporting directly to the board, coordinating all risk control activity, including senior representatives from front, middle and back office. Responsible for portfolio risk, counterparty risk, operational risk, compliance risk, review of insurance arrangements, disaster recovery, contingency planning and systems change control. Many companies now recognise the need for coordinated thinking and behaviours in relation to risk so have created the role of Chief Risk Officer to oversee all the firm's risk activities.

ii) *Portfolio Risk Committee.* Reporting to the Risk Management Committee, responsibilities include portfolio and liquidity risk, ensuring that portfolios are managed within client expectations and mandate restrictions and the approval of new products, strategies and instruments.

iii) *Counterparty Risk Committee.* Reporting to Risk Management Committee, approving counterparties and their credit limits.

iv) *Operational Risk Committee.* Reporting to Risk Management Committee, responsibilities include error monitoring, information quality and change control.

All risk measures ex post and ex ante to some extent rely on historical information which may not include an extreme event; therefore, it is essential in risk management to understand the impact on portfolios of potential extreme events using stress testing (another term borrowed from engineering) and scenario analysis.

Typical historical scenarios include:

- **Black October, 9 September to 13 October 2008**

  In the United States, 15 banks failed in 2008, with several others being rescued through government intervention or acquisitions. On 11 October the International Monetary Fund (IMF) warned that the global financial system was on the brink of systemic meltdown. In the week beginning 6 October the Dow Jones Industrial Average (DJIA) closed lower for all five sessions, falling over 18%, its worst weekly decline ever on both a point and percentage basis. The S&P 500 fell more than 20%. On 14 October after being suspended for three successive trading days, the Icelandic stock market reopened, closing down 77% after the failure of three banks. By 24 October many of the world's stock exchanges experienced the worst declines in their history, with drops of around 10% in most market benchmarks.

- **9/11 Terrorist Attack, 11 September to 21 September 2001**

  The 11 September attacks had unprecedented effects on the financial markets. The New York Stock Exchange, the American Stock Exchange and NASDAQ did not open on 11 September and remained closed until 17 September. When the stock markets reopened, after the longest closure since the Great Depression in 1933, the DJIA stock market index fell 684 points, or 7.1%, its biggest ever one-day point decline. By the end of the week, the DJIA had fallen 1369.7 points (14.3%), its largest one-week point drop in history. US stocks lost $1.2 trillion in value in the week.

- **Sovereign Debt Crisis, 16 April 2010 to 7 May 2010**

  Early 2010 saw increasing fears of a sovereign debt crisis across the European Union including Greece, Ireland, Portugal, Spain and Belgium. A crisis of confidence followed with a significant widening of bond yield spreads and step increases in insurance on credit default swaps between these countries and other EU members. Downgrading of European government debt caused alarm in the financial markets.

- **Sub-prime Crisis, 20 July 2007 to 17 August 2007**

  Early 2007 saw a downturn in the financial sector when the first major sub-prime related losses began to be reported. As 2007 continued, at least 100 mortgage companies either shut down, suspended operations or were sold. The crisis caused panic in financial markets and pushed investors to take their money out of mortgage-backed securities and increasingly volatile equities

- **Lehman Brothers Crisis, 8 September 2008 to 18 September 2008**

  When Lehman Brothers filed for Chapter 11 bankruptcy protection on 15 September 2008, the markets witnessed the largest bankruptcy filing in

US history, with Lehman holding over $600 billion in assets. The Dow Jones reacted by closing down 500 points (-4.4%) on 15 September, at the time the largest drop by points in a single day since 11 September 2001.

Many risk management systems will offer as standard the above historical scenarios as pre-canned stress tests but, given recent events, risk managers would be strongly advised to additionally develop their own tests unless they believe that financial market history tends to repeat itself. Stress tests are a useful supplement to traditional risk measures that may well reveal particular vulnerabilities in turbulent, abnormal markets.

There is a paradox: recent history better reflects the current relationships between securities and instruments, but is less likely to contain an extreme event. In turbulent markets all bets are off, normal relationships break down and all risk measures to varying degrees lose their value.

Risk controllers should guard against complacency; it is a well-rehearsed issue that the calculation of sophisticated risk measures may lead to a false sense of security. Sadly, risk controllers must be permanently cynical, trusting no-one or any calculations particularly their own. It's worth remembering that a performance analyst tells you what happened yesterday, a trader tells you what is happening today and a risk manager fails to forecast accurately what will happen tomorrow.

Glossary of Key Terms

Active risk
Risk relative to the benchmark. The standard deviation of excess return, otherwise known as relative risk, tracking error or tracking risk

Active share
Active share is a measure of the percentage difference of security holdings in the portfolio as opposed to the benchmark

Adjusted M^2
Return adjusted for risk, skewness and kurtosis

Adjusted Sharpe ratio
Sharpe ratio adjusted for skewness and kurtosis

Alpha
Excess return adjusted for systematic risk

Annualised return
The annual return which when compounded with itself will generate the cumulative return over multiple years

Asset manager
Investment advisory firm or financial institution making investment decisions on behalf of, and managing the assets of asset owners

Asset owner
Asset owners are investors, typically pension funds, endowments, sovereign wealth funds, boards of investment trusts and high net wealth individuals.

Autocorrelation
Autocorrelation is the correlation of a lagged return with itself

Beta
Systematic risk

Calmar ratio
The ratio of excess return above the risk-free rate to maximum drawdown

Composite
An aggregation of one or more portfolios managed according to a similar investment mandate, objective or strategy

Conditional value at risk
The average return conditional on the return exceeding the value at risk

Continuous compounded return	The natural logarithm of simple returns
Correlation	A standardised covariance which measures the tendency of portfolio and benchmark returns to move together
Dispersion	A measure of the spread of returns within a composite. Sometimes described as internal risk
Downside risk	Variability of underperformance below a minimum target rate
Drawdown	Any continuous period of negative returns or peak to valley fall in performance
Duration	Systematic risk for fixed income instruments. The average life of the present values of all future cash flows
Ex-ante risk	Prospective or forward-looking risk, based on a snapshot of the current securities and instruments within the portfolio and their historical relationship with each other. An estimate or forecast of the future risk of the portfolio
Ex-post risk	Historical or risk after the event
Excess kurtosis	Kurtosis in excess of 3, the kurtosis of a normal distribution of returns
Excess return	The excess return between the portfolio and benchmark returns. Not to be confused with the excess return above the risk-free rate. The excess return can be calculated either arithmetically or geometrically
Gain at risk	The best expected gain over a given time interval under normal market conditions at a given confidence level. Otherwise known as potential upside
GIPS	Global Investment Performance Standards. Voluntary, ethical standards for investment performance presentations to ensure fair representation and full disclosure of investment performance
Information ratio	The ratio of annualised excess return compared to annualised tracking error

Kurtosis	The 4th moment of the return distribution, a measure of the weight of returns in the tails of the distribution relative to standard deviation. More often associated as a measure of flatness or peakedness of the return distribution
M^2	Return adjusted for risk
Maximum drawdown	The maximum potential loss over a specific time period, buying at the high point in the return series and selling at the lowest
Mean return	The 1st moment of the return distribution, a simple arithmetic average of returns
Portfolio manager	Individual, normally employed by an asset manager or asset owner managing a portfolio of assets
Potential upside	The best expected gain over a given time interval under normal market conditions at a given confidence level
Relative risk	Risk relative to the benchmark. The standard deviation of excess return, otherwise known as active risk, tracking error or tracking risk
Risk-free rate	The rate of return an investor can expect from a theoretically risk-free investment
Risk manager	Risk managers take risk in order to achieve higher return
Risk controller	Risk controllers measure and monitor risk
Serial correlation	See autocorrelation
Sharpe ratio	The grandfather of composite risk/return measures. The ratio of annualised excess return above the risk-free rate divided by the variability of return
Skewness	The 3rd moment of the return distribution, a measure of asymmetry
Sortino ratio	The ratio of annualised excess return above the minimum acceptable return divided by downside risk
Upside potential	Average sum of returns above target
Upside risk	Variability of portfolio returns that exceed a given target
Value at risk	The worst expected loss over a given time interval under normal market conditions at a given confidence level

Variability   The standard deviation of returns

Variance   The 2nd moment of the return distribution. The square
                       of standard deviation

Volatility   Sometimes used to describe the systematic risk of a
                       portfolio but more commonly the variability

Composite Internal Risk Measures

The GIPS standards (4.A.1.i) require the presentation of an internal risk measure to measure the dispersion of annual portfolio returns within the composite. The standards do not mandate a particular method of calculation, although the method used must be described. A low or narrow dispersion implies a tight investment process with less variability of portfolio returns whilst a high or wide dispersion implies weaker controls or other issues such as portfolios allocated to the wrong composite. On balance investors should prefer portfolio managers with a lower dispersion of returns. Dispersion is calculated using the annual returns of all portfolios that are included in the composite for the entire calendar year. Acceptable measures of internal risk or dispersion include:

i) Equal weighted dispersion (this might be described as internal standard deviation or internal risk, although I do not like this term)

$$\text{Equal weighted dispersion } \sigma_p = \sqrt{\frac{\sum\limits_{i=1}^{i=p}(p_i - \overline{p})^2}{p}} \qquad \text{(A.1)}$$

Where:

p_i = individual annual portfolio return
$\overline{p}$ = mean annual portfolio return
P = number of portfolios in the composite for the entire calendar year

ii) Asset weighted dispersion

$$\text{Asset weighted dispersion } \overline{\sigma}_p = \sqrt{\sum\limits_{i=1}^{i=p} W_i \times \left(p_i - \left(\sum\limits_{i=1}^{i=P} W_i \times P_i\right)\right)^2} \qquad \text{(A.2)}$$

Where:

W_i = individual portfolio weight

iii) High and low returns

The high return p_H represents the best annual portfolio return in the composite.

The low return p_L represents the worst annual portfolio return in the composite.

iv) Range of returns

The range of returns is the difference between the best and the worst annual portfolio returns in the composite:

$$p_R = p_H - p_L \qquad\qquad (A.3)$$

v) Inter-quartile range

The inter-quartile range is the range between the 25th percentile and the 75th percentile as calculated by any of the percentile rank methods in Equations 8.1 to 8.5.

$$\text{Inter-quartile range } p_{QR} = p_{25} - p_{75} \qquad\qquad (A.4)$$

Where:

p_{25} = 1st or upper quartile return
p_{75} = 3rd or lower quartile return

For composites with a large number of portfolios my preferred measure of dispersion would be equal weighted standard deviation; asset weighted is perhaps too complex for little added value. The high/low range is of course easy to calculate and useful to clients, but perhaps a little aggressive and too sensitive to outliers. If a standard deviation is not to be calculated the inter-quartile is my preference. If the composite contains five or fewer portfolios for the full years the GIPS standards recognise that a measure of internal dispersion is of little value and therefore does not require it to be presented in a GIPS report.

Bibliography

Abdulali, A. (2006) The Bias Ratio™: Measuring the Shape of Fraud. *Protégé Partners – Quarterly Letter* 3Q.

Adams, A. T., Bloomfield, D. S. F., Booth, P. M. and England, P. D. (1993) *Investment Mathematics and Statistics*. Graham and Trotman.

Agarwal, V. and Naik, N. Y. (2004) Risk and Portfolio Decisions Involving Hedge Funds. *Review of Financial Studies* 17(1), 63–98.

Association of Investment Management and Research (1997) *AIMR Performance Presentation Standards Handbook 1997*.

Akeda, Y. (2003) Interpretation of Negative Sharpe Ratio. *The Journal of Performance Measurement*, Spring, 19–23.

Alexander, G. J. and Baptista, A. M. (2003) Portfolio Performance Evaluation Using Value at Risk. *Journal of Portfolio Management* 24(4), 93–102.

Amenc, N., Goltz, F. and Lioui, A. (2011) Practitioner Portfolio Construction and Performance Measurement: Evidence from Europe. *Financial Analysts Journal* 67(3), 39–50.

Amenc, N. and Le Sourd, V. (2003) *Portfolio Theory and Performance Analysis*. John Wiley & Sons.

Amenc, N. and Le Sourd, V. (2007) A Critical Analysis of Fund Rating Systems. *Journal of Performance Measurement*, Summer, 42–57.

Ang, J. S. and Chua, J. H. (1979) Composite Measures for the Evaluation of Investment Performance. *Journal of Financial and Quantitative Analysis* 14(2), 361–384.

Artzner, P., Delbaen, F., Eber, J.-M. and Heath, D. (1999) Coherent Measures of Risk. *Mathematical Finance* 9(3), 203–228.

Bacon, C. R. (2007) *Advanced Portfolio Attribution Analysis*. Risk Books.

Bacon, C. R. (2008) *Practical Portfolio Performance Measurement and Attribution,* 2nd edn. John Wiley & Sons.

Bacon, C. R. (2015) A Periodic Table of Risk Measures – Version 2. *Journal of Performance Measurement*, Spring, 25–28.

Bain, W. G. (1996) *Investment Performance Measurement*. Woodhead Publishing.

Bank Administration Institute (1968) Measuring the Investment Performance of Pension Funds for the Purpose of Inter Fund Comparison, October.

Becker, T. (2010) *The Zephyr K-Ratio*. Zephyr Associates.

Bernardo, A. and Ledoit, O. (2006) *Gain, Loss and Asset Pricing*. http://www.ledoit.net/gainloss.pdf

Biglova, A., Ortobelli, S., Rachev, S. T. and Stoyanov, S. V. (2004) Different Approaches to Risk Estimation in Portfolio Theory. *Journal of Portfolio Management* 31(1), 103–112.

Bogle, J. C. (1994) *Bogle on Mutual Funds*. Irwin.

Bogle, J. C. (1999) *Common Sense on Mutual Funds*. John Wiley & Sons.

Booth J. (2019) Carney Warns that Woodford-style funds Are "Built on a Lie", *City A.M.*, 26 June.

Boston, W. (2008) Hedge Funds Shorting VW Stung by Porsche. *Time Magazine*, 29 October.

283

Bradford, D. and Siliski, D. (2016) Performance Drawdowns in Asset Management: Extending Drawdown Analysis to Active Returns. *The Journal of Performance Measurement*, Fall, 34–48.

Broeders, D. W. G. A., van Oord, A., and Rijsbergen, D. R. (2019) Does it Pay to Pay Performance Fees? Empirical Evidence from Dutch Pension Funds. *Journal of International Money and Finance* 93, 299–312.

Burke, G. (1994) A Sharper Sharpe Ratio.*The Computerized Trader*, March.

Butler, C. (1999) *Mastering Value at Risk*. Financial Times, Prentice Hall.

Carhart, M. M. (1997) On Persistence in Mutual Fund Performance. *Journal of Finance* 52(1), 57–82.

Chevalier, J. and Ellison, G. (1997) Risk Taking by Mutual Funds as a Response to Incentives. *Journal of Political Economy* 105(6), 1167–1200.

Christopherson, J. A., Carino, D. R. and Ferson, W. E. (2009) *Portfolio Performance Measurement and Benchmarking*. McGraw-Hill.

Clarkson, R. (2001) FARM: A Financial Actuarial Risk Model. In F. Sortino and S. Satchell (eds) *Managing Downside Risk in Financial Markets*. Butterworth Heinemann.

Cogneau, P. and Hubner, G. (2009a) The (More Than) 100 Ways to Measure Portfolio Performance Part 1: Standardized Risk-Adjusted Measures. *The Journal of Performance Measurement*, Summer, 56–71.

Cogneau, P. and Hubner, G. (2009b) The (More Than) 100 Ways to Measure Portfolio Performance Part 2: Special Measures and Comparison. *The Journal of Performance Measurement*, Fall, 56–69.

Coleman, T. S. (2011) *A Practical Guide to Risk Management*. Research Foundation of CFA Institute.

Corbishley N. (2019) Liquidity Crisis at Woodford Equity Fund is Symptomatic of Systemic Problem, Bank of England Warns. *Wolf Street,* 12 July.

Cremers, K. J. M. and Petajisto, A. (2006) How Active Is Your Fund Manager: A New Measure that Predicts Performance. Yale IFC Working Paper No. 04-14.

Cremers, K. J. M. and Petajisto, A. (2009) How Active Is Your Fund Manager: A New Measure that Predicts Performance. *Review of Financial Studies* 22(9), 3329–3365.

Crouhy, M., Galai, D. and Mark, R. (2006) *The Essentials of Risk Management*. McGraw-Hill.

Davanzo, L. E., and Nesbitt, S. I. (1987) Performance Fees for Investment Managers. *Financial Analysts Journal*, 43(1), 14–20.

DeCarlo, L. T. (1997) On the Meaning and Use of Kurtosis. *Psychological Methods* 2(3), 292–307.

Dembo, R. S. and Freeman, A. (1998) *Seeing Tomorrow: Rewriting the Rules of Risk*. John Wiley & Sons.

Dowd, K. (1998) *Beyond Value at Risk: The New Science of Risk Management*. John Wiley & Sons.

Dowd, K. (2000) Adjusting for Risk: An Improved Sharpe Ratio. *International Review of Economics and Finance*, 9(3), 209–222.

Dunbar, N. (2000) *Inventing Money*. John Wiley & Sons.

Eikeland, S. (2016) Fair and Transparent Performance Fee – Part One. *Journal of Performance Measurement*, Fall, 6–14.

Eikeland, S. (2016/2017) Fair and Transparent Performance Fee – Part Two. *Journal of Performance Measurement*, Winter, 30–40.

Eling, M. (2008) Performance Measurement in the Investment Industry: Does the Measure Matter? University of St Gallen, Working Paper Series in Finance No. 73.

Eling, M. and Schumacher, F. (2007) Does the Choice of Performance Measure Influence the Evaluation of Hedge Funds? *Journal of Banking and Finance* 31(9), 2632–2647.

Eling, M., Farinelli, S., Rossello, D. and Tibiletti, L. (2009) *One-Size or Tailor-Made Performance Ratios for Ranking Hedge Funds*, Fakultat fur Mathematik und Wirtschaftswissenschaften, Universitat Ulm.

Elton, E. J. and Gruber, M. J. (1991) *Modern Portfolio Theory and Investment Analysis*, 4th edn. John Wiley & Sons.

Fabozzi, F. (1999) *Duration, Convexity, and Other Bond Risk Measures*. Frank J. Fabozzi Associates.

Fama, E. F. (1972) Components of Investment Performance. *Journal of Finance* 27(3), 551–567.

Fama, E. F. and French, K. R. (1993) Common Risk Factors in the Returns of Stocks and Bonds. *Journal of Financial Economics* 33(1), 3–56.

Farinelli, S. and Tibiletti, L. (2008) Sharpe Thinking in Asset Ranking with One-Sided Measures. *European Journal of Operational Research* 185(3), 1542–1547.

Favre, L. and Galeano, J. (2002) Mean-Modified Value at Risk Optimization with Hedge Funds. *The Journal of Alternative Investments* 5, 21–25.

Feibel, B. J. (2003) *Investment Performance Measurement*. John Wiley & Sons.

Fischer, B. (2010) *Performance Analyse in der Praxis*, 3rd edn. Oldenbourg.

Frazzini, A., Friedman, J. A. and Pomoski, L. (2016) Deactivating Active Share. *Financial Analysts Journal* 72(2), 14–21.

Galton, F. (1989) Kinship and Correlation. *Statistical Science* (Institute of Mathematical Statistics) 4(2), 80–86.

Gini, C. (1912) Variabilità e mutabilità. C. Cuppini, Bologna.

Gini, C. (1921) Measurement of the Inequality of Incomes. *The Economic Journal* 31, 124–126.

Global Investment Performance Standards (2019) CFA Institute.

Goetzmann, W. N., Ingersoll, J. E. and Ross, S. A. (2003) High-water Marks and Hedge Fund Management Contracts. *The Journal of Finance* 58(4), 1685–1718.

Golub, B. W. and Tilman, L. M. (2000) *Risk Management*. John Wiley & Sons.

Goodwin, T. (1998) The Information Ratio: More Than You Ever Wanted to Know About One Performance Measure, *Russell Research Commentary*,

Goyal, A. and Wahal, S. (2008) The Selection and Termination of Investment Management Firms by Plan Sponsors. *Journal of Finance* 63(4), 1805–1847.

Graham, J. R. and Harvey, C. R. (1997) Grading the Performance of Market-Timing Newsletters. *Financial Analysts Journal* 53(6), 54–66.

Gregoriou, G. N., Hubner, G., Papageorgiou, N. and Rouah, F. (2005) *Hedge Funds: Insights in Performance Measurement, Risk Analysis, and Portfolio Allocation*. John Wiley & Sons.

Gregoriou, G. N., Karavas, V. N. and Rouah, F. (2003) *Hedge Funds: Strategies, Risk Assessment and Returns*. Beard Books.

Grinold, R. C. (1989) The Fundamental Law of Active Management. *Journal of Portfolio Management* 15(3), 30–38.

Grinold, R. C. and Khan, R. N. (1994) *Active Portfolio Management: Quantative Theory and Applications*. McGraw-Hill.

Grinold, R. C. and Khan, R. N. (1999) *Active Portfolio Management: A Quantitative Approach to Proving Superior Returns and Controlling Risk*. McGraw-Hill.

Haight, G. T. and Morrell, S. O. (1997) *The Analysis of Portfolio Management Performance*. McGraw-Hill.

Haight, G. T., Morrell, S. O. and Ross, G. E. (2007) *How to Select Investment Managers and Evaluate Performance*. John Wiley & Sons.

Hallerbach, W. G. (2002) Decomposing Portfolio Value-at-Risk: A General Analysis. *Journal of Risk* 5(2), 1–18.

Handzy, D. (2013) Visual VaR – Intuitive and Effective Risk Communication. *Investor Analytics, Thought Leadership Series*, September.

Harris, L. (2002) *Trading and Exchanges*. Oxford University Press.

Henriksson, R. D. and Merton, R. C. (1981) On Market Timing and Investment Performance II. Statistical Procedures for Evaluating Forecast Skills. *Journal of Business* 54, 513–533.

Holton, G. (2004) Defining Risk. *Financial Analysts Journal* 60(6), 19–25.

Hudert, R., Schmitt, M. G. and von Thaden, M. (2018/2019) Portfolio Performance Evaluation: What Difference Do Logarithmic Returns Make? *Journal of Performance Measurement*, Winter, 8–15.

Hussain, A. (2000) *Managing Operational Risk in Financial Markets*. Butterworth Heinemann.

Hymans, C. and Mulligan, J. (1980) *The Measurement of Portfolio Performance*. Kluwer.

Ineichen, A. M. (2003) *Absolute Returns: The Risk and Opportunities of Hedge Fund Investing*. John Wiley & Sons.

Israelsen, C. L. (2005) A Refinement to the Sharpe Ratio and Information Ratio. *Journal of Asset Management* 5(6), 423–427.

Jarque, C. M. and Bera, A. K. (1987) A Test for Normality of Observations and Regression Residuals. *International Statistics Review* 55, 163–177.

Jensen, M. (1968) The Performance of Mutual Funds 1945–1964. *Journal of Finance* 23(2), 389–416.

Jensen, M. (1969) Risk, the Pricing of Capital Assets, and the Evaluation of Investment Portfolios. *Journal of Business* 42(2), 167–247.

Jorion, P. (1997) *Value at Risk*. Irwin.

Kahneman, D. and Tversky, A. (1979) Prospect Theory: An Analysis of Decision under Risk. *Econometrica* XLVII, 263–291.

Kaplan, P. D. (2012/2013) What Is Wrong with Multiplying by the Square Root of Twelve? *Journal of Performance Measurement*, Winter, 16–24.

Kaplan, P. D. and Knowles, J. A. (2004) Kappa: A Generalized Downside Risk-Adjusted Performance Measure. *Journal of Performance Measurement* 8(1), 42–54.

Kazemi, H., Schneeweis, T. and Gupta, B. (2004) Omega as a Performance Measure. *Journal of Performance Measurement*, Spring, 16–25.

Kemp, M. (2011) *Extreme Events*. John Wiley & Sons.

Kestner, L. N. (1996) Getting a Handle on True Performance. *Futures* 25(1), 44–46.

Kestner, L. N. (2003) *Quantitative Trading Strategies: Harnessing the Power of Quantitative Techniques to Create a Winning Trading Program*. McGraw-Hill, Traders Edge Series.

Kidd, D. (2011) *The Sharpe Ratio and the Information Ratio*. CFA Institute.

Klock, M. (2018) A Practical Journey through Risk for Performance Analysts. *Journal of Performance Measurement*, Spring, 37–48.

Knight, J. and Satchell, S. (2002) *Performance Measurement in Finance Firms, Funds and Managers*. Butterworth Heinemann.

Konno, H. and Yamazaki, H. (1991) Mean–Absolute Deviation Portfolio Optimization Model and its Application to Tokyo Stock Market. *Management Science* 37(5), 519–531.

La Grouw, G. (2012) *Effective Dashboard Design: Design Secrets to Getting More Value from Performance Dashboards*. Electrosmart.

Latham, M. (2019) The Neil Woodford Crisis: An Accident Waiting to Happen? *Funds Europe*, July–August.

Lavinio, S. (1999) *The Hedge Fund Handbook*. McGraw-Hill.

Lhabitant, F. (2004) *Hedge Funds*. John Wiley & Sons.

Liang, B. and Park, H. (2010) Predicting Hedge Fund Failure: A Comparison of Risk Measures. *Journal of Financial and Quantitative Analysis* 45(1), 199–222.

Lo, A. W. (2002) The Statistics of Sharpe Ratios. *Financial Analysts Journal*, 58(4), 36–52.

Lowenstein, R. (2000) *When Genius Failed: The Rise and Fall of Long-Term Capital Management*. Random House.

Macaulay, F. (1938) *Some Theoretical Problems Suggested by the Movement of Interest Rates, Bond Yields and Stock Prices in the US since 1856*. National Bureau of Economic Research.

Marrison, C. (2002) *The Fundamentals of Risk Measurement*. McGraw Hill.

Martin, P. G. and McCann, B. (1989) *The Investor's Guide to Fidelity Funds: Winning Strategies for Mutual Fund Investors*. John Wiley & Sons.

Martin, R. D., Rachev, S. T. and Siboulet, F. (2003) Phi-alpha Optimal Portfolios and Extreme Risk Management. *Wilmott Magazine* 6, 70–83.

McCafferty, T. (2003) *The Market Is Always Right*. McGraw-Hill.

Mendeleev, D. (1869) Uber die Beziehungen der Eigenschaften zu den Atomgewichten der Elemente. *Zeitschrift für Chemie* (in German), 405–406.

Metropolis, N. (1987) The Beginning of the Monte Carlo Method. *Los Alamos Science* (Special Issue dedicated to Stanisław Ulam), 125–130.

Modigliani, L. (1997) Risk-Adjusted Performance, Part 1: The Time for Risk Measurement Is Now. *Morgan Stanley's Investment Perspectives*, February.

Muralidhar, A. (2000) Risk-adjusted Performance – The Correlation Correction. *Financial Analysts Journal* 56(5), 63–71.

Muralidhar, A. (2009) Risk and Skill-adjusted Compensation. *Journal of Performance Measurement*, Summer, 40–55.

Muralidhar, A. (2015) The Sharpe Ratio Revisited: What it Really Tells Us. *Journal of Performance Measurement*, Spring, 6–12.

National Association of Pension Funds (2011) *Performance Measurement, Attribution and Risk Made Simple*. National Association of Pension Funds, October.

Pearson, K. (1894) On the dissection of asymmetrical frequency-curves. *Philosophical Transactions of the Royal Society of London* 185, 71–110.

Pearson, K. (1895) Contributions to the Mathematical Theory of Evolution. II. Skew Variation in Homogeneous Material. *Philosophical Transactions of the Royal Society of London* 186, 343–424.

Pearson, K. (1905) Das Fehlergesetz und seine Verallgemeinerungen durch Fechner und Pearson. A Rejoinder. *Biometrika* 4, 169–212.

Perold, A. F. and Alloway, R. (2003) *The Unilever Superannuation Fund vs. Merrill Lynch*. Harvard Business School Publishing.

Pezier, J. and White, A. (2006) The Relative Merits of Investable Hedge Fund Indices and of Funds of Hedge Funds in Optimal Passive Portfolios. *ICMA Centre Discussion Papers in Finance*, icma-dp2006-10, Henley Business School, Reading University.

Qian, B. and Rasheed, K. (2004) *Hurst Exponent and Financial Market Predictability*, IASTED Conference on Financial Engineering and Applications (FEA 2004), 203–209.

Rachev, S. T. (1991) *Probability Metrics and the Stability of Stochastic Models*. John Wiley & Sons.

Rachev, S. T., Menn, C. and Fabozzi, F. (2005) *Fat-Tailed and Skewed Asset Return Distributions, Implications for Risk Management, Portfolio Selection, and Option Pricing*. John Wiley & Sons.

Rachev, S. T., Ortobelli, S., Stoyanov, S., Fabozzi, F. and Biglova, A. (2008) Desirable Properties of an Ideal Risk Measure in Portfolio Theory. *International Journal of Theoretical and Applied Finance* 11(1), 19–54.

Rachev, S. T., Stoyanov, S. V. and Fabozzi, F. (2008) *Advanced Stochastic Models, Risk Assessment and Portfolio Optimization*. John Wiley & Sons.

Record, N. (2003) *Currency Overlay*. John Wiley & Sons.

Reilly, F. K. (1989) *Investment Analysis and Portfolio Management*. Dryden HBJ.

Reynolds Parker, V. (2005) *Managing Hedge Fund Risk*, 2nd edn. Risk Books.

Rockefeller, R. T. and Uryasev, S. (2000) Optimization of Conditional Value at Risk. *Journal of Risk* 2(3), 22–41.

Rogers, D. S. and Van Dyke, C. J. (2006) Measuring the Volatility of Hedge Fund Returns. *The Journal of Wealth Management,* Summer, 45–53.

Rom, B. M. and Ferguson, K. W. (2001) A Software Developer's View: Using Post-Modern Portfolio Theory to Improve Investment Performance Measurement. In F. Sortino and S. Satchell (eds) *Managing Downside Risk in Financial Markets*. Butterworth Heinemann.

Romer, P. (2015) Mathiness in the Theory of Economic Growth. *American Economic Review, Papers & Proceedings* 105, 89–93.

Roy, A. D. (1952) Safety First and the Holding of Assets. *Econometrica*, July, 431–450.

Ryan, T. P. (2006) *Portfolio Analysis*. Risk Books.

Ryan, T. P. (2015) How to Select Investment Portfolios Using Performance Analysis. *Journal of Performance Measurement*, Fall, 7–14.

Schliemann, M. and Stanzel, M. (2008) Performance-based Compensation Contracts in the Asset Management Industry. *Journal of Performance Measurement*, Spring, 61–70.

Shadwick, W. and Keating, C. (2002) A Universal Performance Measure. *Journal of Performance Measurement*, Spring, 59–84.

Sharpe, W. F. (1964) Capital Asset Prices: A Theory of Market Equilibrium Under Conditions of Risk. *Journal of Finance* 19(3), 425–442.

Sharpe, W. F. (1966) Mutual Fund Performance. *Journal of Business*, 39, 119–138.

Sharpe, W. F. (1994) The Sharpe Ratio. *Journal of Portfolio Management*, Fall, 49–58.

Simpson, J. (2015a) Risk-adjusted Performance Ratios: Part 1. *Journal of Performance Measurement*, Spring, 29–47.

Simpson, J. (2015b) Risk-adjusted Performance Ratios: Part 2. *Journal of Performance Measurement*, Summer, 52–63.

Singer, B., Kessler, C., Schwarz, G., Terhaar, K. and Zerolis, J. (1999/2000) Improving Risk Measurement, Analysis and Management (with a Little More Help from Euclid). *Journal of Performance Measurement*, Winter, 58–18.

Smith, K. and Tito, D. (1969) Risk Return of Ex-Post Portfolio Performance. *Journal of Financial and Quantitative Analysis* 4(4), 479–471.

So, S. (2008) *Why Is the Sample Variance a Biased Estimator?* Signal and Processing Laboratory, Griffith School of Engineering, Griffith University, Brisbane, Queensland, Australia, 11 September.

Sopranzetti, B. (2014) Value at Risk and Expected Shortfall: A Primer. *Journal of Performance Measurement*, Fall, 35–39.

Sortino, F. and van der Meer, R. (1991) Downside Risk. *Journal of Portfolio Management*, 17(4), 27–31.

Sortino, F., van de Meer, R. and Plantinga, A. (1999) The Dutch Triangle: A Framework to Measure Upside Potential Relative to Downside Risk. *Journal of Portfolio Management* 26, 50–58.

Sortino, F., Miller, G. and Messina, J. (1997) Short Term Risk-adjusted Performance: A Style-based Analysis. *Journal of Investing* 6(2), 19–27.

Sortino, F. A. and Satchell, S. E. (2001) *Managing Downside Risk in Financial Markets*. Butterworth Heinemann.

Spaulding, D. (1997) *Measuring Investment Performance*. McGraw-Hill.

Spaulding, D. (2005) *The Handbook of Investment Performance*. TSG Publishing.

Starks, L. T. (1987) Performance Incentive Fees: An Agency Theoretic Approach. *The Journal of Financial and Quantitative Analysis* 22(1), 17–32.

Stewart, S. D. (2013) *Manager Selection*. The Research Foundation of the CFA Institute.

Stewart, S. D., Heisler, J., Knittel, C. and Neumann, J. (2009) Absence of Value: An Analysis of Investment Allocation Decisions by Institutional Plan Sponsors. *Financial Analysts Journal*, 65(6), 34–51

Tran, V. T. (2006) *Evaluating Hedge Fund Performance*. John Wiley & Sons.

Travers, F. J. (2004) *Investment Manager Analysis*. John Wiley & Sons.

Treynor, J. L. (1965) How to Rate Management of Invested Funds. *Harvard Business Review* 44(1), 63–75.

Treynor, J. L. (2007) *Treynor on Institutional Investing*. John Wiley & Sons.

Treynor, J. L. and Black, F. (1973) How to Use Security Analysis to Improve Portfolio Selection. *Journal of Business*, January, 66–85.

Treynor, J. L. and Mazuy, K. (1966) Can Mutual Funds Outguess the Market? *Harvard Business Review* 44, 131–136.

Wagner, W. H. and Tito, D. A. (1977) Definitive New Measures of Bond Performance and Risk. *Pension World*, May, 17–26.

Walker, O. (2021) *Built on a Lie*. Penguin Random House.

Waring, B. M., Whitney, D. M., Pirone, J. and Castille, C. (2000) Optimizing Manager Structure and Budgeting Manager Risk. *Journal of Portfolio Management* 26(3), 90–104.

Waring, B. M. and Siegel, L. B. (2003) The Dimensions of Active Management. *Journal of Portfolio Management* 29(3), 35–51.

Watanabe, Y. (2006) Is Sharpe Ratio Still Effective? *Journal of Performance Measurement*, Fall, 55–66.

Watanabe, Y. (2014) New Prospect Ratio: Application to Hedge Funds with Higher Order Moments. *Journal of Performance Measurement* 19(1), 40–52.

Weber, A. E. (2017) Annual Risk Measures and Related Statistics. *Journal of Performance Measurement*, Spring, 50–64.

Wiggins, R. Z., Piontek, T. and Metrick, A. (2014) The Lehman Brothers Bankruptcy. *Yale Program on Financial Stability Case Study*, 2014-3A-V1, 1 October.

Xiong, J. X. and Idzorek, T. M. (2011) The Impact of Skewness and Fat Tails on the Asset Allocation Decision. *Financial Analysts Journal* 67(2), 23–35.

Yitzhaki, S. (1982) Stochastic Dominance, Mean Variance and Gini's Mean Difference. *American Economic Review* 72(1), 178–185.

Young, T. W. (1991) Calmar Ratio: A Smoother Tool. *Futures Magazine*, 1 October.

Zakamouline, V. (2010) On the Consistent Use of VaR in Portfolio Performance Evaluation: A Cautionary Note. *The Journal of Portfolio Management*, Fall, 37(1), 92–104.

Zakamouline, V. (2011) The Performance Measure You Choose Influences the Evaluation of Hedge Funds. *Journal of Performance Measurement*, Spring, 48–63.

Zask, E. (2000) *Global Investment Risk Management*. McGraw-Hill.

Ziemba, W. T. (2005) The Symmetric Downside- Risk Sharpe Ratio. *Journal of Portfolio Management* 32(1), 108–122.

Zipf, R. (2003) *Fixed Income Mathematics*. Academic Press.

Index